Ascetic Practices in Japane Religion

Ascetic practices are a common feature of religion in Japan, practiced by different religious traditions. This book looks at these ascetic practices in an inter-sectarian and inter-doctrinal fashion, in order to highlight the underlying themes common to all forms of asceticism. It does so by employing a multidisciplinary methodology, which integrates participant fieldwork – the author himself engaged extensively in ascetic practices – with a hermeneutical interpretation of the body as the primary locus of transmission of the ascetic 'embodied tradition'. By unlocking this 'bodily data', the book unveils the human body as the main tool and text of ascetic practice. This book includes discussion of the many extraordinary rituals practiced by Japanese ascetics.

Tullio Federico Lobetti is Senior Teaching Fellow in the Study of Religions Department at SOAS, University of London, UK.

Foreword writer, **Hirochika Nakamaki**, is Director of the Suita City Museum and Professor Emeritus of the National Museum of Ethnology, Japan.

Japan Anthropology Workshop Series

A Japanese View of Nature
The world of living things by Kinji Imanishi
Translated by Pamela J. Asquith, Heita Kawakatsu, Shusuke Yagi and Hiroyuki Takasaki
Edited and introduced by Pamela J. Asquith

Japan's Changing Generations
Are young people creating a new society?
Edited by Gordon Mathews and Bruce White

The Care of the Elderly in Japan
Yongmei Wu

Community Volunteers in Japan
Everyday stories of social change
Lynne Y. Nakano

Nature, Ritual and Society in Japan's Ryukyu Islands
Arne Røkkum

Psychotherapy and Religion in Japan
The Japanese introspection practice of naikan
Chikako Ozawa-de Silva

Dismantling the East–West Dichotomy
Essays in honour of Jan van Bremen
Edited by Joy Hendry and Heung Wah Wong

Pilgrimages and Spiritual Quests in Japan
Edited by Maria Rodriguez del Alisal, Peter Ackermann and Dolores Martinez

The Culture of Copying in Japan
Critical and historical perspectives
Edited by Rupert Cox

Ascetic Practices in Japanese Religion

Tullio Federico Lobetti

LONDON AND NEW YORK

First published 2014
by Routledge
2 Park Square, Milton Park, Abingdon, Oxfordshire OX14 4RN

Simultaneously published in the USA and Canada
by Routledge
711 Third Avenue, New York, NY 10017

First issued in paperback 2016

Routledge is an imprint of the Taylor & Francis Group, an informa business

British Library Cataloguing in Publication Data
A catalogue record for this book is available from the British Library

Library of Congress Cataloging in Publication Data
Lobetti, Tullio Federico.
Ascetic practices in Japanese religion / Tullio Federico Lobetti.
    pages cm. – (Japan anthropology workshop series; 22)
    Includes bibliographical references and index.
    1. Asceticism. 2. Japan–Religious life and customs. I. Title.
    BL625.L595 2013
    204'.470952–dc23
    2013007898

ISBN 13: 978-1-138-65206-4 (pbk)
ISBN 13: 978-0-415-83375-2 (hbk)

Typeset in Times New Roman
by Sunrise Setting Ltd, Paignton, Devon

To my parents and godparents, who never tire of waiting

Contents

Figures

Tables

Preface

Mainstream research on religion in Japan adopts historical or theological approaches, and the history of investigations using field sciences such as sociology and anthropology is still relatively limited. Questionnaire inquiries are used in sociology, and participant observation and interviews are the main approaches in anthropology. However, this book distinguishes itself further, though it is an anthropological study, because of the way it addresses the troublesome subject known as religious asceticism.

Ascetic practices may not be understood only by observing from the outside. This is a world which cannot be described without personal experience. And we have to impose all sorts of hardships on our bodies, for without becoming a practioner, we cannot understand the essence of the thing we are observing. What can we understand if we simply take a picture of the places of ascetic practice? Even if we speak to a person practicing asceticism, an interview may not be easily recorded. Practitioners abusing and overworking the flesh can hardly spare time for a researcher.

There is a long tradition of mountain ascetic practice in Japan where more than 80 per cent of the country is composed of mountains and hills. Central among these is the religious practice known as Shugendō. Overflowing with abundant youthful energy, the author of this book, Tullio Federico Lobetti, took on the challenge of its study, literally with his own body. *Dewasanzan*, the three mountains of Dewa province, were the main region for his fieldwork, and it was 'body data' which he collected there rather than simply 'field data'. '*Corporis ascensus*' is the expression he uses, complete with pun, to describe what is gained by the Japanese practitioners as a result of the practice. Perhaps I may suggest that what was being built intellectually by the author during his research was '*cognitus corporis*'.

This book positions the '*cognitus corporis*', grounded in the ideas and practice of '*corporis ascensus*', into spatial, social and religious contexts. It also seeks to make comparisons with asceticism found in Judaism, Christianity and both Theravada and Mahayanist Buddhism. If it is a little short on anthropological generalization, it is surely because '*corporis ascensus*' does not lend itself to abstraction, although it is excellent to find this method of research at the heart of the anthropological endeavour.

Lobetti's fieldwork in Japan was made under the supervision of Keio University's Professor Suzuki Masataka, whose department follows the tradition of Emeritus Professor Hitoshi Miyake, Japan's best-known scholar of mountain asceticism. This school is also the largest base of empirical research on mountain asceticism – in the fields of sociology, anthropology and religious studies – and Lobetti was undoubtedly influenced by the scholarly discipline practiced there.

This book not only offers the reader a path in the direction of experiencing Japanese religious culture, but you will also be able to take some steps towards the discovery of the comparative study of ascetic practice. Please take a look.

Hirochika Nakamaki

Acknowledgements

This book is based on the research I conducted between 2004 and 2008 for my PhD dissertation, and I would like to thank first of all my supervisor, Lucia Dolce, for her constant support and her patience in helping me to transform my twisted theories into more legitimate arguments. None of this would have ever happened without her continuous encouragement and advice.

During my fieldwork period in Japan, I benefited from the help and supervision of Suzuki Masataka, who allowed me to attend his seminars and introduced me to the leaders of many of the ascetic practices in which I participated. Without his support, much of my fieldwork would have been impossible. I also want to express my gratitude to Gaynor Sekimori, who first introduced me to Shugendō and who helped me in settling in Japan. I would also like to remember the leaders of the Shōzen-in, Tōnan-in and Tōshō-ji temples, the head priest of Dewa Sanzan-jinja and the leaders of the Agematsu Jiga Daikyōkai for allowing me to participate in their practices and for their patience in answering all of my endless questions.

My research was financed by the Centre for the Study of Japanese Religions (CSJR) and by the Arts & Humanities Research Council (AHRC), while I was economically supported by the Japan Foundation during my fieldwork period. I would like to express my gratitude for their financial help.

Fellow SOAS students Satomi, Fumi, Benedetta and Kigensan have all helped me along the way. At SOAS, I particularly thank Cosimo Zene for his continuous support and inspiration, and above all for honouring me with his friendship. I also would like to thank my language teacher, Yoshiko Jones, for her patience in teaching me how to communicate proficiently in Japanese.

At home, my mum and dad and godmother and godfather were always very supportive and never failed to show me their affection, despite my long periods of absence. I always found them waiting for me with a smile and a hot meal, which are probably the nicest things to find after a long journey. I would like also to express my gratitude to Federica for her patience and for nursing me back to health after many of my ascetic efforts.

Notes to the reader

All Japanese names are given in the Japanese fashion, with the family name first.

Macrons have been used for long vowels in transliterating Japanese terms, with the exception of well-known places and terms such as Tokyo or Shinto.

Notes on some issues in fieldwork methodology

The recording of data during the performance of an ascetic practice presents some peculiar difficulties. In many of the practices analyzed in this study, constant attention is required in order to follow the practice progress and to keep up with the other participants. Occasionally, the researcher is forced to adapt to highly distressing and unforeseen circumstances, such as fatigue, dangers and injuries. It is thus difficult to apply a consistent methodology in observation, enquiry and interviews.

Observation of the surrounding environment is often hindered by the need to focus on one's immediate performance for safety reasons. It is therefore easy to overlook some details present in the practice locations, such as small statues, inscriptions and small places of worship. In the case of group practices, surveying the actions of the other practitioners is not always possible, since one's view may be impeded by some of the practice requirements, such as facing a wall during sitting meditation. Taking pictures or having pictures taken is even more difficult for two main reasons at least. First, some places or contexts of practice forbid photography; second, there is seldom enough time to pause, focus the camera and take a picture. For this reason, it has been impossible to document some of the participant observations present in this study photographically, while in some other cases, pictures have been taken only in moments of pause or at the end of the practice itself.

Enquiries about the meaning or circumstances of practice need to be conducted carefully, as in all cases the leaders are very busy and not prone to dedicate time to answer direct questions. In some cases, a rigid hierarchical scale is implemented inside the group of ascetics, which makes the participants' upper echelons unavailable to neophytes. Asking questions to one's peers is instead much simpler, and many among fellow participants are readily available to respond. A substantial amount of information about practice lore or its tradition is collected in this way, for instance, while walking in the mountains or during pauses between ascetic exercises. It is, of course, very difficult to systematize one's referent samples, as these kind of interactions occur primarily with the people walking, eating or sleeping in proximity to the researcher rather than with informants methodically selected.

Interviews during the performance of a given practice could not be conducted formally, as all the practitioners were generally very tired and did not wish to spend their little rest time being interviewed. I thus tried to seamlessly slip my interviews inside the informal conversations that spontaneously arose during breaks. It was remarkable how, after an initial period of diffidence, some people actually approached me of their own accord and started telling me their stories. Their accounts were often sincerely heartfelt and moving, and it was clear that they were asking for sympathy and understanding.

Because the use of more sophisticated means of recording, such as cameras and portable recorders, was impractical in the aforementioned circumstances, the vast majority of the fieldwork data has been recorded using small portable notebooks that could easily be carried along during the practice and did not suffer too much from environmental conditions such as damp, sweat and rain. To be used as reference material in this book, I have classified them using the following scheme:

Author (initials)	Date (six figures)	Types of recording:	Progressive number preceded by #
		I: Interview	
		OFN: Observation Fieldwork Notes	
		OFI: Observation Fieldwork Interview	
		PFN: Participant Fieldwork Notes	
		PFI: Participant Fieldwork Interview	

For example, the first notebook of participant fieldwork notes recorded on 24 August 2005 will be quoted as: TL 240805 PFN#1. The practices used as case studies were selected in order to offer a balanced set of accounts pertaining to the various *modes* of Japanese asceticism: occasional performance of ascetic feats (TL 101006 PFN#1; TL 100407 PFN#1; TL 090407 PFI#1); popular practices (TL 220107 PFN#1; TL 280606 OFN#1); and practices in established religious environments (TL 240805 PFN#1 and PFN#2; TL 150706 PFN#1; TL 260806 PFN#1; TL 010407 PFN#1).

Introduction

A white-clad figure emerges from a secluded temple hall on the southern slopes of
Mount Hiei. Groups of people waiting outside are eager to get at least a glimpse
of this man, whom they regard as a living Buddha. He has just spent nine days
in that hall, without eating, drinking or sleeping, painfully rising from his seat
only to offer water to a sacred well once per day. His emaciated look and sunken
eyes seem to belong to a person who exhausted all his physical energies. He did
not seek such extreme austerities to be destroyed, however, but to be transformed
and empowered. Having faced death, he now returns to the world to spread that
power for the benefit of the others, and the crowd salute him as a new-born ascetic
master.[1]

This scene is not taken from a colourful narration of medieval Japan or from
some contemporary exotic fiction; it is real-life, present-day Japan. The person
in the aforementioned account is a *kaihōgyōja* 回峰行者, one of the so-called
'marathon monks' of Mount Hiei. Their practice of long-distance walking over
extended periods of time has attracted the interest of the media on more than one
occasion. This also includes a number of biographies of these practitioners which
have been published with great success, some even becoming best-sellers.[2] The
kaihōgyō 回峰行 is by no means the only case of Japanese asceticism known
to the wider public. Numerous autobiographical and biographical works, largely
written by the practitioners of various ascetic disciplines, are widely available
throughout Japan. This is the case for such books as *Aragyō* 荒行 by Yamada
Ryūshin, focused on the ascetic training of a *shugenja* 修験者 on Mount Kubote
求菩提山, or Shima Kazuaharu's *Gyōdō ni ikiru* 行道に生きる, the biography of
the *kaihōgyōja* Sakai Yūsai.[3]

In Japan, asceticism is not the prerogative of a small group of elite practitioners.
From members of various religious denominations undertaking strict hardships to
commoners walking on the harmless half-extinguished *goma* 護摩 fire at a local
celebration, the use of the body as a means of spiritual empowerment manifests
itself with astonishing richness.

I began this study intrigued by the variety of ascetic phenomena present in contemporary Japan. Rather than focusing my research on a single practice or sect,

I thus decided to attempt a systematic analysis of a number of case studies. This was done in order to avoid considering a certain practice as the exclusive feature of a specific religious environment, and so circumvent the risk of analyzing different ascetic traditions as perfectly discriminated and self-contained. As a result of this research, this book is particularly focused on answering the following key issues:

1   Is it possible to apply the term *asceticism* meaningfully to the various phenomena of bodily practices present in contemporary Japan?
2   What is the role of ascetic practitioners inside the social and religious context?
3   Is it possible to identify a common *theme* (or themes) in Japanese asceticism that can lead to a better definition of asceticism also applicable to other contexts?

On account of its variety, 'Japanese asceticism' cannot be easily identified as a circumscribed intellectual subject, but rather is understood as an umbrella term for various different phenomena involving the use of the body and physical exertion, thus represented in a heterogeneous ensemble of literature. The only scholarly work in western languages explicitly treating 'Japanese asceticism' is Massimo Raveri's *Il corpo e il paradiso* (1992, only in Italian). However, Raveri analyzes a wide range of ascetic practices pertaining not only to Japan but also to the wider context of East Asian asceticism.[4]

Mentions of Japanese ascetic practices can be found in books pertaining to a variety of *genre*s. The first *genre*, one that we may also consider as a primary source, is that of biographies or autobiographies of modern ascetic practitioners, mostly written from the late 1970s until the present day.[5] These books are written primarily for mass diffusion, and in many cases they have met important publishing success. Most of them are narrative works in which the life of the ascetic practitioner is often presented as an example of personal evolution or redemption starting, in many cases, from an initial period of crisis, (Wazaki 1979; Yamada 1988). This kind of work seems to fulfil at least two purposes. The first is the praise of the author for his religious undertaking, with the detailed description of all the benefits provided by the ascetic practice that he undertook. The second is a more general attempt at re-evaluating spiritual life within a modern materialistic context. In fact, nearly all of these authors clearly express their dissatisfaction for the lack of consideration that spiritual life seems to suffer from in the modern world (not necessarily only in Japan) and put forward their life as an example of a meaningful existence built instead on spiritual values and religious practice (Shima 1983). Although these works constitute important evidence of various ascetic practices and of the life of the ascetic practitioners themselves, the style of writing and analysis is, in most cases, excessively unsophisticated and the narrative often assumes rhetorical tones. In some cases, like Yamada (1988), an interesting quantity of data is provided in the appendix but without any form of critical interpretation.

The second *genre* may generally be defined as monographic works centred on a particular practice.[6] The principal characteristic of these works is that the ascetic practice taken into account is analyzed as being completely self-contained; there is no attempt to consider it within a larger phenomenon which we may call Japanese asceticism. Most of these books are academic works with a high degree of sophistication. Unfortunately, only a few of the numerous Japanese ascetic practices still alive today have been covered by such studies. Scholars have mostly concentrated on the study of the self-mummified Buddhas (Naitō 1999) and the Tendai *kaihōgyō* (probably the most studied ascetic phenomena in Japan). Hiramatsu (1982) is a particularly notable case of presenting an academic work written by an 'insider', the author being a *kaihōgyō* practitioner himself. A more recent study is that by Schattschneider (2003), with her detailed and comprehensive analysis of the ascetic practices of the population living near Mount Akakura in the Tsugaru region (Aomori prefecture). Also in this *genre* are the works of Sawada (2004) on personal improvement practices in nineteenth-century Japan and the studies of Reader and Walter (1993) and Reader (2005) on pilgrimages.

The third *genre* is constituted by works devoted to the study of so-called Japanese popular religion(s) (*minzoku shūkyō* 民俗宗教).[7] In these studies, ascetic practices often appear as popular religious practices or as a part of so-called popular religious phenomena. However, the aim of these books is to understand and analyze popular religion and not ascetic practice in particular. In fact, asceticism cannot be understood as just as an element peculiar to Japanese popular religions and consequently dismiss any form of ascetic practices present within established religious movements. Indeed, Stephen Covell has pointed out how these 'popular' practices constitute a relevant part of the life of established religious bodies as well, giving the case of the Tendai school.[8] Neglecting the *kaihōgyō*, for instance, as a marginal component of Tendai religious practice would lead to a false picture of what the Tendai school is today. Many people developed an interest in the life and activities of the school mainly through the works of its most charismatic figures, and among them are many *kaihōgyōja*.[9]

Lastly, some issues about Japanese asceticism are discussed in works not directly pertaining to religious practice or religion in general. Some of them deal with the concept of the human body in Japan or in Asia,[10] while some are totally unrelated to religious studies, such as studies about the traditional customs of rural populations.[11]

Another problem in conducting a systematized analysis of Japanese asceticism emerges not only from the variety of the phenomenon, but also from the difficulties inherent in defining the cultural boundaries of the term *asceticism* itself. Western scholarship seems in this sense particularly keen to vacillate between extreme views. While the theological tradition maintained asceticism as being a characteristic of Christianity alone, eighteenth- and nineteenth-century philosophy began to conceive of non-religious forms of asceticism. For instance, Kant interpreted asceticism in the moral sense as a way to fulfil one's duty, while Nietzsche spiritedly described asceticism's paradoxicality.[12] In more recent times, others, starting from Weber, expanded the significance of asceticism to the secular sphere.[13]

Following Weber's work, asceticism has subsequently been portrayed as an inherent component and cause of art, philosophy and politics, among other disciplines.[14] Some have even argued that 'asceticism and related phenomena in classical India and in Christian antiquity suggest the existence of a universal, shared, innate human predisposition', thus postulating the existence of some form of ascetic universalism.[15] This ambiguity also implies that asceticism as a cultural category could be the object of study in various disciplines, including ethnography, anthropology and philosophy, and thus that a more comprehensive picture can be produced by following a multidisciplinary approach.

This book is divided into five chapters, following an increasingly inductive trajectory. In the first chapter, I will analyze the origin of the term 'asceticism' in order to deconstruct its contemporary western understanding and verify its suitability to the Japanese cases. This meta-analysis of what asceticism has meant, and means, in western culture(s) is necessary in order to justify our choice of terms, precluding the risk of superimposing a western terminology onto a similar but totally unrelated phenomenon present in another culture. I shall thus begin with a critical assessment of the categories *asceticism* and *body*, which will determine the appropriateness of the terms to 'translate' into non-western phenomena. It emerges that the contemporary western understanding of the concept of *asceticism* has been heavily informed by the perception of the human body that originated in the modern period. Deconstructing the origins of this understanding shall bring us to reconsider the concept of 'the human body' and its multi-faceted and diachronic development, acknowledging the variety of its contextual meanings. By taking into account such meanings in their inherent historicity we shall be able to delineate points of contact between different traditions, and continue our analysis of Japanese ascetic practices as a meaningful case inside the broader theme of asceticism.

Chapters two, three and four constitute the central body of this work and are devoted to the examination of Japanese ascetic practices. I shall begin with a description of a variety of specific phenomena, mostly from the data collected during fieldwork, which will be then analyzed and systematized in order to elaborate more general considerations. Following such approach, these chapters start with the systematization of a number of ascetic phenomena in respect to their *mode* of practice (occasional or systematic: Chapter 2), and their relationship with their agents and the ways in which ascetics build their identity (Chapter 3). These chapters employ anthropological methodology to treat the data collected through participant observation in the field, combined with a phenomenological approach derived from my direct performance of a variety of practices. In this respect, I consider the direct experience of the ascetic effort also as a privileged form of hermeneutical approach to an ascetic *text*: the ascetic tradition is, as we shall see, also an *embodied tradition* which needs to be scrutinized by means of one's body. Moreover, in more practical terms, some contexts of practice (like certain secret places or rituals) are only accessible to practitioners, and they would be thus impossible to scrutinize by a mere observer. To these issues, we must add the necessity to partake in the ensemble of inner feelings, bodily sensations and physical expressions constituting the nonverbal traits of the ascetic discourse, a dimension that cannot be experienced if not in the practice itself.[16] Chapter 4 will then explore the meaning of Japanese ascetic practices within their social and religious context. While still employing fieldwork data to delineate significant case studies, here a stronger emphasis is placed on hermeneutical questions regarding the role of the human body in asceticism and its relationship with the spatial dimensions of the ascetic practice. From this analysis emerges how a parallel society can develop in the course of an ascetic practice or retreat, and how this 'ascetic society' can, at certain times, overlap with the ordinary 'extra-ascetic' society. The capacity of the ascetic to navigate between these two social dimensions will be highlighted as one of the fundamental reasons for his/her social significance. In the second part of the chapter, the comparative analysis of two sectarian 'versions' of the same practice will also show how similar ascetic practices can be easily incorporated into different orthodoxies to serve different agendas, while preserving their characteristic of benefit and power-producing activities, regardless of the differences in the doctrinal hermeneutics used to justify them.

The final chapter re-reads the traditions previously examined with the aim of constructing a theory for asceticism as a form of philosophy of the body. In this last part I will individuate some fundamental constants in ascetic practice in the categories *body*, *pain* and *power*. I will also argue that asceticism can be eventually understood in more general terms as a path towards the 'ontological progression' of the practitioner's body, inspired by an ideal perfect condition or 'perfect body'. Consequential to this ontological progression is the production of 'power', understood as an inherent property of the ascetic effort. The analysis of ascetic practices in contemporary Japan conducted in this work thus suggests the existence of an 'embodied ascetic tradition' developed in parallel with the sectarian and doctrinal understanding of the practices themselves: the principal *text* of this tradition is the body of the practitioner, and ascetic performance can hence be understood as a form of bodily hermeneutic of such tradition. This 'embodied tradition' appears therefore to be free to circulate among different religious environments, where it can be re-interpreted following the doctrinal or sectarian agendas of each specific religious body.

Philosophical anthropology

This study begins with a more heuristic anthropological approach and progressively shifts to broader philosophical considerations. I would accordingly like to consider this book an essay in philosophical anthropology. The concept of philosophical anthropology is of course not of my making but is found in existing scholarship by leading scholars from Max Scheler to Maurice Merleau-Ponty, although with some degrees of variation in definition.[17] A commonly accepted definition is:

> [the d]iscipline within philosophy that seeks to unify the several empirical investigations of human nature in an effort to understand individuals as both creatures of their environment and creators of their own values.
> (*Encyclopaedia Britannica, ad vocem* 'Philosophical Anthropology')

This, however, is certainly not an exhaustive description of the whole 'discipline', particularly given the ambiguity and degree of interpretation required by the category 'values', which in this case refers not only to ethical assumptions but also to the ways in which people understand themselves and their environment.[18] Particularly interesting is the approach of Michael D. Jackson, considered the founder of existential–phenomenological anthropology, in which ethnographical fieldwork and ontologically oriented existential theories are utilized in order to analyze modes of being and interpersonal relationships in a variety of cultural settings.[19] Jackson's approach starts from concrete and practical situations and attempts to recreate and explain these situations as they are perceived and experienced by the other. Inspired by these approaches, I thus consider my active participation in many of the ascetic practices analyzed in this study as a necessary prerequisite for their theoretical analysis as well, and I have actively pursued my *performance* in the practices as a hermeneutical activity.

The possibility of moving from an empirical investigation of the field towards more general philosophical considerations, which characterizes the approach of philosophical and existential-phenomenological anthropology, proves to be particularly suited to the analysis of performance-based religious practices, such as asceticism.[20] The fact that asceticism can be conceived as an 'embodied tradition' necessarily prompts us to access such tradition directly, by direct participation in the ascetic efforts object of our analysis. In this process, I used my body as a tool through which I could enact the same degree of bodily hermeneutic performed by other participants in the practices object of my enquiries. This allowed me to translate their bodily texts into terms immediately understandable by my body, rather than my mind.[21]

In hermeneutical terms, practising alongside ascetic practitioners, performing the same acts and undergoing the same hardships, can be compared to reading the scriptures of a certain religious tradition. A book or a script becomes a *text* in the moment in which it is read and interpreted by the reader. The text in this case is not a passive object of enquiry. It 'reacts' to the presence of the reader, returning to life as soon as the reader opens the first page of the script.[22] In the hermeneutical process, the text thus exists in a liminal space between the script and the reader, making the reader a part of the text itself. When reading scripts written by other individuals, who are often distant from us in space or time, we can only hope that the text we produce is equal or similar to the one in the author's original intention. The same process can be said of bodily hermeneutic. Reproducing the performance of ascetic acts by means of one's body generates the *text* in which the body of the performer is part of the text itself. Also, in this case, we can only hope that the text produced by the bodies of the other practitioners is similar to ours. This bodily hermeneutical action is thus not dissimilar from more traditional forms of hermeneutic of oral or written sources, and I believe that it can be used as a recurring methodological approach to address performance-based religious phenomena in a more general sense.

As far as the analysis of the agents of asceticism is concerned, my direct participation in the practices also allowed me to critically assess the declarations of my referents. When the practitioners I interviewed spoke about their feelings of 'gain', 'loss', 'exhaustion' and so forth, I was able to critically evaluate their verbal translation of bodily sensations precisely because I accessed the same bodily text myself. Failing this, it would have been difficult to understand if such utterances were the genuine attempt to translate elements of the 'embodied tradition' of asceticism into words, or if they were just the reinterpretation of doctrinal and sectarian tenets. In other words, it would have been like asking what somebody thought of a book, without having previously read the book myself. The fact that I could rely on bodily texts directly accessed through performance allowed me, for instance, to uncover the existence of the two parallel levels of hermeneutic of the ascetic tradition (bodily and doctrinal), and to use them to explain the phenomenon of circulation and sharing of similar practices inside different religious environments.

1 Translating fundamental categories

The human body and asceticism

In this chapter I would like to critically reconsider whether the term 'asceticism' may be proficiently employed as an umbrella-term to 'translate' phenomena that, in the Japanese context, are indicated instead by a variety of different terms. This elucidation is necessary, since our attempt to analyze the way in which ascetic practice is understood in Japan may at first create a picture which partially clashes with the contemporary meaning of the word 'asceticism' in English. Concepts such as 'self-denial', the contempt for one's body, the 'mortification of the flesh' and so forth appear to be such common-sense characteristics of asceticism that they do not even need to be questioned. Yet if employed uncritically, this definition of asceticism would place the whole purpose of the present work under question. During the course of this analysis, it will become clear how Japanese ascetics consider their bodies as a precious device for empowerment and religious practice, and in no circumstance does a sense of contempt or disregard ever arise. It is thus pivotal to the purpose of this study to establish if the term 'asceticism' can be meaningfully applied to the Japanese context, or if this is only another attempt to superimpose a western category onto a similar but unrelated phenomenon present in another culture.[1]

Research focused on overarching categories like 'family', 'work', 'education' and so on often incur the risk of taking the understanding of such categories for granted, to the point of transforming into 'universals' ideas, modes of thought and theories which are, instead, the product of an historical development in a certain cultural and social area. For instance, the simple idea of 'family' in Europe underwent significant changes through the classic, medieval and modern periods, and none of the archetypes elaborated in modern anthropology can provide a comprehensive and unambiguous definition of what may otherwise be perceived as an 'obvious' concept.[2] Undertaking a similar endeavour in an extra-European environment would only complicate the matter further, raising important epistemological doubts on the actual possibility of employing western historically and culturally constructed categories to describe other cultural contexts. Seemingly simple subjects of study such as the 'Japanese family' or 'Chinese family' imply strong epistemic prejudices on the existence of the entity 'family' in the Japanese or Chinese cultural contexts, and the fact that such entity can correspond – or can be made to correspond – to what 'family' means in the English language and related worldview.

The problem of exchange of ideas between different cultures is inherently connected with the problem of 'translation'. Translating categories between different cultural systems often results in the construction of what Simon aptly defines 'interlingual creation(s)' – interlingual signifiers that, rather than 'translating'[3] a meaning from one linguistic system to another, conceptually mediate between the two different cultural contexts.[4] The intellectual space of such mediation resembles what Pratt called the 'contact zone'; that is, the space 'in which peoples geographically and historically separated come into contact with each other and establish ongoing relations',[5] unfortunately too often in hierarchical and hegemonical tones. A large portion of postcolonial translation theory's concerns are implicitly directed against the monologue of western culture vis-à-vis other cultures, and the imposition of western intellectual categories on different systems of thought and worldviews.[6] A further problem that needs to be highlighted is that the practice of translation tends to consider terms in the target language as monoliths with univocal and unambiguous meaning, without taking into account the fact that they are indeed historical entities, subject to a range of variations and interpretations in the course of their existence. Ricoeur synthesizes this problem with remarkable clarity in the concept of the inherent 'polysemy' of words; namely the fact that, although a particular historical moment can privilege a certain meaning over others, all the other meanings are still embedded in the word, constituting its spectrum of nuances and applications.[7] Translating, thus, does not only mean to individuate the most likely correspondence of terms between two languages, but to mediate between different cultural systems inside a conceptual 'contact zone', where the translation terms are employed as a points of contacts between different systems of thought. This necessarily requires us to take into account the historicity of words in the target language, and to deconstruct their polysemy *before* we consider the possibility of their application to a different situation. This action is indeed a form of translation as well, a translation through the historical existence of a word and its polysemy, what Ricoeur calls 'intralinguistic translation'.[8] For our study, this operation is necessary in order to unveil which of the many meanings of the terms 'body' and 'asceticism' are given precedence in the contemporary understanding of such terms, and then to reconsider its suitability as a *point of contact* between different traditions. This last operation, the interlinguistic translation, is not only a semantic problem, but it will define the epistemological interspace within which our study is conducted.

Terminological problems in the definition of 'asceticism'

In Japan, the religious practices that may be defined as 'ascetic' are generally indicated by terms like *kugyō* 苦行 (painful practice), *aragyō* 荒行 (dreadful practice) and more often with *shugyō* 修行 (practice, in general). All these words are constituted by two separate segments. The last character *gyō* that occurs in all the words has a wide range of meaning; the original pictogram depicts a stylized crossroad ╬ giving the character the primary meaning of *travel*, *move* and, by extension, *act*.[9] The character *gyō* is often employed to create terms that have a meaning close to 'practice', 'act', as in the following examples,

水行   *suigyō*: literally the practice/technique of water, indicating water ablutions
一行   *ichigyō*: the 'single practice'
寒行   *kangyō*: the practice in the cold.[10]

In Japanese, *gyō* is also used in words that have the more neutral meaning of *skill*, *technique* or, more generally, *deeds* and with no implicit religious overtones,

興行   *kōgyō*: (to give) a performance, a show
難行   *nangyō*: difficult deeds
悪行   *akugyō*: bad deeds.

The character *gyō* acts in all these cases as a general marker for the word-set 'practice/activity', while the specific meaning of each whole term is given by the first character. It must be noted how there is no word in Japanese indicating 'asceticism' in an abstract sense; instead, there is a generalized use of the suffix *gyō* 行 to mark all the specific practices' names.[11] This marker (*gyō*) is utilized to convey the meaning that bodily practices are indeed something to be *done*, to be experienced in a practical, physical form.[12] The marker also acts on the practice agent itself, as a very common term to indicate the ascetic practitioner is indeed a *gyōja* 行者 (person who acts). The term *gyōja* does not identify any sectarian figure, however, as it is widely employed in both 'popular' and established religious environments. At the same time, there are some people engaged in austerities who do not identify themselves as *gyōja*, such as in the case of the *rōhatsu sesshin* 臘八接心 that we will examine in Chapter 2. These ambiguities are reinforced by the general lack of doctrinal explanations surrounding the practices themselves. In many cases, the theoretical meaning of an ascetic feat is not explicitly explained; and even when an explanation is given, it is often something that has been attached retrospectively onto a practice having a much more ancient tradition.[13] The transmission of the 'ascetic tradition' seems instead to be based on a somewhat high degree of what I would like to term 'technical empiricism'. In other words, bodily practices are enacted because of their practical functionality, and to the extent that they have some practical effectual result, from simple bodily purification to possible huge personal empowerment.

Another function characterizing 'asceticism' as a cross-cultural phenomenon seems to be that ascetic practice can be understood as the process or the construction of a *holy person*, and this is true of many Japanese ascetic phenomena as well.[14] As we shall see, the practitioners acting within an established religious body find themselves generally more highly ranked at the end of the practice, while the training of people like *itako* イタコ (blind mediums) and *gomiso* ごみそ

serves the purpose of (re)configuring their social and professional position.[15] Thus, no practice is apparently done without purpose.

Based upon these premises, a fundamental question needs to be asked: What makes a religious bodily practice an ascetic practice? The obvious answer would be 'the use of the body' – but this still leaves a number of doubts and contradictions to be resolved. A number of practices, particularly within Buddhism in Japan, require the use of the body in order to be enacted, such as the *odori nenbutsu* 踊り念仏[16] and *zazen* 座禅,[17] but these acts or series of acts are never perceived or officially sanctioned as being 'ascetic'. It seems that what may be labelled as 'ascetic' should be something *extra-ordinary*, in contrast with the *ordinary* bodily practices present within a certain religious body. The difference from normality is, in this case, the quantity of effort and austerities used to 'malleate', to reshape, the human body for a spiritual purpose.[18] The presence of 'pain' then becomes the specific marker of the ascetic experience, although not pain for its destructive power. Quite the contrary, it is for its power to transform the practitioner and to awaken in him unknown energies.[19] Indeed, the presence of pain seems to connect all the ascetic experiences of the world, regardless of their different socio-historical contexts. Many explanations for this 'need for pain', mostly by physiologists and psychologists, are strongly biased, however, by the clear-cut distinction between body/matter and mind/spirit belonging to modern western culture. Works like Glucklich (2001),[20] for instance, tend to put all possible phenomena of self-damage on the same level without any effort to individuate a possible correlative taxonomy among the different groups of acts. Comparing the self-mutilation of stressed American teenagers to the practice of Zen monks, for instance, is like understanding the two sentences 'John eats the apple' and 'the apple eats John' as being the same simply because they contain exactly the same words.[21]

In the case of the ascetic, 'pain' must be understood in relation to its context as a culturally influenced category rather than as merely a physiological absolute. The word *kugyō* is thus better understood as a *relative* (e.g. the harder, more painful practice) rather than as the *absolute* concept of 'hard, painful', which is much more difficult to define unequivocally. In fact, even ordinary religious practices may be painful. Everyday *zazen* or extended chanting of the *nenbutsu* or of the *Lotus Sutra* may be distressful and challenging; however, in these cases, pain is more a by-product rather than a consciously employed tool. The purpose of the ascetics is to go a step further than the 'ordinary' level of pain so as to grasp and control its power and thus utilize it as a tool for their own benefit.

Body, pain, power and eventually asceticism are the categories that we thus need to 'translate' for the purpose of our study.

Asceticism and the human body: an intralinguistic translation

Alphonso Lingis' opening words for his seminal work *Foreign Bodies* – '[t]he human body is a product of natural evolution, but also of our own history'[22] – suggests how, far from being an 'obvious concept', the attempt to define such a fundamental thing as 'the (human) body' is in fact paradoxically daunting. A basic feature that unquestionably seems to belong equally to everybody appears to be impervious to conceptual generalizations, and it is remarkable how the attempt to outline a *History of the Human Body* ended up as no more than a gargantuan collection of *fragmenta*.[23] Our process of 'translation' will thus start from 'the body', by exposing the inherent polysemy already present within the European cultural contexts where its contemporary understanding developed.

The body and its contemporary meaning

Although, as modern people, we have been brought up in a cultural environment that claims that all human beings are equal, the bases of this equality paradigm are founded not in the physicality of being *man*,[24] but on something transcending it. Humans are thus equal because they possess a common constitutive essence (or more eloquently, a *substance*) that is indeed the same for everybody.[25] The *substance* of humanity, whether called spirit, soul or mind, is hidden in this 'fleshy bag' and thus the physical differences we may find in individual human beings do not undermine the basic equality of the human condition. In other words, we are all human beings, regardless of how our (human) body may appear.

This assumption is firmly consolidated in western thought well beyond the limits of religious beliefs. Even a materialist thinker like Hobbes, for instance, organized his theory about human nature around the immaterial categories of imagination, speech, reason and mind.[26] At the same time, considering man purely from the perspective of his flesh body seems to have been perceived by Hobbes as a gross understatement, denigrating humanity to a mere thing.[27] Having interiorized this kind of cultural legacy, when modern men and women try to think about the generic expression 'human body', what almost instinctively arises in their mind is an image resembling a picture or drawing in a medical book: an 'organism', namely a set of biologically constituted parts that work together in a series of mechanical processes. The failure of one of these processes may result in disease or even death. Healing, therefore, means nothing more than 'fixing' the bodily failure, the same way that a mechanic may fix a broken engine. This conception of the body is eminently *analytical*: the various organs are seen as semi-independent entities and often the dysfunction of one part of the body is considered to be unrelated to the others.[28] The attitude of modern men and women towards their own bodies in the last two centuries appears to have been shaped by this basic position.[29] Although the body is still the object of many concerns, these are mostly of a utilitarian nature. The body must be healthy; otherwise the 'spirit' residing in it will not be able to move or act according to its desires. It must be kept in good condition because a dirty or poorly maintained body could act as a major obstacle in social relationships. In other words, the body must be maintained with care in order to employ it most effectively to fulfil the spirit's desires.[30]

What we were not taught to think is that *we are* our bodies. The underlying assumption is that being a 'human being' means something different from being merely a body; more precisely, it means to be something more than it.

If something more than the merely physical exists in the human being, that *thing* is implicitly supposed to be subtle and to transcend our ordinary physical reality. The 'realm of the soul' is thus conceived of as having a parallel but clearly distinct ontology, as the soul inherently possesses a set of durative qualities that the body seems instead to lack: i.e. perfection, purity and permanency. When the two terms are juxtaposed in the common expression 'body and soul', the impression is that this phrase is trying to reconcile two opposites, two natural enemies. Something 'good for body and soul' seems to mean something good for all possible manifestations of the human being in a hierarchical order, from the lowest to the highest.[31]

Judaeo-Christian dualism

This clear-cut dualistic and incompatible stance between body and spirit is generally advocated in Christian culture, with its alleged antagonistic dualism between body and soul, material and spiritual. The structure of this dualism and its relationship with Christian asceticism is, however, much more complex.

Simply saying that Christianity resolved the relationship between body and soul by emphasizing the primacy of the latter and forgetting the former would represent a blunt oversimplification of a much richer tradition. Also, it would be inappropriate to think that this dualistic perception involving matter/body and spirit/soul has its roots only in Christian beliefs. Indeed, if we try to describe the figure of the ascetic practitioner using these conceptual tools alone, the natural result is the image of a religious zealot seeking nothing but complete and destructive self-denial. Let us examine for a moment the following definitions of *asceticism*:

> From the Greek *askesis* meaning 'self-denial'. The view, which has been an important theme of both Eastern and Western religion and has played a minor role in philosophy, that the body is to be denied, possibly mortified, in order to make possible the purification of the soul in its progress towards salvation.
>
> (William L. Reese, *Dictionary of Philosophy and Religion*:
> *Eastern and Western Thought*: 34)

and

> A variety of austere practices involving the renunciation or denial of ordinary bodily and sensual gratifications. These may include fasting, meditation, a life of solitude, the renunciation of possession, denial of sexual gratification, and, in the extreme, the mortification of the flesh.
>
> (David Crystal, *The Cambridge Encyclopedia*: 75)

These examples come from two widely diffused encyclopaedic works – one about religion and one on more general knowledge – that are clearly inspired by the same dualistic distinctions affecting our general perception of the human body. In both cases, it is taken for granted that *asceticism* involves, above all, the negation of the body. Moreover, in both definitions the original meaning of the word ἄσκησις itself seems to be forgotten. Ἄσκησις means 'training' and, more specifically, 'physical training', as it was originally used in reference to the athletes training for the Olympic games in ancient Greece.[32] In the Christian religious environments of the first centuries of the Common Era, the same term was employed with a wide spectrum of nuances, among which just a few exceptions may be considered to be utter self-denial.[33] It is true that those practices were projected onto the pre-existing, well-consolidated background of a clear dualism between body and soul. However, the body/soul or matter/spirit dualism alone does not necessarily justify the idea that a deeply religiously committed person must deny his physicality as a whole in order to obtain spiritual benefits.

The problem of this sharp dualism between body/soul arises well before Christianity; it is found in Judaism and is reflected in its strict normative law, developed mostly to prevent bodily pollution, as both body and soul were going to be subject to the 'Judgement of God'.[34] In this respect, it is interesting to note how many sources of pollution come from the human body itself, such as menstrual blood or contact with a corpse.[35] However, the biblical view is not free from contradictions. *Body* and *flesh* are treated like synonyms throughout the books of the *Tanakh*, yet their meaning changes widely, from the long series of prohibitions in Leviticus[36] and Numbers[37] up to the Psalms, where, interestingly, the body is often portrayed as the inseparable companion of the soul.[38] The frequent juxtaposition of the two terms 'body' and 'soul' is indeed remarkable, and it is meant to express the harmonic wholeness of the human being rather than its irreconcilable dualism.[39] Although the *Tanakh* vacillates between varied definitions of the human body – of the *flesh* – from impure hindrance to exalted object, at least one fact seems to be consistently clear: the body is an integral component of what we call 'the human being', not an accessory object. It would therefore be quite inappropriate to affirm that Judaism promoted the total negation of the body for the sake of the soul. Indeed, it is the body that bears the irrevocable sign of the alliance between man and God in the circumcision.[40]

Many of the most important changes in the understanding and conceptualization of the human body that we can find in Christianity, vis-à-vis the Old Testament biblical tradition, have arisen in relationship to the question of defining the human nature of Christ. *Human nature* in this context means that a distinctive characteristic of Christ was the fact that he possessed a true human body. In Christian soteriology, the body of Christ is the vehicle of salvation, as his passion is possible only through his physical sufferance. Christ's body is also an exalted body. It is resurrected, *perfected* to become an ontological bridge between the present world and the kingdom to come. The mystical unity of the Church is therefore represented by the participation of the believers in the mystical body of Christ: '[He] will change our lowly body to be like his glorious body, by the power which enables him even to subject all things to himself'.[41] In the Acts of Paul, the apparent desire for the complete negation of one's physical dimension does not arise from Paul's wish for the annihilation of the human body, but from his quest for its exaltation from coarse matter to a body of perfection.

> Since we have these promises, beloved, let us cleanse ourselves from every defilement of body and spirit, and make holiness perfect in the fear of God.
>
> (2 Corinthians 7:1)

> As it is my eager expectation and hope that I shall not be at all ashamed, but that with full courage now as always Christ will be honoured in my body, whether by life or by death.
>
> (Philippians 1:20)

Paul's cry – 'Wretched man that I am! Who will deliver me from this body of death?'[42] – does not express his desperation for a condition without remedy, but rather the contrary; the harshness of the labour necessary to fashion his body as the perfect temple for the perfect soul.[43]

Gnostic critique

A significant part of early Christian apologists sought to exalt the human body to a higher dimension.[44] What then emerges from this brief summary is that the idea of *body* and *soul* as two antagonists forever stuck in an irreconcilable fight was not a fundamental position of Christianity either. It is thus not surprising that excessive behaviours and ideas against the human body were already viewed with suspicion in the early centuries of Christianity, to the point of being proclaimed heresies. The Gnosticism of the early centuries of the Common Era is one of the most notable cases among a number of early *quasi*-Christian ascetic movements that was oriented on this kind of dualistic/self-destructive stance. In Gnostic soteriology, the path of the soul towards liberation was an ascending path towards God that unavoidably had to leave the world behind. The contraposition between God (perfect, unlimited) and the physical world (defiled, limited) led necessarily to a pessimistic view of 'matter' in general, and not only of the human body. Matter was uncompromisingly identified with evil, while liberation from sin and defilement came to coincide with liberation from matter and the material world itself.[45] The human body was confined, in this case, to the realm of matter and thus was conceived as a mere physical obstacle to the achievement of a superior dimension. In this sense, the works of the Gnostic, Valentinus (*c*.100–*c*.155), and his mythical cosmology were particularly influential in widening the irreconcilable fracture between spirit and matter.[46] Reality pertained to the spiritual universe, the *Plérôma*, while matter was no more than a 'grotesquely distorted mirror of the spiritual riches of the 'Place of Fullness [the *Plérôma*]'.[47] Moreover, in regard to this 'keeping the distance' with the material world, the Gnostic soteriological process itself is often compared by Gnostic writers to a journey.[48] The spatial element of the journey, even if understood as merely symbolical, enhances the idea of distance from the material and earthly dimensions. The ontological dualism finds its strongest expression in this kind of spatial dislocation. Death, the point of no return, is therefore to be identified with the final liberation from the material realm, the apotheosis in the life of the dedicated person.[49] All Gnostic adepts were somehow dedicated ascetics. They attempted to neglect physical reality through the passive negation of their bodies and bodily needs, especially sexual drive.[50]

Christian ascetic narratives

As noted earlier, the Gnostic clear-cut dualism should not be taken as representative of the early Christian ascetic attitudes towards the human body, even in the rigidly controlled monastic environment of the first centuries of the Common Era. The Gnostic attitude towards body and matter in general was in fact considered somewhat excessive, even in those times. Criticism of Gnostic ideas came from numerous contemporary saints, from Clement of Alexandria to Origen.[51] In their critique, it is easy to recognize the same effort to reconcile the two dimensions of body and soul which we saw as an underlying theme in the Judaic and Christian traditions in general. This can also be clearly seen in the attempt to build a less antagonist distinction between body and spirit in the narratives portraying the life of the saints belonging to the most extended group of desert-dwelling ascetics in the Eastern Roman Empire: the Desert Fathers.[52] Although they were to all effects 'renunciants' of this world, such renunciation did not imply the complete withdrawal from matter, and from one's body as a whole. The role model for this generation of ascetics was Saint Anthony the Great (251–356); a few passages from *The Life of Anthony*, compiled by Athanasius of Alexandria, provides us with a sense of his importance.[53]

> Anthony spent almost twenty years alone practicing his ascetic discipline this way, neither going out, nor being often seen by anyone … This was the first time that he came out of the barracks and appeared to those who came to see him. When they saw his body they marvelled at his sweetness, for he had not exercised yet he was not weak as though he had come out from fasting and fighting with demons … They saw that the thought of his soul was pure, and he was not sorrowful and suffering.
>
> (Athanasius of Alexandria, *The Life of Antony*: 91–2)

The *exempla* from *The Life of Anthony* became highly inspirational for the following generations of Eastern Christian ascetics.[54] What they probably saw in his example was a possibility for the redemption of their body, rather than the Gnostic pursuit for absolute withdrawal. Being used to seeing the strict practices of Gnostics and the excesses of the Stylites, the crowd waiting at the exits of Anthony's voluntary exile was probably expecting a completely different person to emerge from his solitary retreat. What they were waiting for was the emaciated and putrid body of a man who had finally succeeded in neglecting his own materiality. What they saw instead was the fresh, young body of a newly born saint. In Anthony's *persona*, body and soul stopped their endless fighting. The soul was exalted but the body was not destroyed; indeed it was purified, made a perfect vessel for the perfect soul. Through his ascetic efforts, Anthony changed the role of his body, transforming it into the image of his soul, a tool permitting him to reveal the invisible as a visible form. It is true that the body was still 'matter', but the ascetic practice brought a substantial change in that matter. Anthony's body 'received a portion of that spiritual body which is to assume in the resurrection of the just'.[55] In the case of Anthony, his spiritual achievements are hence definitely manifested in his flesh as well.

The communities of mountain-dwelling Fathers that later settled near important urban centres like Antioch also adopted a milder, non-destructive stance towards their bodies.[56] The motto of their monastic *regulae* was indeed the word 'moderation' rather than 'annihilation'. The target of their practices was to win back the body to its former perfection rather than destroying it, to 'undo the sin of Adam'[57] which, in their understanding, was primarily greed for forbidden food.[58] The Gnostic-inspired quest for abandoning and neglecting the body was here reinterpreted as a process to 'perfect the body' so as to make it a more suitable place for the soul of a saint.[59]

Despite their ambiguous relationship, we must, however, admit that body and soul never achieved a completely equal status within the Christian religious context. In this regard, *The Life of Anthony* tells us that:

> [h]e used to say that it is necessary to give all one's time to the soul rather than to the body, but to concede a little time ['a little bread' in the Coptic version] to the body for its necessities; all the rest of the time, however, one ought to devote to the soul and what is profitable for it.
>
> (Athanasius of Alexandria, *The Life of Antony*: 155)

In other words, the physical appearance of Anthony was an external 'symptom' of his holiness, but not the cause. In his case, the human body is still the object of a 'passive' kind of asceticism: letting go, letting things be as they are. For the Fathers, the body did not reach, and would never reach in Christianity, a status equal to the spirit. The perfect unity of soul and 'spiritual body' was not achievable in the present, but belonged only to the future life in the Kingdom of God.

Modern dualism

From this brief sketch of early Christian positions about the body/soul dualism and asceticism, we have reasons to believe that the understanding of the human body as something distant or unrelated to one's soul or mind – what we have noted as constituting our proper *substance* as human beings – did not straightforwardly stem from the nonetheless clear dualism present in the Judaeo-Christian culture.

As mentioned earlier, the idea that instinctively comes to the mind of modern men and women when they think about the 'human body' is something resembling an illustration in a medicine book. Modern medical science has heavily redefined our view of our own bodies in an attempt to provide an effective response to what has been for centuries the major bodily problem known to humanity: disease. In Foucault's words, 'the human body defines, by natural right, the space of origin and of distribution of disease'.[60] Enlightenment's scientists and medical doctors fought a battle 'against what they saw as the ignorance and superstition of both the entrenched politico-religious establishment and folk traditions'[61] and eventually won. Starting from the seventeenth century, medical science became more and more identified with the sciences of the body *par excellence*, while philosophy, literature and religion had to renounce their theories about bodily physiology as they were apparently unable to compete with this new kind of 'scientific' knowledge. It is only at this point in history that the perception of the human body turned into what it is now: the body as an organism, a fleshy machine deserving a range of studies comparable more to mechanics than philosophy. When the human body was dissected, analyzed and recorded in the first attempts of practical pathological anatomy, it ceased to be the 'temple of the spirit' and it was reduced to a mere *thing*.[62] Modernity, thus, rather than creating a new meaning for the body, exalted one aspect of its polysemy (its materiality) above the others. In this process, much of the rich and fluid relationships between the physical component of the human being and its more subtle counterpart (however conceived) were lost. Moreover, the aspects of the body polysemy that proved to be pivotal in religious practice (the ideas of 'sacred', 'perfect', 'spiritual' as attributes or conditions of both body and soul) were then ascribed exclusively to non-bodily entities, like the soul or the mind, thus widening the gulf between the two.[63]

For our study, this means that since that time, any activity involving the body for spiritual election was regarded with suspicion, and the effort of the ascetic came to be regarded as close to the desperate attempts of a lunatic.[64] To modern men and women, the efforts of ascetic practitioners of different places and times, from the solitary life of the Stylites to the excesses of the infamous Indian *aghorīs*,[65] seem to be nothing but mere acts of senseless violence towards our physical being, a physicality that has no purpose other than to support the existence of our mind or spirit in this world.[66] The Enlightenment's primacy of mind over body redefined the otherwise fluid and vast spectrum of interactions between these two entities as a one-way relationship. It is the body that can benefit from the mind deeds, as in the case of modern medicine, but not the opposite.[67]

I would argue that the 'modern' sense of repulsion and marvel in regard to ascetic exertions derives from this medico-scientific stance towards the human body and not from any innate disregard of the body inherent in Judaeo-Christian culture. As we have seen, although Judaism and Christianity maintained body and soul as two separate entities while clearly pointing out the primacy of the latter, they never tried to conceive of the 'human being' without the presence of the 'human body', Gnosticism being the notable exception. This would have been impossible in a cultural-religious environment in which the body was still believed to be a thing shaped by the hands of God. Disregard towards the body would therefore have represented an unacceptable negation of the goodness of a portion of God's Creation.

Asceticism and the body: interlinguistic translation issues

If we take into account the development of the meaning(s) of the term 'body' in a diachronic sense – namely, if we recognize the polysemy inherent in the historicity of the term – we can attempt a more conscious interlinguistic translation, together with the concurrent translation of meanings from different cultural contexts. From the Indian *sādhus* and *śramanas* up to the Chinese Taoist ascetics and Japanese 'marathon monks', although the relative cultural-religious background may differ greatly, the idea of the human body as a possible 'tool' that can be employed for spiritual empowerment underlies a variety of disciplines that can – in light of the above premises – be proficiently *translated* as 'ascetic'. Rather than building a systematic comparative argument, I would like here to 'chart a map of viewpoints' on body and asceticism, in order to individuate 'point of contacts' that can help us in delimiting the conceptual space within which our study is conducted.[68] Issues about the human body present in Theravāda, Mahāyāna and Tantric Buddhism will now be examined in order to extend the range of views that we may apply to our polysemic understanding of the entity 'body' in cross-cultural terms.

Theravāda themes

The set of rules that underscores the spirit of the *Patimokkha*[69] about bodily needs draws an ethical and meta-noetical picture of the entity 'body' remarkably not so distant from that of the Desert Fathers. Food, sexual and appropriate social behaviour are the same fundamental issues which the regulations for the life of monks in Theravāda Buddhism addressed.[70] Here is an extract from some of the principal rules in the *Patimokkha*.[71]

> Whatsoever Bhikkhu who has taken upon himself the Bhikkhus' system of self-training and rule of life, and has not thereafter withdrawn from the training, or declared his weakness, shall have carnal knowledge of any one, down even to an animal, he has fallen into defeat, he is no longer in communion (Pārāgika 1).

> The emission of semen by design, except by a person sleeping, is a Samghādisesa (Samghādisesa 1).

> Whatsoever Bhikkhu, being degraded, shall, with perverted mind, come into bodily contact with a woman, by taking hold of her hand, or by taking hold of her hair, or by touching any part of her body- that is a Samghādisesa (Samghādisesa 2).

> Whatsoever Bhikkhu, being degraded, shall, with perverted mind, address a woman with wicked words, exciting to passion as those of a young man to a maid – that is a Samghādisesa (Samghādisesa 3).

Now those medicines which may be used by the sick Bhikkhus – to wit, ghee, butter, oil, honey, molasses – when they have received them, they may enjoy them, storing them up to the seventh day. To him who exceeds that there is a Pākittiya offence involving forfeiture (Nissaggyā Pakittiyā 23).

These are also complemented by a number of minor rules.[72] The discipline here is clearly meant to foster the use of the body in the correct way, not to neglect it permanently. The traditional narrative of the life of the Buddha is inspired by this same effort in finding a middle way between two excesses: the sensual life of pleasures of the young prince Siddhārtha in his palace and the harsh austerities of the first part of his life as a wandering *Sraman□a*. These two phases in the life of the Buddha are strongly connected with the physical condition of his body as well. They mark the two opposites that should be avoided by the genuine truth seeker: blind enjoyment of one's body and blind negation of it. Again, the role of religious practice is not to destroy the body but to maintain it properly in order to make it the perfect vehicle for salvation. In the words of the *Vinaya*, 'devotion to indulgence of pleasure in the objects of sense is inferior, low, vulgar, ignoble and leads to no good',[73] and at the same time, 'devotion to self-torment is painful, ignoble and leads to no good'.[74] As in the case of Anthony mentioned above, the physical appearance of the religious practitioner is a symptom of his holiness, though not its direct cause. The attitude of Theravāda Buddhism towards the human body also represented the attempt to reconstruct the social significance of the practitioner, in addition to the body being a 'tool' for religious practices. The body is in fact first 'desocialized' through the privation of its fundamental physical needs – food, sexual intercourse and shelter – and then 'reconstructed' in the parallel but distinct social environment of the Sangha.[75] It becomes a perfect body for the perfect collective body of the monastic community in which the ideology is physically actualized.[76]

Mahāyāna themes

As in the Theravāda tradition, a consistent number of verses throughout Mahāyāna literature seem at a first glance to openly denounce the weakness and burden of the human body. The *Vimalakīrti Nirdeśa says*:[77]

Friends, this body is so impermanent, fragile, unworthy of confidence, and feeble. It is so insubstantial, perishable, short-lived, painful, filled with diseases, and subject to changes. Thus, my friends, as this body is only a vessel of many sicknesses, wise men do not rely on it.[78]

But few lines later in the same *Vimalakīrti Nirdeśa* we also read:

Therefore, such a body should repulse you. You should despair of it and should arouse your admiration for the body of the Tathāgata …

Friends, the body of a Tathāgata is the body of Dharma, born of gnosis. The body of a Tathāgata is born of the stores of merit and wisdom. It is born of morality, of meditation, of wisdom, of the liberations, and of the knowledge and vision of liberation.[79]

Following the *Trikāya* doctrine,[80] Mahāyāna Buddhism constructed what we may define as a new form of 'reconcilable duality' between two different dimensions of the same body: the material and the sacred, the 'vessel of many sickness' and the body 'of merit and wisdom'. The body is therefore considered capable of potentially becoming the perfect expression of the *Dharmakāya*. In the same way, it may also become the utmost and most precious offering. One passage of the *Lotus Sutra* about the Bodhisattva Medicine King appears to be inspired by the tension towards the exaltation of one's body that conversely makes the capacity of voluntarily renouncing it the highest possible merit:

'Though by resort to supernatural power I have made an offering to the Buddha, it is not as if I made an offering of my own body'. Straightway then he applied [to his body] various scents … and then burnt its own body.[81]

The example of the Bodhisattva Medicine King fostered a number of self-sacrificing ascetics, particularly in China. A variety of evidence proves that their biographies were well distributed and widely read[82] and that they were regarded by many as the ultimate example of the exaltation of the Dharma, despite some criticism by Confucians and Taoists.[83]

It is consequently possible to draw a parallel between these two conceptions of the human body in Theravāda and Mahāyāna Buddhism with that in Judaism and Christianity respectively. Theravāda Buddhism is, in Collins's words, 'conceptually dualistic' and its treatment of the body and conscience seems to come close to the Jewish idea of the human being as constituted by body and soul altogether.[84] In both cases, the religious effort is a *normative* one; the *Vinaya* and Leviticus share the same concern with the body – to make our 'fleshy vessel' a dignified dwelling for a properly dedicated religious person. The normative framework is enacted to nurture the human being as a whole and not to deprecate its physical constituency. What it is still missing is the possibility to actually (and thus physically) reform one's body so as to allow it to reach the same ontological subtle level advocated for the soul or for the condition of perfect non-attachment that is Nirvana.

A leap forward is achievable in Tantric Buddhism, thanks to the presence of a *perfect body* ideal in which the two dimensions are reconciled into their final perfection. Here, the ascetic practitioner is no longer the 'properly behaving' dedicated man, but a man that enacts through his body a redefinition of his own ontological constituent elements. An important development of this theme about the human body in Japanese Buddhism is the possibility of 'attainment of Buddhahood in this very body' (*sokushin jōbutsu* 即身成仏). A clear explanation of its doctrinal base is offered by Kūkai's interpretation of the *Trikāya* doctrine. In Kūkai's thought, the totality of the *Dharmakāya* (Jp. *hosshin* 法心)[85] is seen in the four manifestations of Mahāvairocana (Jp. Dainichi 大日) as expressed by the fourfold mandala system constituted by:

a   The *daimandara* 大曼荼羅 (Skr. *Mahā-mandala*, the great mandala) in which Mahāvairocana is seen in his physical extension,

b   The *samaya mandara* 三昧耶曼荼羅 (Skr. *Samaya-mandala*) representing the omnipresence of Mahāvairocana's intention (*samaya*),

c   The *hō mandara* 法曼荼羅 (Skr. *Dharma-mandala*) representing Mahāvairocana's preaching of the Dharma and

d   The *katsuma mandara* 羯磨曼荼羅 (Skr. *Karma-mandala*) representing the activities, actions of Mahāvairocana.[86]

From this basic scheme, Kūkai developed a highly sophisticated cosmology based on the mandalization of the whole of reality: the *daimandara* representing sentient beings, the *samaya mandara* the environment and non-sentient beings, the *hō mandara* rules and precepts and the *katsuma madara* the Tathāgata salvific activities in the world.

This mandalic system should not be seen as merely a symbolical representation of the Tathāgata but as the true nature of all phenomena, and in this sense it can also be understood as a cosmological theory. In the case of the *daimandara*, we have Mahāvairocana and the other deities represented in their bodily forms, which correspond to sentient beings in their bodily forms. That all the mandalas and bodies are, in Kūkai's words, 'inseparably related to one other' means that 'in any of these four the remaining three are present'.[87] This also implies that, via bodily practice, it is possible to interact with all the dimensions that constitute reality. Kūkai points out that the practice of the body is the performance of *mūdras*.[88] As the bodies of Mahāvariocana are distinct but at the same time 'inseparably related to one other', when the practitioner performs the correct sequence of *mudras*, his bodily gestures, and by extension his body as a whole, is identified with Mahāvariocana in its wholeness. He therefore truly becomes a 'Buddha in his very body'. The notion of *sokushin jōbutsu* underlies more or less explicitly a great part of the ascetic practices still alive in Japan. Some practitioners actually do express their sense of achievements with the expression 'while doing this, I am a Buddha',[89] implicitly identifying performance with an ontological condition.

To summarize, in all the examples sketched so far, the human body seems to be endowed – or it has the potentiality to be endowed – with supernatural forces, and is consequently capable of handling such supernatural powers as well. This is indeed the tool that the ascetic practitioner employs in ascetic practice. Ascetic practices can be thus understood as methods aimed to trigger the body's potentiality for power in order to achieve a wide range of results. This concept opposes the dualistic, Gnostic-like vision of the antagonism between soul and body in which the ascetical aim should be the annihilation of the latter for the monistic exaltation of the former. Instead, each of the examples provided show how the final aim of the ascetic practice is to resolve a different kind of opposition – that between the ordinary body and the sacred body. The dichotomy that we must take in account is hence between these two bodily dimensions: material and sacred, imperfect and perfect, unclean and pure etc., all referring to a common entity – the body of the practitioner. The ascetic practice works in this case not as a moral repressive action but as a sort of unwritten and unspoken epistemological process allowing the practitioner to 'access' his own body and to grasp and direct its full potentiality.

This understanding also dismisses doubts about the suitability of the term asceticism for the present research. It is possible to aptly translate the term 'asceticism' interlinguistically if we focus on those meanings in its polysemic spectrum where different traditions do converge; namely on the dignified and powerful figure of the ascetic, as well as on the determinant role of the body in religious practice. The contempt for our physicality that informs our present understanding of asceticism as 'self-denial' seems to rest mainly on its modern (mis)understanding alone.

Body and society: meanings in context

If we try to understand the ascetic practitioners only through the emphasis they place on their physical dimension and the meaning given to the body, we may be tempted to see them as self-centred individuals whose practices led them to drastically reject 'non-holy' society as a whole and eventually to 'wander alone as a rhinoceros'.[90] Moreover, the very idea of polysemy rests on the assumption that meanings are diachronically developed inside a context, at the same time following and influencing its historical being.[91] In Ricoeur's words we are now moving 'from the word to the sentence',[92] where the *word* is the ascetic's body and the society where we find it 'thrown'[93] represents the social *discourse* where we are trying to situate the meaning of the categories pivotal to our study.

The heading of this section intentionally draws from the title of Brown's masterpiece about early Christianity: *The Body and Society*.[94] Indeed, the most basic interaction of a human being with the society or community surrounding him unquestionably has at its very base the need for the presence of the body. By its mere physical presence, the body performs the basic function of affirming one's existence, while other manifestations of the self must rely instead on what we can generally define as 'performances'. Speaking, moving, shouting: any phenomenon that may show our presence as individuals to a possible 'other' necessarily passes through what, in the most general way, may be defined as an 'act' or its results.[95] The body, in this case, seems to be the only notable exception. We can acknowledge the existence of the 'other' by simply looking at his body without any need of further performances to prove his actuality. Even a corpse still performs a number of functions; it is the physical witness of the past life of a human being. This property of the body can also be seen as a sort of inherent performance as well. The social function performed by the body is first of all to visually and physically discriminate the individuals that eventually form the group or society at large. This form of discrimination is apparently perfectly defined between the individual beings themselves (no middle point or series of infinitesimal points exists between two individuals, between two bodies), while liminal or superimposed space exists between the entities and their environment (the body is instinctively seen as something different from the environment in which it is acting).

The major problems that our body gives us are seen primarily in terms of its wide variety of desires. It is not surprising that, as the body is a material thing, all its desires are material as well. As we have seen, the 'codes of rules' of the ascetics, from the Desert Fathers' *Regulae* to the *Vinaya*, are specifically aimed at upsetting the natural cravings of our bodies. The desire for food is offset by the practice of fasting, the desire for sex is offset by extreme sexual continence and so on; in Flood's words, asceticism is 'the reversal of the flow of the body'.[96] What I want to point out here is that society seems instead to be based on the efforts to both satisfy *and* discipline those same needs. Money and economic systems were born in order to regularize the basic supplies for everyday living – originally, mainly food – while the family started taking shape as a form of regulation of the sexual impulse, eventually becoming a standardized archetype for the relationship between men and women.[97] Accordingly, we may say that society took shape as a solution to the practical needs of human beings, with most of these needs being physical. Consequently, it is nearly inevitable that a person who withdraws completely from those basic needs may find himself an outsider from civil community entirely. An unmarried, not materially producing nor consuming person is easily relegated to the ranks of marginality, carrying little or no impact on society as a whole.[98]

All ascetics pertain, in various ways, to this 'desocialized' category of human beings. One may then be misled to classify the ascetic as a marginal person who voluntary rejected society so as to live in a parallel world of his own. Surprisingly, the evidence we can produce about the lives of these people brings this apparently obvious conclusion into question.

Ascetics and societies – ascetic societies

The relationships of 'solitary' ascetics, from the Desert Fathers to the *pratyeka-buddhas* of early Buddhism, show a variety of rich patterns of interaction with both their respective local communities and society at large.

In the first centuries of Christianity, for example, we can see the development of monastic communities on the margins of rich urban environments, particularly in the eastern area of the late Roman Empire. The followers of those monastic orders achieved freedom from the secular patterns of life by systematically upsetting all of its components. To the hard work of late empire cities, they preferred – indeed insisted upon – the total renunciation of any manual labour; to the noisy crowds, the solitude of their mountain dwellings; to the craving for richness, their total poverty.[99] And, what is important for our study, to the hedonistic indulgence of urban life they chose abstinence: abstinence from food, sexual intercourse and body care in general. Their message was clear: 'we are not of this world', we are 'holy persons'. Since, as we have seen, the body is the 'thing' that discriminates individual entities within the social context, they neglected their own relevance to the secular world by neglecting the needs of their bodies as a whole.

However, an indirect consequence was the constitution of a parallel and new kind of society: the world of the ascetic community. This society was supposed to be the reflection of the qualities of the soul on Earth: perfect, incorruptible, holy. A sacred city made up of sacred men.[100] Not surprisingly, the secular city was not indifferent to the nearby ascetic community. Bishops and priests used to visit the ascetics' caves for short periods of training, sometimes to enhance their spiritual awareness, but more frequently to ask for the powerful intercession of the Fathers.[101] The people of cities like Antiochia were well aware that the nearby community of mountain ascetics was a sort of safeguard for their secular life.[102] Society, therefore, was not indifferent to the figures of the ascetics but was actually eager to incorporate more and more 'holy persons' into its ranks.

In the late fourth century, when Christian communities had clearly consolidated in cities, we can in fact observe the emergence of a new caste of 'urban' ascetics: the dedicated virgins. There were two main circumstances for the ordination of a dedicated virgin. In the first case, the ordination and what it represented was deeply desired by the family, with the will or aspirations of the girl playing little or no part. In the second case, there were a number of self-dedicating virgins that apparently took the decision by their own choice.[103] In what we may call a 'forced dedication', the basic issue underlying such an act seems to be the will to 'fabricate' a 'holy person' for the sake of family, community and society progressively. In the words of the *Canons of Athanasius*: 'In every house of Christians, it is needful that there be a virgin, for the salvation of the whole house is that one virgin'.[104] Therefore, the dedicated girl works as a salvific means, regardless of her true inclinations and will. She is merely a sort of 'human ex-voto'.[105]

By contrast, the intentions of the self-dedicating virgins were often in sharp opposition to the girl's family will, with this tension frequently assuming spectacular tones. The virgin often pronounced her vows in front of the entire community assembled in the church; this public expression of religious zeal was frequently accompanied by miraculous manifestations that eventually confirmed the sanctity of the girl's choice.[106] A number of issues may lay behind the decision to remain a virgin against one's family will. I would not dare, of course, to question the genuine religious commitment of many of these girls, but an analysis of this phenomenon may lead us to relevant conclusions. It is useful here to refer to the concept of social freedom. Despite the fact that, to our modern eyes, a life of prayer and seclusion may not seem appealing at all to a person looking for 'freedom', we should bear in mind that the married life of a fourth-century girl generally offered circumstances that were little better. Seclusion would have taken place in the house of the husband rather than in the father's, while *pietas* and proper religious behaviour were considered a must-have characteristic for a married woman as well. Thus, the choice for the future was apparently within a very narrow spectrum: be a wife or not, have sexual relationships or not. This was the only freedom allowed to a 12-year-old girl; from this point of view, that many wanted to opt for the religious seclusion is not unreasonable. The real issue at stake was again sexual abstinence, and that was the only point on which, perhaps for the only time in her life, a teenage girl could have the last word.

Sexual abstinence is indeed one of the main points of schism between the ascetic renunciants of all times and places and their societies. Sexual matters are the important underlying element of a progressive social scale that runs from the couple to the family, village or city up to society in general. Sexual intercourse is the basic engine from which extensive social relationships are developed.[107] Moreover, begetting children was also a vital requirement for ancient societies; with their short life-expectancies, they were always fighting against the threat of death and extinction.[108] It is not surprising then that the first arguments proposed by mostly non-Christian writers against chastity stressed how this kind of extreme sexual continence was undoubtedly capable of being 'disruptive of the human race' as a whole.[109]

As put forward by Brown, because society was so dependent on marriage and sex for its survival, pursuing a different pattern of sexual behaviour was a viable way of pursuing personal freedom from those same social institutions – and was not simply a way to constrain the flesh for spiritual purposes.[110] The point at stake was not just spiritual election but also something almost equally valuable: freedom from secular institutions. Renunciation of sex and marriage was the most important means that the ascetic could employ in order to free himself from the traditional pattern of life.

We have, then, a somewhat ambiguous and fluid relationship between early Christian ascetics and the secular society surrounding them. On the one hand, the desire for social freedom as the prerogative of a dedicated religious life was counterbalanced by the constitution of a new kind of 'holy society'. On the other, secular society proved to be reluctant in letting go of the palpable amount of power that the presence of a 'holy person' may represent. It consequently developed devices to maintain relations with the renunciants' holy world, to the point of producing and nurturing some of them inside its very bosom. In the large spectrum of possibilities that such an interactive picture may offer, it is indeed their reciprocal negation that seems to be the least and most improbable option.

The fluid and ambivalent relationship between the figure of the ascetic and its social context seems to be present in a variety of other cultural contexts, from the India of the early Buddhist monastic communities to China and Japan as well. For example, in Mahāyāna environments, the term *pratyekabuddha* (Buddha only-for-himself, a term designating the solitary practitioner) gained the negative nuance of a sort of 'second-class Buddha' capable of attaining enlightenment for himself but unable to teach the Dharma to others. In the literature of the early *Pali* canon, he is in fact placed second, after the *sammāsambuddha* (the Buddha Teaching the Dharma), in the ranking of the 14 kinds of people worthy of receiving offerings.[111] This also means that, before the birth of a *sammāsambuddha*, the *pratyekabuddha* is the highest form of human being. These two typologies of Buddhas are understood as incompatible, in fact, at the birth of a *sammāsambuddha*, all the *pratyekabuddhas* must enter *parinirvāna* immediately, as previously advised by the *devas*.[112]

However, the idea that there is no place for *pratyekabuddhas* when a *sammāsambuddha* is present in the world seems to imply that *pratyekabuddhas* were somehow performing part of the roles or duties of a *sammāsambuddha*. This may seem contradictory, because the *pratyekabuddhas* do not generally preach; indeed, they hardly even speak. Rather, it is their physical presence that makes the difference. Although they were supposed to dwell alone in the forest for most of their time, these ascetics also had to beg for their alms (*bhikśa*) and this inevitably led them to be near settled areas.[113] The very act of begging places them 'in a social context' and permits them to fulfil their unspoken teaching and salvific actions. We may understand the act of receiving *bhikśa* from laypeople as working primarily in two ways. First, it performs a moral discrimination between *good* and *bad* men: the good ones are those who can understand the status of the *pratyekabuddha* and so give him alms willingly, while the bad men scold or despise him.[114] Second, after receiving a proper offering, the pratyekabuddha often gives a demonstration of some sort of supernatural power.[115] This supernatural 'show' confirms the status of the donor as a proper believer while at the same time may elicit faith in the non-believers witnessing it.

All of these 'social functions' are generally performed without the need for the *pratyekabuddha* to speak even a single word. He performs his duties merely through his presence and the performances of his body. He does not communicate verbal or intellectual concepts. He is, in himself, a living witness of the power of the Dharma, and his presence is indeed his social function; the moment in which he is identified as something extra-ordinary is thus relevant for the ordinary. The final purpose of his 'renunciation' is not to cut all forms of relationship with society for good; what the practitioner is seeking in his extra-mundane effort is indeed freedom, personal freedom from secular institutions and from a secular way of life. As in the case of the Desert Fathers, the solitary ascetic seems to be not so lonely. Once again, it appears that we cannot easily identify him and his role if we do not superimpose his figure onto the background of the 'normal' society or community which he is supposed to renounce. Even ascetics that apparently try to escape this kind of background-related definition eventually find themselves deeply entangled in a complex web of relationships between society and their own figure as 'holy person'.

All of the efforts of the Taoist Immortals, for instance, seem to be directed at preserving their bodies for eternity in a condition of total non-dependence on their environment and on other people.[116] The appearance of the Taoist Immortal is therefore one of a human monolith: totally excluded (or better yet, self-excluded) from the passing of time that characterizes the normal world, and from the basic needs of normal people (food, shelter and so on).[117] A closer look at or, rather, inside his body, however, will reveal a completely different picture. Some examples from the *Lingbao* scriptures may clarify this point.

> Inside the human body there are the 36,000 gods of the Three Palaces and Six Bowels. When the human body does evil, the bodily deities report it to the Three Officials. When the human body does good, they recommend the person for selection as an immortal …

> If you contemplate internally and guard what is Perfect, what is Perfect will
> not depart from the body … If you lose your jing and lose your qi [instead],
> your myriad [bodily] gods will escape and fall out. Your gods will wander
> and your qi scatter, and your [bodily] form will perish as an empty corpse.
>
> (*Gong quizhong jing*, 21a, quoted in Eskildsen,
> *Asceticism in Early Taoist Religion*: 125)

These deities inhabit an inner spatial dimension that is compared to no less than
a full-fledged country, including mountains, fields, streams, lakes and, of course,
inhabitants.[118] The Taoist Immortal is, for this reason, by no means a loner but
entertains instead a full set of social relationships with a completely featured spatial and social context that happens to be not outside his body but inside.

The ascetic process through which a man can become immortal is inspired by
this conception of oneself. The progressive refusal of food up to complete abstinence is not a 'cause' or 'symptom' of sanctity, a visible manifestation of inner
spiritual qualities, but instead no more than a method, a technique aimed at get-
ting rid of all possible external influences and restoring the body to its intrinsic
perfection.[119] This perfection, however, does not escape the need to be confronted
with a referent in order to affirm itself. The referent, in this case, is the Inner
Country, and for that country the Immortal performs the same duties of protection and nurturing that, as we examined in the other context, an ascetic performs
for an external country, city or kingdom. Moreover, although many Immortals
simply 'disappeared' into the woods, many others were seen living at the margins of settled areas in a fashion not so different from the Desert Fathers of early
Christianity, pursuing altruistic deeds for the welfare of the local communities.[120]
Their effort may be seen as an attempt to harmonize external and internal space to
reach the ultimate unity that is the Tao.

Furthermore, the particular diet of the Immortals may give us another sugges-
tion about their idea of their relationship with the environment. The first step for
immortality was abstinence from cereals. This did not mean, however, complete
and immediate abstinence from any kind of food, as cereals were replaced by pine
needles, sesame, tree bark etc.[121] Besides being informed by doctrinal issues, this
kind of diet has a practical basis: the preferred retirement place for the aspiring
immortal was, in a very general sense, 'the mountain'. Pine needles, tree bark etc.
are in fact the only kind of food that can be easily found on a mountain; the manner of their consumption was also a part of popular knowledge, a sort of survival
lore for times of famine.[122] Cereals and pine-derived foods are also closely linked
with two different kinds of spatial environments. The former are grown by man's
labour in cultivated land while the latter grow spontaneously in wild mountains.
Taking this into account, I think that it is possible to trace an existential paradigm
between the path of the Immortals and their land.

What the Immortal practically does is to renounce any artificial way of life
(cereals, cooked food, clothes) in order to restore the proper, essential condition
of his body, a body that, if purged by all accumulated impurities, is intrinsically
immortal. This belief is reflected in the Immortal's diet as well. He gives up all

food that maintains some relationship with the 'artificial' world and embraces a diet made of food coming spontaneously from the 'world as it is' and therefore closer to the Tao.[123] None of the food that can be found on a mountain is culti- vated. To the choice of food itself is applied the same principle of 'letting things [be] as they are', which the Immortal tries to apply to his very body. This also triggers an identification between him and the environment. The Immortal is, in fact, not just 'the man of the mountain', but also the 'mountain man', the man-became-a-mountain.[124] With the mountain, the Immortal shares all the char- acteristics of thusness, stasis and spontaneity that make the non-settled wild land (and the food that it produces) closer to the Tao than any other place. Again, the efforts of the ascetic seem meaningless if they are not projected onto some sort of background. Once more, the meaning of the 'ascetic' gains his value of exception- ality in confrontation with normality.

Conclusions

In this preliminary chapter, we have outlined some fundamental points involved in the definition of 'asceticism' and 'ascetic practitioner, and considered to which extent the meaning and concept of Ἄσκησις can be employed to translate other form of religious practice based on bodily exercise. Our attempt necessarily brought us to reconsider the central concept of 'the human body' not only as a given physical fact, but also as a culturally-developed form of self-awareness, which we have taken into account in its polysemic diachronic development. Paraphrasing Kuriyama, instead of reducing the subject of asceticism to a par- ticular synchronic 'definition', we have tried to 'chart a map of viewpoints on the body'[125] from varied times and places, taking advantage of the inherent polysemy of the concept to bridge between different cultural contexts, where '[n]either tradition can be reduced to a single viewpoint'.[126] Rather than a stiff comparative exercise, this chapter was meant to synthesize the 'point of contact' where our study is conducted: the body as the cultural *locus* where the ascetic tradition is preserved and through which it is transmitted, its social functions and contextual meanings.[127] By taking into account such meanings in their inherent historicity we may indeed find points of contact between different traditions, and continue our analysis of Japanese ascetic practices as a meaningful case inside the broader theme of *asceticism*.

2 Modes of ascetic practice

In Japan, it is possible to witness the performance of bodily religious practices that can be labelled as 'ascetic' in a variety of circumstances. Further, it is not unusual to see the same kind of practice as part of the activities of various often unrelated religious groups.[1] It is therefore necessary to somehow rationalize the observable phenomena in order to pinpoint common practice trends which may help us in individuating themes and tendencies in Japanese asceticism. The purpose of this chapter is first to provide a broad classification of Japanese ascetic phenomena by taking into account the circumstances or *modes* of practice, which will be divided thus:

1 Occasional borrowing of ascetic acts by various religious practices
2 Practices taking place outside an institutional religious body
3 Practices taking place within an institutional religious body.

These three *modes* are ordered in a progressive scale of physical commitment and doctrinal complexity; significant case studies will be proposed for each *mode*. We shall then undertake an analysis of occasional ascetic feats that can be witnessed, for instance, in local festivals (*matsuri* 祭) or as a part of the so-called 'popular religion' (*minzoku shūkyō* 民族宗教) activities. We will then examine more structured ascetic practices held by organized 'popular' religious groups, such as Ontake-san 御岳山 devotees. Lastly, we will examine some highly refined practices carried out in established religious environments, such as Shugendō 修験道 and Sōtō Zen 曹洞禅.

In order to provide more detailed conceptual tools for our analysis, I would like to first break down the category 'asceticism' into two distinct elements: *ascetic acts* and *ascetic practice*. Ascetic acts, such as standing under a waterfall, walking on fire, fasting etc., if considered only as bodily activities, possess no contextual meaning; they represent mere bodily actions in which the meaning corresponds to the action itself. If we want to attempt to analyze ascetic acts from a hermeneutical perspective, they represent the visible signs pertaining to the objective referent arbitrarily associated to them.[2] In other words, they occupy the same function that individual words have in language. Shouting a series of words merely juxtaposed one to the other does not mean one is speaking, as simply hurting oneself without method and purpose does not mean practicing any kind of asceticism.

Those methods and purposes are indeed what constitute the *practice*, namely a series of ascetic acts ordered and motivated by a complex and structured internal taxonomy.

An ascetic practice can accordingly be read as we can read a book: by knowing the meaning of its individual words (the *ascetic acts* involved), referring it to a syntax and a grammar (the *taxonomical disposition* of the acts), thus obtaining as a final result the whole text itself (the *practice*). Uncovering the meaning of an ascetic practice therefore requires a proper hermeneutical effort aimed at understanding a coordinated set of bodily activities rather than the mere analytical enquiry of the individual acts per se.

Occasional borrowing of ascetic acts in various religious practices

The occasional borrowing of ascetic acts in various religious practices represents a widely diffused mode of practicing asceticism in Japan. This is often the case with various ascetic experiences in so-called 'popular religions' (*minzoku shūkyō*). The picture here is thus extremely heterogeneous and difficult to systematize.[3] The implementation of *extra-practice* ascetic acts, that is, the use of *isolated* ascetic acts within an ordinary religious practice, may be seen at local festivals, harvesting rites, New Year's rites, occasional retreats of laypeople and so forth.[4] In these circumstances, the use of ascetic feats might be functional but not central to the main purpose of the religious event, such as performing water ablutions (*mizugori* 水垢離 or *suigyō* 水行) before a *matsuri* or a sacred dance (*kagura* 神楽) performance, or it can represent the culminating moment of an otherwise non-ascetic religious event. Lastly, a series of ascetic acts can be incorporated more or less loosely into popular forms of worship, particularly in pilgrimages related to sacred mountains.[5]

Ascetic acts in festivals and sacred dances

The most widespread representative of this first type are sizable ascetic acts acting as a part of the preparations preceding a *matsuri*. People closely connected with the *matsuri* organization, such as those who carry the portable altar (*o-mikoshi* 御神輿), prepare the food and offerings, play music etc., generally perform a simple set of ascetic acts which have a cleansing effect, such as the aforementioned *suigyō* or *mizugori*. Purificatory water ablutions have been documented in *matsuri* preparation all over Japan, and they are still a common sight at these occasions.[6]

Kagura performances also often require the performers to undergo similar purificatory rituals, and occasionally embed a few other ascetic acts as well. The following considerations are based on a fieldwork observation conducted in April 2007, about a *kagura* performance held from 7 to 9 April in Iwakuni, Yamaguchi prefecture (see Figure 2.1). Simply named *Iwaguni kagura* 岩国神楽, the event is held only once in seven years and constitutes a major occasion for collective celebration for the local area.

The *kagura* dancers – all male, ranging from 10 to 20 years old – perform water ablutions every day around 6.30am at the river near the *kagura* stage.[7]

Figure 2.1 Iwaguni *kagura*, Iwakuni, Yamaguchi prefecture (7–9 April 2007)

Figure 2.2 Iwaguni *kagura gyōja* (8 April 2007)

Their technique is very simple and unorganized; each participant simply pours a number of buckets of water from the river on his head before rushing back to the stage dressing room. Although this event was held in early April, the weather was still bitterly cold and even standing in the open completely dressed was a somewhat uncomfortable experience. When briefly interviewed, all dancers agreed that the *mizugori* were unpleasant at first, but also agreed that they became more accept-able after the first few buckets as the body started to react; in their words, 'energy is drawn out of the body'.[8] Then, a pleasant sensation of 'heat' and 'mental sharpness'

Figure 2.3 Iwaguni *kagura gyō* (8 April 2007)

would accompany the dancers during their very long daily performance, which lasted from early morning until late at night (about 7.00am until 10.00pm).⁹

The climax of the event is marked on the second day (8 April) by another ascetic-flavoured performance, where a white-clad *gyōja* climbs a 20-metre-high pine trunk set next to the stage area (see Figures 2.2–2.4).

The climbing itself can be understood as a form of ascetic feat, in the sense that it involves physical effort and a certain amount of personal risk; and indeed, it was called '*gyō*' by many of the people attending.

Figure 2.4 Iwaguni *kagura gyō* (8 April 2007)

However, the risk factor is definitely diminished by the steel security belt that the *gyōja* attaches to the long rope that he will climb – not without a certain exhibitionist gusto – to the top of the pine.

Once there, he will break small twigs from the tree branches and throw them to the people below, who will treasure them as powerful amulets (*o-mamori* お守り). The *gyōja* I interviewed after the performance, about the way in which he prepared himself for the day's feat, simply said that he 'did *shugyō* in the mountain' in the weeks before, without further explaining what kind of *shugyō* he performed. Pressed by further questioning, he eventually explained it as 'walking in the mountain' but without hiding a certain surprise for my lack of knowledge of what '*shugyō*' is.[10]

This is possibly one of the simplest examples of the use of asceticism within a religious practice that I had the occasion to observe in Japan. The ascetic acts have no direct connection with the theme of the *kagura* itself and seem to serve very simple circumstantial purposes: bodily purification in the case of the *mizugori* and the production of amulets from the tree together with a somewhat proud display of supernatural qualities (which we shall see in other cases shortly). Even more interesting is the uni-dimensional understanding of asceticism which collapses the whole category '*gyō*' into a single form – mountain-walking practice – and the ascetic (the *gyōja*) as its performer.

We may wonder if such cases – particularly the simple pre-*matsuri suigyō*, so widespread throughout Japan, and so univocally understood as a purificatory practice – may be considered a form of asceticism at all or if a sub-category of *quasi*-ascetic feats is required. However, following the premises for this chapter, it seems inappropriate to break down the category 'asceticism' into further subcategories, since this can lead the concept of bodily practice as meant by ἄσκησις to blur with other forms of bodily agency. For the purpose of this work, it is more appropriate to maintain the use of the term 'asceticism' in relation to this kind of simple phenomena as well: bodily practices involving/requiring/producing a certain degree of physical effort and possibly pain.[11]

We can also assume that, in this kind of 'popular' setting, the awareness of the doctrinal meaning of the ascetic act is so faint that the act itself is not understood as such by its performer, as the vague answers to some of the interviews referred to earlier on confirm. The distinction between *popular* and *established* does not seem to be a determining factor for the understanding of the ascetic phenomenon. Indeed, asceticism appears to be a sort of 'transversal' activity that is not in direct relationship with the complexity of the doctrinal background of its relevant environment. In other words, simple, unexplained and empirically-focused practices appear in both popular and established religious environments, as we shall see later on, while the opposite also proves to be true: more demanding feats are part of the ascetic traditions of both popular and established religious groups. Pertinent to this last point are the ritual and ascetic events accompanying the celebration of the *Ontakegyōja harumatsuri* 御岳行者春祭, annually held on 10 April at Ontake-san jinja 御岳山神社 in Honjō 本庄, Saitama prefecture.

Paths of embers and ladders of swords

Religious beliefs and practices associated with Mount Ontake in Nagano prefecture have been documented since the Kamakura period. Mount Ontake worship remained primarily a local cult activity until the seventeenth century, when the number of pilgrims began to increase because of the popularity of mass pilgrimages in the Edo period.[12] This led to the formation of a great number of devotee confraternities (*kō* 講) which benefited particularly from the performance by local mediums of shamanic practices called *oza* 御座, where a kami possesses the body of a medium and speaks through him (*kamigakari* 神憑り).[13] By the middle of the nineteenth century, there were around 500 large and small confraternities scattered all around the Japan. Following the religious policies of the Meiji government, in 1882 local confraternities were unified into a religious sect called Ontakekyō 御岳教, while the confraternities allied themselves with other official Shinto sects. Nowadays, some Ontake confraternities are still affiliated with Ontakekyō while others are attached to pre-war Shinto sects or Shugendō groups. A number of new Ontake groups also formed after the Second World War.[14]

The Ontake-san jinja *harumatsuri* of Honjō gathers Ontake devotees mostly from the Saitama area, but many participants also belong to a variety of confraternities from other areas of Japan, as well as those who attend on an individual basis.

The richness of the *harumatsuri* is such that it would require a work of its own to describe all the numerous rituals and activities that take place more or

Figure 2.5 Hiwatari (fire-walking) practice at Ontake-san shrine in Saitama (10 October 2006)

less simultaneously on the shrine grounds. For example, in a corner near a small Inari shrine, it is possible to see a small group performing a rice-pot (*kamado* 竈) divination ritual, where a small quantity of rice is cooked in a pot heated by a fire fuelled and controlled by enchantments (*kaji* 加持). The rice is then divided into small sachets and distributed to the attending crowd to be added to the following day's family rice in order to ensure good health.[15] In another corner, a young participant performs a simple esoteric ritual, empowering the purificatory wand (*gohei* 御幣) to be used later by tracing the nine syllables of the *kuji* 九字 spell in the air with the aid of a wooden *vajra*. At the same time, in the centre of the shrine precinct, a number of older practitioners are blessing the wooden sticks (*goma-ki* 護摩木) to be used in the fire ritual (*goma*) with a few simple spells. All of this activity is drenched in screaming, laughter and a general sense of expectation for the two main events to come.[16]

Walking on fire: hiwatari

In contrast to the *Iwaguni kagura*, here two ascetic performances constitute the main event of the *harumatsuri*. They are the *hiwatari* 火渡り (fire-crossing) and the *hawatari* 刃渡り (climbing of the ladder of swords). The *hiwatari* is possibly the most common Japanese ascetic feat, together with water ablutions and the

Figure 2.6 Hiwatari (fire-walking) practice at Ontake-san shrine in Saitama (10 October 2006)

mountain-walking practice. Fire-walking events are very common in *matsuri* all over Japan, such as the *Daihiwatari matsuri* in Hachiōji (Tokyo) or the *hiwatari matsuri* on Takao-san (Tokyo).[17] They are often performed on the embers of a spent *goma* fire, such as in the case of the Ontake-san jinja *harumatsuri*. In the first hours after lunch, the *goma* pyre is prepared with a quantity of fuel approximately four by two metres, which is subsequently set ablaze (see Figures 2.5–2.7).

The *ontakegyōja* then start to circle the *goma* fire while chanting the Fudō Myōō 不動明王 mantra, occasionally alternating with the recitation of the *Heart Sutra* (*Hannya shingyō* 般若心経), using their cymbals to keep the pace while throwing the *goma-ki* previously blessed onto the pyre. In about half an hour, the flames are spent and the remaining hot embers are spread out to cover a path about five metres long. A circular sacred rope (*shimenawa* 注連縄) adorned with numerous white paper strips (*gohei*) is set at the beginning of the fire path, mark-ing the limit where the *shugyō* begins – and from which, once passed through, is not possible to turn back, as I was told by the people around me while queuing for our turn.[18] The first to cross are the Ontake devotees, in order of rank and senior-ity; the first few people apparently faced the scorching heat from the charcoals not without injury and they had to be carried away in the arms of other practition-ers. When the time to cross comes, it is necessary to put one's feet first on a heap of salt set right after the *shimenawa* 'door'; it is then possible to stride forward

Figure 2.7 Hiwatari (fire-walking) practice at Ontake-san shrine in Saitama (10 October 2006)

across the burning path.[19] After the crossing, one can collect a few spent embers, considered to be powerful talismans (*o-mamori*).

Since I was one of the first laypeople to cross, the charcoal was still very hot but the walk was definitely not impossible. There had been no formal 'instructions' on how to cross safely, but from the chit-chat of the people in line to cross the embers, I received a variety of valuable information: 'First, try to have some salt sticking to your soles, that will protect you from the heat'; 'then keep your feet flat, try not to move the surface of the embers – the external layer is in fact quite cool'; 'and walk without pausing, or you will get burned'.[20] As I have often observed during my fieldwork, the transmission of a great part of the ascetic 'lore' and practical techniques is left by the practice leaders to the informal training offered by senior practitioners on a voluntary base (see Figures 2.8 and 2.9). Following these practical instructions, I crossed the fire path without injury and with no more than a sensation of slightly annoying heat under my feet.[21] Was this no more than fumbling over burning ashes, with just enough technique to make it to the other side without unwanted blisters? While pondering this issue, I was about to wash my feet with the help of a water hose when an old lady came to scold me gently: 'If you wash your feet, you also wash away the power (*chikara* 力)! Keep them as they are at least until bath time!'[22] I thanked her and then slipped my socks over my dirty feet without further complaint.

This balance between what we earlier called the 'technical empiricism' of an *ascetic act* and the more subtle meanings and powers associated with it remains a constant feature of the ascetic experience, apparently unaffected by the level of complexity of the surrounding religious environment, the awareness of the performer or the doctrinal justifications supporting the act itself. Certainly, as we will encounter later, there are incredibly articulated ascetic practices in which layers of meaning and doctrine enrich the whole experience exponentially. Yet from these very early examples, one characteristic of the ascetic phenomenon emerges that we can associate with the term 'performativity'. Performativity has become a recognized term in ritual theory, and I feel that it is possible to apply its many overtones to the analysis of asceticism as well.[23] One feature of asceticism is that it is supposed to produce some kind of 'real' effect. Asceticism is clearly not created solely for the symbolizing of doctrinal meanings or cognitive traditional values.[24] Rather, this equation seems to be reversed: it is doctrine that participates as an 'added value' to the enactment of an ascetic act, on the same level of 'technical empiricism', to add performative power to the ascetic act itself. The people performing the *hiwatari* were in fact managing all the available parameters (the context of the *jinja*, the *goma* ritual, the skills needed to cross the fire safely, the use of spent embers as amulets etc.) with the purpose of maximizing the practice performance. What 'popular' asceticism such as this is lacking is not an 'ascetic theory' but rather an officially established set of meanings.[25] Each one of the participants was in fact able to formulate his own 'theory' regarding how the practice 'works' and its significance. These theories were quite disparate but all of them shared the basic tenet that the practice is performative, that it produces effects and that through its performance, these effects could be maximized.

Figure 2.8 Hiwatari (fire-walking) practice at Ontake-san shrine in Saitama (10 October 2006 – picture courtesy of Andrea Castiglioni)

Figure 2.9 Hiwatari (fire-walking) practice at Ontake-san shrine in Saitama (10 October 2006 – picture courtesy of Andrea Castiglioni)

Climbing the ladder of swords: hawatari

The second event in the *harumatsuri* – the *hawatari* – seems to rely on this same tension between empirical and symbolical/doctrinal elements. The practice of climbing the sword-ladder (*hawatari* or, perhaps more commonly, *katana-watari*) is one of the ascetic feats that Miyake Hitoshi classifies as *yamabushi*'s *genjutsu* 山伏験術[26] (demonstration of magico-spiritual powers) and was at one time believed to be lost.[27] True enough, it is very difficult to prove a historical continuity between the *genjutsu* traditionally performed by *yamabushi* and the current practices of the various groups of Ontake devotees.[28] The introduction of the *hawatari* into the celebrations of the Ontake-san jinja *harumatsuri* dates at most from the post-war period and has been performed regularly only in the last 20 years.[29] However, the Saitama confraternity leader (*daisendatsu* 大先達) seems to offer a certain historical perspective by offering for the practice his own collection of *katana* 刀 (Japanese swords); the oldest date from the late Edo period until the newest, offered to the *kō* as recently as 2007. If this arises from the desire to create a bridge between past and present practices or simply to highlight the high price of proper *katana* blades, it is difficult to tell. What is clear is that the preparation of the ladder is by no means casual but follows a complex procedure aimed at achieving both structural solidity and an acceptable degree of safety, together with a manifest symbolical richness.

A four-metre-high platform is permanently set up in the inner grounds of the Ontake-san shrine; for the *matsuri*, a small altar dedicated to Ontake Daijin 御岳大神 is prepared on its top.

Figure 2.10 Spring Festival, Ontake-san shrine, Saitama. Preparation of the ladder of swords (10 April 2007)

Two long square-section poles lean on the platform, each of them displaying a number of three-centimetre-deep notches engraved along their total length. The notches are 13 in number, made to hold exactly 13 swords. Senior *ontakegyōja* start preparing the ladder by matching the blades with the notches, all with the sharp edge up, the tip on the left side and the tail on the right (see Figures 2.10 and 2.11).

Figure 2.11 Spring Festival, Ontake-san shrine, Saitama. Preparation of the ladder of swords (10 April 2007)

Then sheets of folded white paper are inserted between the metal of the blade and the wooden pole, both to secure the sword against unwanted slips and to keep the blade clean from impurities (see Figure 2.12).

As we have said, the *katana* belongs to the personal collection of the *daisen-datsu*, and their age ranges from the late Edo period until the present day. This factor is also considered when arranging the swords on the ladder: the oldest swords are set at the bottom, comprising the ladder's first rungs, while the others follow in age order, with the newest – merely one year old – forming the two top rungs. In this case, symbolism and subtle meaning leave room for more practical issues. The two newest blades are also the sharpest, so it is safer to place them as the last ones; this way, the person climbing the ladder can more easily lean on the wooden poles, and on the platform itself, while stepping onto such dangerous rungs. Older *katana* provide a good start, as they are less sharp and more easily manageable even by inexperienced feet. Also, they are better when one's balance is still hard to maintain and the only other place to put one's hands is on another sharp sword a few feet above.[30]

When all the swords are set, they are securely tied with a twisted rope using numerous knots to hold them firmly in place; then a symbolical tie is made with long white and red ribbons following a precise criss-cross pattern. Again, the empirical approach to concrete solidity manifests alongside symbolical and aesthetic representations. The ladder of swords is, in a sense, an *ascetic object*,

Figure 2.12 Spring Festival, Ontake-san shrine, Saitama. Preparation of the ladder of swords (10 April 2007)

charged with both symbolism and empirical performativity: it leads upwards, both as a symbol and as an actual means for the *gyōja* election, but it is also frightening and potentially dangerous, as all ascetic practices – even the mildest of them – *should* be in order to achieve any effect. To mitigate this inherent danger, the ladder is clad in the shrine's colours and kept pure by the same paper from which the *gyōja*'s *gohei* are made. Man's hand also intervenes with powerful knots of an ordinary but sturdy rope to make the whole ascetic object safe enough to actually be used. The sword-ladder stands as a powerful symbol of the ascetic effort; it is an instrument of torture in disguise, but indeed a self-inflicted torture, aimed at a positive outcome and not at the destruction of the practitioner. It is a torture that can still be managed.[31]

Climbing the ladder is a short but intense process that thrives on this same tension between what is physical and what is magical. The first step is the hardest and is carried out while still on the ground: one has to beat one's fear and place the first foot on the first blade. When I personally undertook this practice, I was the first person in line, so I had no example before me that could provide an idea of what I was about to face. True enough, prior to me and the other ordinary people who attempted the climb, the *ontakegyōja* elders who prepared the sword-ladder climbed it up and down – and not without an ill-concealed glimpse of pride! – but they were all too skilful and experienced to constitute a model that could actually be followed. As in the case of the *hiwatari*, instruction on how to climb came from the other people in line, including some personal friends who were something of 'professional' *gyōja* and to whom we shall return later.[32] Their advice was practical enough: keep one's foot parallel to the blade, balancing one's weight on the line between the toe and the heel. In this way, the body weight is best distributed and the risk of being cut is minimal.[33] As I placed my right foot on the first blade, magical help also came to my aid (see Figure 2.13). The older practitioners were all standing around the ladder, their sights firmly concentrated on my feet while they performed simple protective *kaji*.

The array of spells of popular *ontakegyōja* is not that vast; they were simply using the syllables of the *kuji* spell, focusing them with their index and middle fingers and releasing their power with a sharp hiss. This is the same technique used to control the flame in the *kamado* ritual and in the preparation of the *goma-ki*. Their attention was, however, remarkable and not for a single instant were my lower extremities without magical protection.[34] The whole climb does not take more than a few minutes as it is very uncomfortable. The edge of the sword is still very painful and the feeling is that of one's flesh being cut into deeply so one is pushed to finish the practice as soon as possible. The practical technique I was instructed to follow worked and my feet suffered no injury even on the sharpest of the blades. Having reached the top of the platform, respect is paid to Ontake Daijin with a simple bow. It is then possible to reach the ground by coming down an ordinary ladder.

I have suggested earlier on that the *hawatari* is understandable more as a single *ascetic act* rather than a complex practice. It is, however, a very powerful act, in which the mind and body of the practitioner are concentrated uniquely on

Figure 2.13 Spring Festival, Ontake-san shrine, Saitama. The author climbing the ladder
   of swords (10 April 2007 – picture courtesy of Erica Baffelli)

the edge of a sword. The participants interpret it in a variety of manners. Some
practitioners say that the *hawatari* is a way to display the powers accumulated
during the various *gyō* on Mount Ontake. Additionally, in a sense, demonstrating
them publicly is also a way to show the power of Ontake Daijin to other people, thus acknowledging his benign influence and demonstrating their gratitude.[35]

This explanation, however, seems to exclude the people that attempt the feat without being *ontakegyōja* or having undergone any other kind of ascetic training beforehand. Contrary to the *hiwatari*, there are a number of restrictions limiting those who can actually attempt the *hawatari*. People who are clearly overweight, drunk, too old or too young, in poor physical condition or evidently too scared are not permitted to climb.[36]

Besides myself, another western man was allowed to climb the ladder, followed by an old woman from the neighbourhood and few other occasional participants. Being questioned about the benefits that they may obtain from the *hawatari*, their answers were rather casual. The old woman plainly stated that she was an Ontake devotee who received many benefits from the *kami*, and that this was her way of paying him back. One man told me that it makes him feel stronger and healthier. In the midst of this conversation, one of the older practitioners broke in to point out that 'you see, this is very difficult, walking on the edge of a sword, the most difficult thing of all. If you can do this, you can do anything!' All the people around nodded in agreement.[37] Here again it is possible to observe how the 'meaning' or 'purpose' of an ascetic act or practice is somewhat unclear and very often left to the personal understanding and intention of the individual practitioner. We can also anticipate that this does not appear to depend on the complexity of the practice or on it being carried out in a 'popular' versus 'established' environment. These *ontakegyōja* are perhaps not too distant from the *hijiri*-type practitioners that Shinno consider pivotal in the transmission of religious values and experiences to urban populations. Shinno also points out how the heterogeneity of meanings I had the occasion to observe in these circumstances, can be considered the product of equally unstable concurring factors:

> The organized religions that try to manage and control sacred meaning; the hijiri-type figures who actually come in contact with and attempt to supply this meaning to believers and followers; the bloated urbanization of modern society that continues to erode the sense of community – all three of these factors lack stability in the present world. Thus, the system of meaning that runs through these three unstable factors is also unstable, undergoing constant growth and change.
>
> (Shinno Toshikazu1993: 203)

We shall encounter this same tension again between a precisely determined way of *acting* and a blurred and variable layer of *meaning* in far more articulated ascetic practices held in established environments, such as Shugendō.

Although none of the examples described thus far have proven to be a complex ascetic practice, we must not be tempted to consider this a consequence of them being 'popular' religious manifestations. As we shall see in the following section, non-established religious environments are indeed perfectly capable of giving birth to articulated practices and of justifying their deeds with significant layers of meaning.

Practices taking place outside an institutional religious body

There is a sort of intermediate category of practices that stands between the occasional ascetic acts and performances examined at the beginning of this chapter, and the complex and multi-layered ascetic practices belonging to long-established religious traditions. This is the case of ascetic experiences presenting some degree of organization, often driven by specific purposes, and offering a limited amount of what can be called an *ascetic tradition*. In this section, we will move away from the simple use of single or unrelated ascetic acts to explore those *practices* taking place in non-established religious environments which also portray a complexity and richness of meaning and purpose close to the ascetic activities of more prestigious traditions.

Samugyō: *the cold practice*

One valid example of this is the Ontake *samugyō*[38] 寒行 (cold practice) held by the Jiga Daikyōkai 滋賀大教會, an Ontake group based in Agematsu 上松 village (Nagano prefecture), set at the foot of Mount Ontake itself. The Jiga Daikyōkai itself is a religious group displaying some degree of coherent tradition. Initiated by the father of the current leader in the immediate post-war period, the Daikyōkai is a family-run Ontake-*kō* led by the Okamoto 岡本 family. Okamoto males are thought to have a particular predisposition for being possessed by the Ontake deities. Despite the fact that none of them is an ordained Buddhist or Shinto priest, they work full-time for the Daikyōkai, making their living from the believers' support; thus, they can be legitimately identified as *religious professionals*.[39] Their role and powers are not very different from those of a *miko* 巫女 or *itako*, but unlike the latter who normally train alone or in small groups with a teacher and then perform the *kamigakari* by request at local *matsuri* or celebrations,[40] the Daikyōkai also display many of the characteristics of a *kō*, involving its followers in pilgrimages and other organized religious events.[41]

The winter *samugyō* lasts from 22 until 24 January. This is the Daikyōkai's main annual event and it draws a consistent number of participants from many areas of Honshu, particularly from Saitama (especially as the Okamotos are particularly close to the Saitama Ontake-*kō* (indeed, the Okamoto brothers were the acquaintances who helped me with the *hawatari* feat) while almost half of the participants came from the Nagano area. The 2007 group numbered about 40 people, most of whom were in middle age, with the majority women, although there were also a number of people in their thirties present, including a recently married young couple.[42] Most of them were long-standing members of the Jiga Daikyōkai and in close personal relationship with its leaders. It was clear from the very beginning that the Okamotos knew all the vicissitudes of the lives of most of their followers, who, in turn, came to participate in the practice with great expectations.[43] More than a routine pilgrimage to already well-known places, the Ontake *samugyō* is in fact a collective ascetic practice, led by 'professional' leaders with particular training on whom the group of participants places sensible hopes of actual effectiveness.[44] Results and purposes have to be sought after the active participation of the believers in the *gyō*, and the degree of commitment they displayed during the course of the practice over two days leaves no doubt as to their awareness of undertaking a well-structured and necessarily demanding *shugyō*.

The *shugyō* itself actually started three days earlier than the day of the participants' meeting in Agematsu. Abstention was recommended by the leaders in order to prepare oneself to meet the mountain deities: consumption of meat, fish and alcohol was forbidden from 20 January, although plenty of these same foods were made available during the practice itself.[45] Once in Agematsu, the participants were briefly greeted by the leaders and then travelled to the base of Mount Ontake by bus. The practice starts with a series of water ablutions under the Fudō Myōō waterfall (*takigyō* 滝行) performed only by the leaders (see Figures 2.14 and 2.15). When the Okamotos appeared wearing only their traditional white underwear (*fundoshi* 褌) in the early afternoon, the outside temperature was nearly minus five degrees Celsius. The three nearly naked people strode quickly towards the waterfall and, once in front of it, they started cutting the air with the traditional gesture of the *kuji* spell, reciting the Fudō Myōō mantra loudly. When they stepped into the waterfall, a new series of *kuji* followed, followed again by the Fudō mantra. Although their voices were raised high, as if in an effort to counter the cold, their countenances remained firm and their movements never gave way to unwanted shivering.

Figure 2.14 Samugyō (cold practice) Mt Ontake (22–24 January 2007)

Figure 2.15 Takigyō (waterfall practice) during the *samugyō* on Mt Ontake (22 January 2007)

Interviewed shortly after the practice, they described their sensations with these words: 'The body reacts to that, you feel warmth coming from the inside of your body. After few minutes it is not cold anymore!'[46] The other participants are not required to do this, but it is mandatory for the leaders; they need both the power arising from the *gyō* and to have their body purified in order to become acceptable to the *kami* during the *kamigakari*.[47] From this moment on, the *samugyō* takes the shape of a collective walking practice in the cold, as the following two days are dedicated to reaching various places of worship on Mount Ontake (see Figure 2.16).

As an ascetic act, the walk itself did not feature particularly difficult or dangerous routes, except perhaps on the last day when the practitioners' group visited Kyotaki-Fudōson 清滝不動尊 shrine, which is located right under a frozen waterfall dedicated to Fudō Myōō (see Figure 2.17).

The last portion of the climb must be conducted on solid ice with the help of ice racks; only the younger participants attempted this part of the trail. On previous days, all the routes were far more accessible and every participant, including the oldest, could follow with ease (see Figure 2.18).

The main ascetic act in the *samugyō* practice seems to be the passive endurance of quite cold temperatures for long periods. On the evening of the first day, having climbed up Mount Ontake for about 1,000 metres, the company of pilgrims reached Ontake shrine 御嶽神社 where the first *kamigakari* took place. The Jiga Daikyōkai leaders began to prepare themselves shortly after the group arrival at

Figure 2.16 Climbing Mt Ontake during the *samugyō* on (22 January 2007)

Figure 2.17 Worship at Kyotaki-Fudōson shrine during the *samugyō* (23 January 2007)

Figure 2.18 Climbing Mt Ontake during the *samugyō* (23 January 2007)

the shrine; nonetheless, it took a few hours for the *kamigakari* to properly start. The deity possessing the medium also took at least two more hours to call each one of the participants to his feet in order to communicate advice and personal messages to each of them and to receive the proper worship.[48] Overall, we spent around five hours standing still on a small, snow-covered plateau at temperatures that I might estimate reached minus 15 degrees Celsius.[49] The practitioners are unanimously aware that this endurance is granting them the 'right' to encounter the deity and to benefit from his advice (see Figure 2.19). They gladly remarked to me how they felt cleansed by the cold, a feeling that also many other practitioners seemed to share enthusiastically.[50]

Despite the fact that the *samugyō* is in itself doctrinally rather unsophisticated, and also that it is primarily focused on the single ascetic act of cold endurance, the practice is unanimously understood by the participants as being a form of *gyō*, as the term often appears in their discourses about the *samugyō*. Interestingly enough, however, none of them would describe themselves as being *gyōja*, ascetics. The leaders of the Jiga Daikyōkai are, on the contrary, considered *gyōja* because they regularly participate in a number of *gyō* all over Japan in order to sharpen their powers. Many of the lay practitioners still consider themselves as 'pilgrims', in spite of their clear awareness of the *samugyō* as being a *gyō*, while some had no particular definition for themselves.[51]

The Ontake *samugyō* is clearly a step ahead of the previously mentioned borrowing of ascetic acts in religious events, as the performance of a series of *gyō*

Figure 2.19 Worship on Mt Ontake during the *samugyō* (23 January 2007)

is central to and not merely tangential to the event. Moreover, the practice is organized following a precise and recursive taxonomy, involving 'professional' practice leaders. However, a boundary between the leaders as *gyōja* and the lay practitioners still persists. This is made evident by a certain disparity in the practice commitment: leaders perform the *takigyō* (while the lay members do not), are less heavily dressed to protect themselves from the mountain cold, perform simple rituals and lead the worship. Moreover, as the *samugyō* is carried out in a non-established environment, there is no certificate, no initiation or any form of official acknowledgement at the end of the practice which declares the practitioner to be a *gyōja*. In some other cases, such as the Saitama Ontake-*kō*, where there is a link to an official religious institution, such as Ontake-san jinja, there is an upper rank of *sendatsu* (guide) who can eventually provide a practice certificate to rank the devotees.[52] The Jiga Daikyōkai is possibly too small and peripheral to have proper internal ranking, so the self-awareness of the devotees remains at the level of pilgrims, regardless of the fact that the practice itself is seen as a *gyō*.

Nanao-san shugyō

A similar case in which the performance of a *gyō* does not lead to the practitioner being considered a *gyōja*, an ascetic, is a brief walking practice that laypeople can undergo at Nanao-san 七尾山 (Mount Nanao) near Dorogawa village, close to the more famous Mount Ōmine. Nanao-san is the object of a relatively recent worship starting from the post-war period.[53] Its main feature is an internal grotto, which used to be enshrined in a much older Shinto shrine, in which three anthropomorphic rocky formations can be seen.[54] Walking the path to reach this sacred place is called '*shugyō*' by the shrine attendant and involves a simple, but authoritative, set of rules to be followed. First, one must not be drunk or under the influence of any intoxicant. Then, before starting to climb the long stone stairs leading to the grotto, the pilgrim must purify himself following the traditional Shinto manner. A short white kimono can then be donned to present oneself as clean as possible in front of the deity.[55] The climb is long and quite tiring; upon reaching the grotto, the pilgrim is welcomed by one of the shrine *gyōja*. The person I met there was very kind and eager to explain every aspect of the worship of the Nanao-san deities, with a particular emphasis on the fact that the mountain is not forbidden to women (perhaps a veiled polemic against Mount Ōmine?). The last steps of the *gyō* require one to free climb a narrow vertical tunnel leading to the sacred grotto with only the aid of a chain hanging from above. Nanao-san is indeed open to everyone, but the difficulty of this last segment limits access to the sacred cave to only the strong and able. After having worshipped the deities manifesting in the form of human-shaped rock formations, and having enjoyed some refreshments, it is possible to return by following the same way back. At the bottom of the mountain, the *miko* at the entrance takes back the white garment and then congratulates the visitors for having completed the '*kami no shugyō*' (*shugyō* of/for the deity).[56] A money offering is made at this point, although not explicitly requested, and in exchange it is possible to receive few *o-mamori* and the calendar of the shrine's activities for the year.

In virtue of its quite simple but sound structure, this basic practice also deserves to be considered as more than a simple borrowing of ascetic acts. First of all, the *shugyō* is considered as a 'stand alone' religious practice, without the need for it to be incorporated into other religious events; the behaviour of the *miko* at the shrine entrance and of the *gyōja* at the cave clearly shows an awareness of this. Moreover, the *gyō* has a clear purpose and this communicates to the practitioner a clearly discernible sense of achievement. In the previous examples of simple borrowings, the dimension of the ascetic act is much more fluid; it is only part of a larger, ongoing religious event but is not fully legitimate by itself. In the case of the Ontake *samugyō*, however, this achievement does not include the fact that the practitioner can consider himself a *gyōja*. The term *gyōja* still seems to belong only to a select few, such as the person guarding the entrance of the mountain grotto who told us how he was practising regular austerities in the surrounding mountains, including at Mount Ōmine, and how he considered himself to be a properly trained *yamabushi*.[57]

Practices taking place within an institutional religious body

The third general *mode* that we have identified in Japanese asceticism comprises those practices organized by institutional religious bodies and led by officially ordained practitioners. In some cases, the practices are reserved for fully ordained religious professionals in that same institution (as in the Tendai *kaihōgyō* or the Nichiren-shū *daiaragyō*). However, it must be noted that 'practices taking place inside an institutional religious body' are not synonymous with 'practices for religious professionals'. Indeed, in some other cases (like the *okugake shugyō* 奥駈修行 and the Haguro *akinomine* 秋乃峰, both discussed below), laypeople practice alongside fully ordained practitioners, sometimes acting as minor leaders and participating in the celebration of rituals and religious services. Lastly, as in the case of the *rōhatsu sesshin* taking place in Tōshō-ji 東照寺 temple in Tokyo, a practice is carried out in an established environment – here, a Sōtō Zen temple – under the guidance of temple officials but the participants actually practicing are only laypeople. As the *shugyō* taking place in Shugendō environments are possibly the most common representatives of this *mode* in contemporary Japan, this analysis will begin with the Haguro *akinomine* practice. This particular practice has been selected among the wider spectrum of Shugendō ascetic practices still well alive in Japan, because it exists in two different doctrinal 'versions' (Buddhist and Shinto) that will allow us to conduct a comparative analysis in the latter part of this work.

Haguro akinomine

The Dewa Sanzan mountains – Hagurosan 羽黒山, Yudonosan 湯殿山 and Gassan 月山 – are located in Yamagata prefecture and constitute a major pilgrimage locale. Their cultic centres used to be affiliated with the Shingon school of Buddhism, but in the Edo period, Haguro changed its affiliation to the Tendai school. Until 1873, Hagurosan was primarily a Buddhist shrine-temple complex but in the late nineteenth century become a Shinto cultic centre under the government policy of Separation of Kami and Buddhas (*shinbutsu bunri* 神仏分離). Much of the Buddhist tradition was lost at that time and only a few Buddhist temples survived at the foot of the mountain. In 1946, the Haguro Shugen Honshū 羽黒修験本宗 was established as an independent Shugendō organization having the Hagurosan Kōtaku-ji Shōzen-in 羽黒山荒沢寺正善院 temple in Tōge 手向 as its headquarters.[58]

The *akinomine* is the annual mountain-entry practice at Haguro, which is still practiced in its traditional form from 24 August to 1 September by the Haguro Shugen Honshū. Another 'version' of the *akinomine* exists, held by the Dewa Sanzan-jinja at almost the same time of the year. For the moment, however, we will concentrate on the 'Buddhist version' organized by the Shōzen-in 正善院 and Kōtaku-ji 荒沢寺 temples.[59]

The practitioners initially meet on 24 August at Shōzen-in where the day is mainly spent in practical tasks such as the purchase or loan of some element of the *yamabushi* attire, the payment of training fees and so forth. The practice starts officially on that same day with the ceremony called *oikaragaki* 笈からがき (the ceremony of 'decorating' the *oi* 笈, the portable altar), during which the *shugenja* spirits are shaken from their bodies (thus virtually killing them) so as to be hosted in the *oi* during the practice period.[60] From the very beginning, the *akinomine* displays a number of characteristics that can lead us to understand it as a practice carried out in an established religious environment, and where the presence of religious professionals is crucial to its undertaking. The practice leaders (*sendatsu* 先達)[61] are in fact the temple heads, all of them fully ordained Tendai priests, and they are in charge of the performance of the religious rituals during the practice. The lay participants can be *shugenja* of proven experience and indeed many of them are acting as *sendatsu*, but the 'official' ritual part is of course in the hands of the temple heads only. Among the participants, there may be some ordained priests from other temples; if so, they are allowed to help in the performance of rituals when the necessity arises. Unlike the cases we have examined so far, there is a remarkably solid and articulated doctrinal structure underlying the whole practice and this, coupled with the presence of a fully 'legitimate' leadership, enhances the sense of orthodoxy of all the ascetic acts that are about to be performed. This sense is so strong that the influence of lay practitioners during the course of the practice becomes virtually nonexistent. Lay *shugenja* let themselves be led, passively assist with rituals that they often do not understand entirely and follow a strict hierarchical order in their relationship with other participants and the leaders.

After a last night of sleep at the Shōzen-in, the practice actually begins on the second day. In the early morning, the attention of all practitioners is concentrated on the preparations for the Ritual of Conception to be held in the Kogane-dō 黄金 堂, the temple in front of the Shōzen-in (see Figure 2.20).[62]

Figure 2.20 'Buddhist' *akinomine*. Ritual of conception at Kogane-dō, Tōge (25 August 2005)

Although the *akinomine* itself officially started the day before with the *oika-ragaki*, the rite at Kogane-dō is the one that really marks the beginning of the practice routine. It is first of all a doctrinal mark, since the rite symbolizes conception, the conception of the embryos of the *shugenja* that will be held in the *oi* and nurtured through the practice until their full development. But it is also a powerful spatial mark. The sensation of setting out from Shōzen-in is sharp, clear and perfectly understandable. It is the setting out from the 'normal life', made of everyday meals, water-flushed toilets, bathrooms, bedding, electricity and so on, for the unknown world of the mountain where none of those amenities will be available. The transition through space at the same time springs from, incorporates and actuates the symbolic death of the preceding ritual, allowing the participants to 'perform' meanings of which they may not necessarily be completely aware.

After the ritual at the Kogane-dō, the column of *shugenja*-in-training passes through the village of Tōge until it arrives at the outer precinct of the Dewa Sanzan-jinja (see Figure 2.21).

During this walk, the *yama no nenbustu* 山の念仏 (short invocations to the mountains' deities and Buddhas) is chanted in a responsorial form, following a leading voice. The walk lasts for around 30 minutes, during which the atmosphere loosens up a little bit. People start chatting between mantras and many enjoy the nice landscape of the village surroundings. No particular order is kept during the walk and everybody feels free to change his or her position in the procession.[63]

Figure 2.21 'Buddhist' *akinomine*. Shugenja leaving Shōzen-in temple, Tōge (25 August 2005)

Upon entering the precinct of the *jinja*, the atmosphere becomes more serious, a conscious acknowledgement of entering a sacred space. The way to the 'First Lodging' is an enjoyable walk in the forest. The pace is slow in order to allow the older practitioners to follow the procession with ease, and the only demanding part is the 2,600-step staircase leading to the top of the mountain. At the top of the stairs, the *shugenja* can enjoy a brief rest and some simple refreshment. Upon arriving at Kōtaku-ji, a number of practical tasks are performed. First, the participants are assigned to their 'room' in the temple. The word 'room' is used provisionally, because many of these 'rooms' are actually divisions of the main hall and other smaller halls, divisions made in a very theoretical way, since nothing marks the boundaries between one 'room' and the others. All the 'rooms' are named after the Chinese zodiac signs, for example, *ushi no heya* 牛の部屋 (room of the ox), *ki no heya* 己の部屋 (room of the snake) etc.[64]

The following days will be marked by a number of ascetic feats undertaken following tradition and enforced by the leadership. The underlying purpose of the whole practice is the 'practice of the ten realms' (*jukkai shugyō* 十界修行), the practical experience of the 10 realms of existence in one's present body. In this practice, the *shugenja* are led from the realm of hell to that of the hungry ghosts, animals, demons (*ashuras*), human beings and heavenly beings by a series of ascetic exercises matching the main characteristics of each realm. Hell beings live in darkness, smoke and pain, and this condition is replicated through a practice called *nanban ibushi* 南蛮いぶし, where the group of *shugenja* has to endure pungent smoke produced by herbs and peppers burnt on braziers set in the sealed main hall.[65] The practice of the hungry ghost is the *danjiki* 断食, the fast of the first three days of practice, when no food is allowed. The practice of animals is the prohibition of any form of personal hygiene; for the entire duration of the practice, no one is allowed to wash. The demons' nature is based on violence, and in order to experience that, a fierce *sumō* competition is held among the practitioners on the third day. The practice of human beings is confession and repentance and this is experienced through extended sessions of prostrations and the confession of transgressions (*zange* 懺悔). The practice of heavenly beings is instead a joyous celebration called *ennen* 延年, where an extensive amount of *sake* is drunk. As can be seen, the Haguro *akinomine* provides practices for only the first six realms of existence (the realms of sufferance), while no practice is explicitly associated with four remaining realms: *śrāvakas* (voice-hearers), *pratyekabuddhas*, *bodhisattvas* and *Buddhas*.

Together with this series of ascetic acts, motivated by their analogy with the realms of existence, is a constant practice of *shugyō* in the mountains that involves many hours of daily mountain walking and leads the practitioners to the most sacred places in the Dewa Sanzan, including the Sankozawa 三鈷沢, Gassan 月山 and Yudonosan 湯殿山 shrines (see Figure 2.22).

Finally, daily religious services, beginning in the early hours of the morning, contribute to the general lack of sleep that the practitioners experience during their stay at Kōtaku-ji.

Figure 2.22 'Buddhist' *akinomine*. Shugenja on the slopes of Gassan (27 August 2005)

Possibly the most important ritual moment is the *saitō goma* (fire sacrifice) rite, which also marks the passage to the Third Lodging and, at the same time, the deliverance from the status of hungry ghosts. It is an important moment in the progress of the practice and, for many, represents the opportunity to benefit from the power and good influences emanating from the *goma* pyre. On a more practical level, it is also the moment in which the practitioners are allowed to eat again, and for this reason marks a peak in the practitioners' weariness. After three days of incessant fasting and practice, and having spent one's last energies in building the *goma* pyre and on more than 400 prostrations that same morning, the participants are all but exhausted. Regardless of the doctrinal importance of the *saitō goma*, most of the people are visibly nodding, including myself, and a few fall asleep completely.[66]

The whole course of the practice seems to have been carefully planned to push all the participants to the edge of their physical endurance.[67] The presence of a strong doctrinal background seems to play a part in this, since the more complex the taxonomy of the practice is, the more efficacious the techniques aimed at bodily *malleation* prove to be. The presence of a well-trained and officially recognized leadership and of an established tradition provides deeper doctrinal background and more articulated justifications for the ascetic experience, but it does not per se make the individual ascetic acts more difficult. The difference between this mode of practice (in established religious environments) and those examined in the previous paragraphs (occasional borrowing and non-institutional practices) seems not to reside in the harshness of the individual ascetic acts but in the richer and more structured practice taxonomy that makes each act more efficient in terms of its performative and transformative power. Many of the acts employed in the *akinomine* can indeed be seen as part of other religious events: fasting and vigil is a frequent component in *matsuri*; the *nanban ibushi* is also part of other Shugendō practices in the Dewa Sanzan, as we shall see later; *sumō* or other forms of wrestling are sometimes featured in festivals, and mountain walking, as we have already said, is possibly the most common ascetic experience of all.[68] The legacy of tradition and the work of religious leadership combine all these elements into a form which is both doctrinally justified and purpose-efficient.[69] The fact that the physical commitment – resulting in a barely bearable fatigue and sometimes even danger – eventually increases must be seen as consequence of this different and more efficient structure rather than being the result of a *different* asceticism as a whole.

Another thing that an established religious environment adds to the ascetic practice is the sense of officially-sanctioned accomplishment, something that we have seen as somewhat lacking in the non-institutional forms of ascetic experiences. During the *akinomine*, a new *shugenja* name is given to all first-time practitioners. This name will remain the same in case they decide to repeat their participation in the following years. Moreover, on the third day, a ceremony of transmission is held when all newcomers receive the initiation to the 'secret' *goshinpō* 護身法 and *kuji* mudras directly from the *daisendatsu*.[70] Lastly, on completion of the practice, an official certificate is issued to each participant, bearing the date of the current *akinomine*, their name and rank. All the practitioners consider the completion of the practice a remarkable accomplishment, and all of them would indeed call themselves *shugenja* – not without some well-deserved pride.[71]

In the case of the *akinomine*, as in most of the Shugendō practices (such as the *okugake shugyō* examined later), the leadership practices alongside the lay *shugenja*, following all of their steps and sharing the same harshness. Shōzen-in leaders endured the fast and vigil, undertook mountain walking and kept themselves unwashed like everyone else. The *daisendatsu* does benefit from few privileges, such as separate private quarters, but for the rest he shares the practice with the group. In some other cases of ascetic practices in established religious environment, however, the leadership guides the lay practitioners without participating directly in the practice itself. One such case is the *rōhatsu sesshin* held twice a year at Tōshō-ji temple in Tokyo.

Rōhatsu sesshin

Tōshō-ji is a Sōtō Zen temple in the Harada Roshi 原田祖岳老師 lineage located in Shinagawa, Tokyo. The temple was established in 1941 by Harada Daiun Sogaku Roshi[72] as a branch of the Hosshin-ji 発心寺 temple in Tokyo; it was initially named Daiun-kai *dōjō* 大雲会道場. Later in 1943, it was registered as

Tōshō-ji temple. The temple was destroyed during the Second World War and reconstructed in its present form in 1948.[73]

Like many other Zen temples, it hosts a special seven-day *zazen* retreat in commemoration of the Buddha's awakening (*rōhatsu sesshin* 臘八接心) at the beginning of December, which is repeated with the same modalities in early April under the name of 'Spring *sesshin*', lasting in both cases a full five days.[74] Although the modalities of the *sesshin* are virtually identical to all Sōtō Zen temples, a few important characteristics allow us to understand this particular *sesshin* as an ascetic practice. The present master, Deguchi Tetsujō, following the tradition passed down from his master, Ban Tetsugyō, and from Harada Roshi himself, places a strong emphasis on maximizing the efficient use of the body during *zazen*. This is done primarily in two ways: first there is the use of the voice as a way to focus one's thoughts single-pointedly, and second, the use of physical pain as an aid to transcend one's conscious ego.

The simple *kōan* '*mu*' 無 is assigned to each of the participants from the second day of practice for the purpose of concentrating one's energy and will on that *kōan* while carrying the effort throughout one's body. In practical terms, the participants have to shout the syllable '*mu*' during the whole *zazen* period, which totals nearly eight hours per day, divided into four sessions, two in the morning and two in the afternoon. Additionally, to 'help' this already considerable effort, a senior lay member of the temple constantly hits the practitioner's right shoulder with the *kyōsaku* 警策 stick.[75] As is well-known, a *kyōsaku* blow during *zazen* is generally a mild but firm blow to each shoulder, which benefits stiff backs and aching legs resulting from long hours of sitting still in *zazen*. In this case, however, the blow is localized always on the right shoulder and it is delivered with uncommon strength, with the unique and openly stated function of causing pain. The mechanism of interaction between the *kyōsaku* blow and the incessant shouting of the '*mu*' *kōan* was efficaciously explained to the participants using the image of a rising mountain ridge. The effort put into emitting the sound '*mu*' pushes you away from yourself, from your conscious ego. At the end of the emission of the voice, however, your burst of strength has ended and you are at risk of receding to your ordinary level of self-awareness.[76] It is at that point that the *kyōsaku* blow intervenes, with the pain distancing you from your conscious ego for the time needed to inhale and start the whole process again. In the words of one of the practitioners, you are 'pushed up, up, up!' with his finger following the ridge of a *sumi-e* painted mountain hanging from the wall.[77] Resolutely handled, the *kyōsaku* delivered such blows to the participants' shoulders that from the third day, many people's backs, including mine, were already copiously bleeding. This, coupled with the incessant shouting and the strict discipline in every aspect of our daily life in addition to *zazen*, made the *rōhatsu sesshin* a most exhausting experience, certainly deserving to be considered an ascetic practice.[78]

Contrary to the *akinomine*, the temple leaders in this *sesshin* do not share the practice with lay practitioners but their presence is nonetheless continuous. While the person handling the *kyōsaku* constantly keeps an eye on discipline during *zazen*, the master waits in a separate room to have private interview sessions with each participant (*dokusan* 独参). This is an important element of the *sesshin*, as it provides the opportunity for the master to check if the practitioner has obtained an initial awakening experience (*kenshō* 見性). The master can, for instance, challenge the practitioner to answer a *kōan* or other questions; in case of failure, the participant can be harshly rebuked. At the end of the *zazen* sessions, the master comes once again into the *zendō* 禅堂 to guide the recitation of the *Hannya shingyō* and to explain the stages of the practice. Before the afternoon *zazen*, he also holds a lecture, in which he explains some principles of Zen practice or the meaning of a particular passage in a certain scripture.[79]

As we can see, the leaders here are acting as a guide for others but are not participating in the practice themselves. A remarkably modern and non-monastic understanding of the *zazen* practice motivates his behaviour: the master is holding the *sesshin* for the benefit of others, a benefit that he already experienced in the past and that does not need to be repeated.[80] The same is true for the practitioners themselves. Because the intense use of the *kyōsaku* is aimed at helping the participant to obtain *kenshō*, the beating ceases once a practitioner achieves the experience of enlightenment and such experience is officially sanctioned by the master during *dokusan*.

We will now conclude this brief examination of the *rōhatsu sesshin* by considering some interesting terminological issues. In describing the *sesshin* activities, the master often used the term *shugyō* in everyday expressions such as 'our practice' (*wareware no shugyō* 我々の修行) or 'today's practice' (*honjitsu no shugyō* 本日の修行) and other similar phrases. He was clearly using the term in its widest meaning of (physical) practice as outlined in Chapter 1 with no specific sectarian references in order to emphasize the importance of bodily practice in the *sesshin*. Interestingly enough, however, none of the practitioners considered themselves to be *gyōja*. When interviewed, they actually remarked how the term is unsuitable for the *sesshin*, as 'it is well-known that *gyōja* practice in the mountains'.[81] They considered the designation *shugyōsha* 修行者 more appropriate, although not many people actually used it.[82]

Conclusions

From this preliminary classification, a few elements seem to coalesce into a definition of an ascetic 'theme' in Japanese religious practice, regardless of the circumstance or *modes* of practice and of their more or less complex doctrinal justification. The first element is the idea of *performativity* of the ascetic practice, which we have seen expressed in the technical empiricism that constitutes so much of the ascetic tradition. The second element is the centrality of the human body as both the main tool and object of the ascetic practice. The third element is the fact that ascetic practices, no matter how simple or brief, appear to possess a degree of *transformative power*. This transformative power seems to be the result of the union of the performativity of the ascetic act with the object of that performative power, namely the body of the practitioner. In order to maximize this effect, a precise taxonomy of agency is called upon. In other words, the transformative power of asceticism depends on the unspoken identity of the practitioner's physical and non-physical dimensions: by acting with and on his own body, the practitioner changes the status of at least part of his self. The defiled becomes pure, as in the water ablutions, cold practice and other purificatory activities. The weak becomes stronger, as some of the people interviewed remarked. Ordinary people become enlightened beings, as with the *akinomine* and *rōhatsu sesshin*. The agency of asceticism extends, then, from being mere bodily training to an active *malleation* of the practitioner's state of being as a whole, that is to say a conceptual transition from praxis to ontology.

To stress the various kinds of efficacy of such agency, it is possible at this point to put forward a preliminary breakdown of these ascetic taxonomies in order to stress the place, meaning and purpose of the individual ascetic acts involved (see Table 2.1).

The first distinction is drawn between *passive* and *active* ascetic acts. The former are generally characterized by unresisting endurance of some kind of bodily stress (e.g. the endurance of extreme cold) for prolonged periods of time or the negation of more normal bodily habits (e.g. eating) for unnatural periods of time (several days or months). Active acts represent instead the energetic pursuit for some kind of bodily exercise and effort, like the cold waterfall practices, the mountain walking or the repetition of a *kōan* for endless hours.

On a first level of symptomatic analysis, all of these acts have some kind of visible effect on the human body. Some, like the progressive weakness on account of extreme fasting, are obvious, while others are more subtle, like the changes in the perception of cold which is experienced after spending a long period of time in a very cold environment. I used the vague word 'subtle' to indicate another set of effects that are not explicitly visible in the bodily reactions of the practitioner but that constitute the real essence and purpose of the ascetic act itself. In this regard, it can seem contradictory that the word 'body' appears so often in the column for 'subtle effects', particularly when referring to the cleansing of the body. Following the earlier discussion, however, this partial overlapping of bodily with 'spiritual' effects can be seen to have an underlying logic. It refers, in fact, to the role of the ascetic body as a liminal space between the material and the spiritual, one which I have outlined as a common feature of all ascetic efforts and the *locus* where praxis and ontology merge into each other.

The role of pain and suffering in bodily practices is therefore part of an empirical tradition in which the final aim of ascetic techniques seems to be to push the practitioner 'over the limit' or, in Carmen Blacker's words, to allow him 'to reach a breaking point', to go to the extremes of one's bodily ability only to discover the supernatural outflow of energy that arises upon passing that limit.[83] The harder the practice, the more functional this purpose seems to be. Committed ascetic practitioners, regardless of their religious denominations, generally agree on at least one point: the practice is really effective if it can bring one near the brink of complete exhaustion, a point of no return from which it appears to be impossible either to come back to normal life or to advance to any successive stage but death.[84] This seems to be the ultimate purpose of all practices, creating a fluid space between the two worlds of life and death where the practitioner can look at both from some

Table 2.1 Ascetic acts and effects

Passive acts	Bodily effects	Subtle effects
Abstention from certain foods (grains, alchohol)	Deprivation of nutrients Cleansing of the body	Bodily purification Preparation of the body to host the deity
Fasting	Starvation, near break-down conditions	Bodily purification Experience of the condition of Hungry Ghosts
Cold endurance	Change of the perception of cold Exhaustion	Bodily purification Preparation of the body to host the deity

Active acts	Bodily effects	Subtle effects
Water ablutions	Change of the perception of cold Surge of heat	Surge of 'energy' or power
Prolonged repetition of *kōan* or formulas	Change of bodily function through the use of the voice Exhaustion	Accumulation of power or merit Weakening of the self
Prolonged walking	Exhaustion Physical danger	Partaking of the holy dimension of the mountain

Table 2.2 Types of distress and effects

Environmental distress	Effect	Physical distress	Effect
Practising in a cold or uncomfortable environment	Environment unsuitable to life	Fasting or abstentions	Diet unsuitable to sustain life
Practising in an alien or secluded environment	Loss of the normal social dimension of life	Cold water ablutions Prolonged walking Prolonged sitting Sleep deprivation	Habit unsuitable to normal life
		Prolonged recitation of *kōan* or other formulas	Unusual vocal effort, unsuitable to everyday life

sort of middle point. What the ascetic does empirically experience in that moment is a massive return of force and energy apparently from nowhere; this marks the moment in which the person becomes a 'holy person'.

If we assume that death is the most 'transforming' event for the human body, as it is the event that negates the human body as a whole, an experience so close to physical death thus enables the ascetic to understand his body as a new body, i.e. the body of the 'holy person'. Just as syntax in a sentence is aimed at conveying meaning from the speaker to the listener, the inner taxonomy of the ascetic practice seems to be aimed primarily at reaching this extreme point. If we re-read the basic circumstances of practice in the case studies analyzed thus far from this perspective, we can discern a clearer picture of the underlying motivations for all these ascetic acts (see Table 2.2).

Thus, the taxonomy of an ascetic practice is aimed at putting oneself in conditions (including environment and bodily and mental habits) that are understood as unsuitable for life itself. Unsuitable for life means to be close to death, not with the intention of reaching death but rather a liminal condition between the two that is indeed experienced at what we have defined as the breaking point. The taxonomy of a practice does not only shape the relationship between the individual ascetic acts, but it can also trim the amount of pain required to fit the purpose, much as the engine of a car always works by the same principles, regardless of the actual speed of the car. This also leads us to conclude that there is no ground on which we can understand some forms of asceticism as being 'lesser' practices: all can be legitimately understood as being 'ascetic' if they serve their purpose by employing the body and pain as tools. Once again, *performativity* seems to be a key word.

3 The ascetic practitioner

Identity and motivation

This chapter will examine a variety of ascetic practices having a range of meanings, with particular attention on the people actually involved in such practices. Our analysis will thus be focused on the *agents* (*who*) and their motivation and purposes (*why*). A more in-depth discussion about the social, theoretical and doctrinal backgrounds will be conducted in the fourth chapter. The purpose of this chapter is to offer a phenomenological overview of significant case studies in order to provide a first-hand account of what ascetic practice means to its agents, mostly in terms of performance and results. I argue that 'meanings' are often arbitrarily ascribed to a series of acts that were initially understood as simply 'profitable' performance, that is to say a performance aimed at obtaining a certain result.[1] As we have seen in previous chapters, ascetic practices and acts are not always the practical implementation of doctrinal knowledge. This is particularly the case with practices taking place in non-established religious contexts, where meanings are often obscure to, and overlooked by, the practitioners themselves,[2] but it is also an important factor in the 'practices for religious professionals' we shall describe in the chapter. The underlying level of what we defined in the previous chapter as 'technical empiricism' often is motivating enough for the practitioner to make the need for further theoretical explanation almost negligible. This does not mean, however, that participants leave their aims and techniques unexplained. We will see how a variety of motivations and reasons are elaborated by practitioners during the practice itself, thus creating a body of '*ascetic* lore' that, in most cases, coexists with the more 'official' ascetic tradition.

Who? The people involved

This part will be divided into two sections, with the first examining lay participation in ascetic practices and the second focusing on those practices exclusive to religious professionals. It must be noted that these two categories do not necessarily correspond to the 'practices taking place outside an institutional religious body' and those carried out 'within established religious organizations', which we have outlined as two of the principal modes of practice in the second chapter. Laypeople can indeed participate in institutionalized practices alongside fully ordained priests, as in the cases of the Haguro *akinomine*, the *okugake* and the *rōhatsu sesshin*. On the other hand, religious professionals can achieve their status, or an improvement in their status, through ascetic training outside the boundaries of religious institutions, as in the case of the *itako* (blind mediums) or the leaders of popular religious group such as the Jiga Daikyōkai.

Laypeople asceticism

Who are the laypeople involved in ascetic religious practices in contemporary Japan? The answer can be *everybody* and *nobody*. Despite a certain popular interest in a few well-known ascetic figures, as mentioned in the introduction, the number of those who actually engage in some form of associated bodily practice represent only a fraction of the people religiously active. It is difficult to produce precise figures here. Some of the practices analyzed in this work are experiencing a period of crisis while others are thriving.[3] Within this group of active practitioners, however, it is possible to identify representatives of almost all contemporary Japanese social groups. From the young to the old, the rich businessman to the humble labourer, the range of laypeople undertaking some forms of *shugyō* within one of the *modes* of practice previously outlined display a remarkable and exciting heterogeneity. This, however, does necessarily imply a commonality of purposes, and it can in some case reinforce existing social division and competition, or create new ones within the practice environment.[4] The motivations urging laypeople to engage in ascetic exercises are various and deserve a deeper analysis, that will be conducted in Chapter 4. For the moment, we will briefly analyze the different frameworks in which laypeople find themselves while participating in a practice as well as how they understand and justify their own participation.

'Strong' lay practice

The first model that I would like to propose may be understood as a 'strong' lay practice framework. By this term I wish to indicate all those practices in which the lay component is 'strong', namely all the people involved do not belong to any recognizable institutional religious group (as trained priests or monks, or shamans etc. – in short, they are not 'religious professionals'). In these cases, there is also little or no difference between the practitioners and the practice leaders in terms of religious status. The practice leaders are thus better understood as simply more experienced practitioners who can help others by virtue of their experience but they possess no special 'powers' or religious initiations that distinguishes them from the others.[5] This framework sometimes overlaps with the previously mentioned *modes* of practice 'outside a religiously established environment' or in the cases of simple borrowing of ascetic acts. For instance, such is the case of many of the practices taking place before or during a *matsuri*, as in the aforementioned Ontakesan-jinja *harumatsuri*. In that case, although ascetic feats like the *hawatari* and *hiwatari* are taking place in the grounds of a Shinto shrine, the instructions about ascetic techniques come mostly from practitioners, with the practice leaders playing no role in this. Lacking an organic doctrinal background – and possibly by

virtue of that – the practice itself is subject to a number of often divergent interpretations and understandings. The practice lore therefore has a life of its own; it
is also susceptible to being influenced by contingent issues and agendas similar to
those influencing the lives of its practitioners. To support this last consideration,
I conducted a series of demoscopic-oriented interviews at Ontakesan-jinja at both
the October and April festivals.

My informants can be divided roughly into three groups: old men, young
men and women.[6] The old and young men are kept separate because they display remarkably different patterns of behaviour and understanding. The proposed
questions were tailored to be concise enough to be efficiently uttered in the noisy
context of a feasting crowd and simple enough to require no more than a short
answer from people who may be too busy to stop for an extended interview. The
questions here were generally posited in the following sequence:

a   Where are you from?
b   Do you come often to the *matsuri*?
c   Do you do this [ascetic practice] every time?
d   What is the meaning of this *gyō*?

Old men tended to belong to local confraternities, so in this specific case they were
mostly from Saitama area and generally attended the festival on a regular basis.
Many of them were indeed very proud to point out that they had participated in the
matsuri every year for the last 20 years or more.[7] They were also quite regular in
the performance of ascetic feats, including the demanding *hawatari*. The question
about the meaning of the ascetic exercises was, not surprisingly, the one eliciting
the widest number of interpretations. To a few of them, as I have already mentioned, this represented a symbolic achievement: 'if you can do this, you can do
everything'. Some others, perhaps the more doctrinally conscious, remarked how
this was a way to 'concentrate all your energy and all your thoughts on a single-
minded effort [*isshin* 一心]', in order to keep your faculties clear and sharp. But
the overwhelming majority agreed on the fact that this was a way to thank Ontake
Daijin for the benefits enjoyed during the year and to ensure the continuation of
this relationship between the *kami* and his devotees. In other words, for old men
this was a sort of 'ascetic routine' aimed at sustaining an uninterrupted flow of
this-worldly benefits (*genze ryaku* 現世利益).[8]

On the contrary, young men displayed a quite different understanding. A relatively larger number of them came from areas other than Saitama, although not so
distant, such as Tokyo, Mito or Utsunomiya. Several of them were from Nagano,
following the Okamoto family, the leaders of the Agematsu Jiga Daikyōkai mentioned in the previous chapter. Their answers to my questions revealed a far lower
degree of regular commitment to the event and the practices when compared with
the old men. Most of them told me that they came only occasionally, 'because too
busy with their job' and, while all of them had practised the *hiwatari* regularly,
only a few had ever attempted the ladder of swords. It was indeed possible to
notice how the group of people performing the *hawatari* was a considerably small

portion of the total participants (15–20 people out of about 200 total participants in the *matsuri*). Most of them were old practitioners, while perhaps no more than five or six of them were the younger ones. Questioned about this, many young men were unashamed to admit that they avoided the *hawatari* because it looked too dangerous. However, most of them agreed that they should attempt it one day. Everybody also agreed on the fact that the ascetic exercises produced a number of tangible this-worldly benefits, ranging from a good job or a good wife to better business performance.[9] Remarkably, none of them had 'deeper' or more 'religious' explanations to offer.[10]

Women proved to be more homogeneous in their behaviour and understanding, which is the reason why they have not been divided in 'old' and 'young' subcategories. They were similar to the old men regarding provenance and attendance: they were mostly from Saitama area and regularly attended the *matsuri*. Almost all of the women attending, judging from a mere visual survey, were avid fire-walkers and queued up eagerly for the *hiwatari* as soon as the *goma* fire was extinguished. Only one middle-aged woman, however, successfully attempted the *hawatari*. But the difference between female and male behaviour and understanding was evident from the divergent purposes urging them to take part in an ascetic feat. Nearly all of the women were practising for the sake of their family, parents, children, husbands and so on. In other words, they were taking part in an ascetic exercise in order to benefit *others* rather than themselves, and in this there was no distinction between the older and younger women.[11]

As noted at the beginning of the chapter, the lack of doctrinal support and absence of a proper leadership allow people to fashion their understanding of an ascetic practice based upon their personal agendas. Personal agendas are, in turn, very often shaped by social issues and customs, so that specific intentions in specific circumstances may be the reflection of a more general understanding of one's place in society at large.[12] Moreover, generational issues also come into play. Men, as we have seen, display a more 'self-centred' attitude, while their understanding of the purpose of the ascetic practice mimics their contingent temporal collocation in the course of everyday life, namely the need to obtain benefits for the present and future. Old men are more 'thankful' and want to 'preserve' an existing relationship between themselves and the deity.[13] They are, in other words, more *past-oriented*; they look back at past benefits with gratitude while managing an already long-standing relationship with the deity. Young men are more *future-oriented*; they often mention goals in a more or less distant future and for them the practice is a way to shorten the time to reach that goal. They do not seem to care too much about a 'continuous relationship' – as proven by their discontinuous attendance – since their mind is still open to change; hence the practice could as well be a part of their future as not. Women are instead taught to care for others; their mindset is more prone to being selfless, already oriented towards a life of service and respect. For them, this ascetic practice is just another way to fulfil this duty.

All this could radically change – and indeed it does change in other examples that we shall examine shortly – if the theoretical background of the ascetic practice is strong enough to provide explanatory and behavioural frameworks alternative to those of everyday life.[14] This shift would require an emphasis on *religious-oriented* results, such as the attainment of *kenshō* in the case of the *rōhatsu sesshin* or the experience of the 10 realms of existence in the *akinomine*. In the examples of 'strong' lay asceticism provided, however, this is not yet possible because of the simplicity of the participants' doctrinal background; hence the practice ends up reflecting the aims and concerns of the participants. Horizontal solidarity, *camaraderie* and also a good handful of genuine will for diversion also constitute a substantial part of the glue that keeps the group together.

'Weak' lay practice

The second main division of ascetic practices involving laypeople relates to what we can define a 'weak' model of lay practice. Here the term 'weak' is employed to emphasize the fact that in this case the laypeople's influence in the practice is weak, as they are practising alongside religious professionals, generally under their leadership. This category does not necessarily overlap with the third *mode* of practice ('practices taking place within an established religious environment'), because such religious leaders do not necessarily belong to any established religious movement. Such is the case, for instance, of the Jiga Daikyōkai *samugyō*, which we examined in Chapter 2. Nonetheless, the circumstances in which laypeople undergo ascetic training under the supervision of religious professionals within an established religious environment is by far the most common way of practising asceticism in Japan. The most diffused form of this 'weak' lay asceticism involves the practice of *shugyō* in the mountain, and this is very often carried out by Shugendō groups. The above discussed *akinomine* practice in the Dewa Sanzan provides a valuable example of this form of lay involvement. In this section, I would like to briefly analyze another Shugendō practice: the *okugake shugyō* 奥駈修行 (practice 'inside the mountain'). My reason for using this highly demanding practice as an example of lay asceticism is to demonstrate how the term 'lay' does not necessarily imply a sloppy standard of the ascetic effort. The *okugake* is indeed a most demanding physical and psychological commitment and it is reasonable to infer that the participation of laypeople does not occur casually.

The *okugake shugyō* takes place generally in late July or early August on the famous pilgrimage route from Yoshino to Kumano.[15] There are many versions of this practice. Some, particularly those held by the Kinpusen-ji 金峰山寺 temple, are reserved for the training of fully ordained priests, while others are closer to a form of pilgrimage rather than a *shugyō*.[16] In yet other cases, laypeople are permitted to undergo the full route (*zenkō* 全航) under the guidance of a Ōmine *sendatsu*.[17] One such case is the *okugake shugyō* organized by Tōnan-in 東南院 temple in Yoshino. Tōnan-in is one of the temples located in the precinct of Kinpusen-ji temple in a southeast direction (hence its name). Popular lore attributes its foundation to En no Gyōja, and the main object of worship is indeed En no Gyōja Jinben Daibosatsu itself.[18]

The *Ōmine okugake route* (*Ōmine okugake-michi* 大峯奥駈道) from Yoshino to Kumano is about 100 kilometres long. This means that in order to cover the distance in five days, as the Tōnan-in version requires, the participants need to walk an average of 20 kilometres per day. A small part of the route is constituted by mountain paths, streets and even staircases, but for most of the way the participants have to walk following steep mountain trails, climb on rock walls barehanded or follow the line of a rocky cliff holding onto an iron chain set into the cliff (see Figure 3.1). To add more distress, no shoes are permitted during the practice, with the only acceptable footwear being the traditional *jikatabi* 地下足袋,[19] whose very thin soles offer little protection from the asperities of the mountain.

The daily walking, tiring and dangerous in itself, is often interrupted by other additional practices, simply called *gyō,* performed at various sacred places known as *nabiki* 靡 set along the road.[20] The first series of these practices takes place on the top of Mount Ōmine[21] (Sanjōgatake *nabiki* 山上ケ岳靡) and it starts at the very well-known Nishi no Nozoki 西の覗, a protruding rock formation looking

Figure 3.1 The author on the *Ōmine okugake* route

westward. Here the practitioner is suspended by a rope head-down towards the valley below and is then asked to confess his sins.[22] Upon arrival at Ōmine-san-ji, the main temple at the top of the mountain, another *gyō* known as *ura no gyōba* 裏の行場 or *uragyōba* takes places in the path among the rocky formations behind the temple. This practice is also known as Sanjōgatake *nabiki* or simply Sanjōgatake, and involves a high degree of physical stress and even potentially fatal risk. First, all of the *gyōja* are asked to climb a steep cliff barehanded, on the top of which a narrow natural stone corridor, known as the 'inner womb' (*tainai kuguri* 胎内潜), leads to a small clearing. From here, a narrow path between the rocks leads to the 'ants' crossing' (*ari no towatari* 蟻の門渡り), where in the past the last part of the trail needed to be covered by a short jump. Now, however, the gap has been spanned with a very narrow stone bridge that needs to be crossed by walking on all fours. At the end of the bridge, a most demanding test awaits the practitioner: 'the rock of equality' (*byōdō no iwa* 平等の岩), a massive boulder almost the size of a small car, protruding from the *higashi no nozoki* 東の覗 cliff. To complete the ascetic act known as '*ishimawari*' 石周り, the *gyōja* must 'circumambulate' the boulder around its entire perimeter. The portion leaning on the edge of the cliff can easily be covered but the remaining half requires the practitioner to hang from the rock by his bare hands alone, while looking for a place to stick his toes in order to slowly advance around the boulder. A slip at this moment would mean certain death, as there is nothing between the cliff and the valley below but hundreds of metres of thin air.[23]

These are but just a few examples of the level of austerities that the participants to the *okugake shugyō* are required to face. Further *nabiki* require the practitioners to climb steep cliffs, cross unstable bridges and plunge themselves into cold streams. Although the road becomes somewhat easier after Zenki (*nabiki* no. 29), the walking practice always remains a formidable challenge and the *shugenja* eventually reach Kumano utterly exhausted.[24]

From this brief overview, we can observe how the organization of this practice resembles the structure of the *akinomine* as described in Chapter 2: an ascetic practice of laypeople under the guidance of religious professionals, where both participants and leaders undertake more or less all the same ascetic exertions. In the *okugake*, however, the boundaries between laypeople and priests seem to assume particular and somehow contradictory overtones. Two distinct factors come into play: *leadership* and *practice*. Regarding the first, the *okugake* is possibly one of the cases where the leadership shows the highest degree of specialization and, at the same time, the strongest emphasis on the leader's authority. While the boundaries between the leadership and the participants in the *akinomine* tend to be more relaxed, in the *okugake* every step is carefully planned by the leaders and enacted accordingly to a rigidly structured hierarchy. The Tōnan-in *daisendatsu* leads the practice with the help of some Kinpusen-ji priests and a number of senior practitioners who are entitled to play various roles.[25] His decision is unquestionable and one is supposed to follow the seniors' instruction to the letter without complaining. The leaders stay in separate rooms during overnight stops and it is not possible to address them directly (particularly the *daisendatsu*) without requesting proper permission.[26] Referring to our preliminary classification, then, this practice appears to be a very 'weak' lay practice, portraying lay practitioners as no more than 'guests' in a 'professional' ascetic environment. On the other hand, this gap is dramatically reduced during the periods of actual practice on the mountain. The *daisendatsu* indeed shares all the practices performed by lay participants, walking the same road as well as leading religious services and offering occasional brief doctrinal explanations on the meaning of specific places. In this sense, the role of laypeople becomes a rather strong one, particularly if we look at the harshness of this practice.

Concurrently, lay practitioners seem to display a certain awareness with regard to the different 'levels' of endeavour that a practice might require, and they attempt to match their specific abilities to the practice requirement. In other words, people seem to be aware that there are 'easier' and 'harder' practices and that the benefits obtained are often proportional to this scale of difficulty.[27] Indeed, many of the discussions of the practices' participants revolve around their experiences of other *shugyō* and they spend lengthy conversations comparing the features of each practice so as to sort out the easier from the harder ones.[28] However, all are equally considered *shugyō* and no practice is thought to be 'less ascetic' than the others. The *okugake* practitioners, as well as those of other 'advanced' lay practices like the *akinomine*, also clearly understand that the practice is not merely a pilgrimage but that they are undergoing a *shugyō* and that they are to be called *gyōja* and not *junreisha* 巡礼者 (pilgrims): '*Junreisha* are old women climbing Mount Fuji!', as someone told me half-jokingly.[29]

This 'sense of *shugyō*' (to paraphrase Bell's 'sense of ritual'), however, does not necessarily seem to stem from doctrinal awareness. It is indeed astonishing to see how wide the gap between the levels of doctrinal awareness within the same *gyōja* group can be, nor does this gap seem to follow any particular pattern.[30] Older practitioners are generally more prepared – some of them know the whole series of *nabiki* by heart – but this is not necessarily a rule. There were a few seasoned practitioners who were remarkable for their mountaineering ability and practical knowledge, remembering, for example, all the places where fresh water could be found along the route. They were at the same time almost completely unaware of any doctrinal meanings but this did not seem to undermine their authority. The same can be said for the younger participants; while most of them were completely unaware of the meaning of the practice, at least two young participants had a specific interest in Shugendō which they also wanted to pursue at academic level. And yet the 'sense of *shugyō*' was equally sharp in all of them. The answers to my question, 'what is *shugyō*, in your understanding?' listed mostly a mere series of acts and circumstances: *shugyō* is walking in the sacred mountain, is the *hiwatari*, is effort, is risk and danger etc. In other words, *shugyō* is *performance, shugyō is what shugyō does.*[31] And *who* does the *shugyō* is a *gyōja*. In this sense, the category *shugyō* is understood as a Boolean variable that can be marked TRUE only when performance is enacted. The variable is binary and displays no middle points; a certain practice either is *shugyō* or it is not, as there is no middle point between performance and non-performance. Other variables may change – place, time, religious environment, doctrinal awareness, physical strain etc. – but once the body of the practitioner is engaged in the performance of an ascetic feat, that performance becomes *gyō* and is perceived as such. Once again, then, we can find the performative use of the human body as the core object of the *shugyō* hermeneutic, which not surprisingly works as a constant within a system of other variables.[32]

Practices for religious professionals

Religious professionals, such as Buddhist and Shinto priests, probably constitute a more homogeneous category of practitioners and portray a narrower range of motivations for their ascetic activities. A first sub-category is represented by those who undertake ascetic practices in order to legitimize their roles within their social community or religious order. This is the case of the Ontake leaders we examined earlier on, who undertake practices, or sets of practices, specific to their roles, such as winter solitary retreats and extended period of water ablutions.[33] Another significant example of the first category is the training of local shamanic figures, which both *fabricates* and legitimizes them as professional mediums.[34] In this case, the ascetic practice operates a permanent change in the religious, and sometime also social, status of the successful practitioner. One such case is the training of the blind mediums generally known as *itako*.[35] Although forms may vary from region to region, the training pattern of a female blind medium generally takes place as follows. The aspirant *itako* undergoes a preliminary training for the duration of one year. She starts her day performing a number of ablutions with cold water, regardless of the season and temperature. Generally, the *itako* is also supposed to practice some dietary rules (the so-called 'three abstentions': from cereals, salt and hot food) and some periods of abstention from sleep as well. The training is generally conducted in a small, generally unheated hut or wooden house, often far away from a settled area. Besides these abstentions, the *itako* is also required to memorize a large number of sutras and invocations, from the *Hannya shingyō* to specific invocations for Fudō Myōō and other local deities. This memorization may be seen as an ascetic practice as well because, from all accounts, the girls are literally forced to repeat the texts hundreds of times a day and are also severely scolded by their teachers in case of error.[36] The end purpose of this whole effort is to put the body of the *itako* in a condition so that it can be possessed by a deity, often Fudō Myōō. Once the possession takes place, the trainee is regarded as a fully legitimate *itako* and she can finally exercise that profession within her community.[37] Thus, while she does not gain the title of *gyōja*, at the end of the practice the trained girl is indeed legitimated as a religious professional. However, it is very difficult to determine if the aspirant *itako* perceives the practice as affecting her identity or if the training is just a form of professional requirement or qualification. As noted earlier on, the absence of a complex doctrinal framework is not per se an obstacle to ascetic practice. However, when this framework is weak, the identity of the ascetic is also weak as a result.

Nevertheless, we can find the most striking examples of practices reserved for religious professionals in established environments, such as Nichiren-shu's *daiaragyō*[38] and the famous Tendai *kaihōgyō*. I would like to highlight the latter as a pre-eminent case of 'highly-exclusive' practice, since it is carried out in a long-established religious institution – the Tendai school – by specially authorized individuals who are already fully fledged members of that institution and will remain as members at the end of the practice, although with some change in their status. No layperson is permitted to attempt such practices nor does the ascetic practitioner allow any group or individual layperson to share his practice in its whole.[39]

Tendai kaihōgyō

A shorter version of the *kaihōgyō*, lasting 'merely' 100 days, is a compulsory practice for any monk wanting to become a Tendai *zasu* 座主 (abbot).[40] However, for our study, I will concentrate on the 1,000-day practice (*sennichi kaihōgyō* 千日回峰行), which represents a more complex ascetic phenomenon. For the sake of clarity and brevity, I will utilize here the brief but efficacious summary of the whole *sennichi kaihōgyō* proposed by Stevens, following which I will explain its various points (see Table 3.1).

The *gyōja* starts off in his white robe and straw sandals, with the *tefuni* (the list of holy places to worship on his way) and various supplies including two candles, matches, a paper lantern and a straw raincoat. Some of the most important items that he carries with him are not just functional but also hold a powerful symbolic meaning. Around his waist are tied the *shide no himo* 死出の紐 (the 'rope of death') and the *goma no ken* 護摩の剣 (a kind of knife). These objects are, as is well known, two attributes of Fudō Myōō, but in this case they also symbolize the absolute will of the practitioner to complete the course or, failing this, to die by his own hand by hanging or disembowelment. I could not find any significant evidence of *kaihōgyōja* who have committed suicide, and when I interviewed the current Mudō-ji *ajari*, Uehara Gyōshō 上原行照, he was rather elusive about this topic.[41] However, an event in recent history proves that this meaning is still alive today. After the occupation of Japan by the Allied forces in 1945, any kind of personal weapon was forbidden; in particular here, the *kaihōgyōja* were asked to stop carrying the *goma no ken*. They refused by stating that the knife was only meant to hurt oneself and not others.[42]

Everything in the *gyōja* appearance seems to represent the fact that he is embarking on what may be his last journey. The white colour of the robe, the traditional colour of death, and the fact that he also carries a coin to be used as toll for the passage into the afterlife, are powerful signs of his determination. In his left hand, he carries his rosary and, later, a wooden staff. The rosary will be used not just for reciting mantras or for the worship at holy places but also to bless the people that the *gyōja* will encounter along the road with a gentle tap on their heads.[43] The main distinctive sign of a *kaihōgyōja* is the characteristic *higasa* 日傘 hat. It is

Table 3.1 Summary of *sennichi kaihōgyō*

Year	Days of practice	Distance	Kaihōgyōja *titles and notable facts*
First year	100 days	30[a] (40)[b] km each day One-day *kirimawari* (54 km)	*Shingyōja* ('new *gyōja*') No *tabi*, hat carried
Second year	100 days	Ibid.	Ibid.
Third year	100 days	Ibid.	Ibid.
Fourth year	100 days 100 days	30 (40) km + *kirimawari*	*Tabi* permitted; hat worn from the 301st day. Upon completion, *Byakutai Gyōja*
Fifth year	100 days 100 days	Ibid.	Wooden staff permitted from 501st day; on 700th day *dō-iri*. Completing the *dō-iri*, the *gyōja* becames *Tōgyōman Ajari*
Sixth year	100 days	60 km each day	*Sekizan Kugyō*
Seventh year	100 days 100 days	84 km each day 30 (40) km, *kirimawari*	*Kyoto Ōmawari* Upon completion, the *gyōja* becames *Daigyōman Ajari*
Total	1,000 days	38,632 (46,572) km	

Source: John Stevens 1988: 71.

Notes

a This number refers to the course starting from Mudō-ji and going through the Eastern Precinct, Western Precinct, Yokawa, Sakamoto and then returning to Mudō-ji.
b This number refers to the Imuro Valley course, starting from Sakamoto and passing through the Eastern Precinct, the Western Precinct, Yokawa and back.

exceedingly long and, strangely, does not offer significant protection from the sun or rain. In the opinion of some *gyōja*, its length is good for removing the small branches and hedges that may wound the *gyōja*'s face, especially while walking at night.[44] On the other hand, a *gyōja* stated in a recorded interview that the hat is important because it is possible for the practitioner to understand from its movement if his pace and body trim are the correct one.[45] The *higasa*, in fact, should be 'flying' straight into the air and not bouncing at every step. Beside its practical use, the shape of the hat is quite clearly the shape of a lotus blooming on the surface of water. This image traditionally represents the blooming of the Buddhist law in the world of illusions, untouched and unscathed like a lotus blooming in muddy waters. The symbolic importance of the *higasa* is such that the *shingyōja* 新行者 (the freshmen) cannot use it until their 301st day of practice; until that day, the hat is carried on their left forearm.

A fundamental feature already present in the early years of the practice is the *kirimawari* 切回 which breaks the incessant walking of the practitioner around Mount Hiei. This longer run goes throughout Kyoto and involves a number of stops to worship at various holy places around the city. Generally, the *gyōja* starts the *kirimawari* between the 65th and 75th days of practice, when they are invited to 'practice for the sake of the others in the world'.[46] This involves not just the worship of selected places but also the direct blessing of the people waiting by the road for the *gyōja* to pass by. During the fourth and fifth years of the *kaihōgyō*, the route remains virtually the same, the only difference being that the days of practice are doubled from 100 to 200. In order to undertake this endeavour, the *gyōja* is permitted to wear the *tabi* and the *higasa* for the first time (from the 301st day), two things that make the continuous walking considerably more comfortable. Then, on the 501st day of practice (a sort of partial turning point), he is finally permitted to use the wooden staff. At this point, the *gyōja* has reached his peak physical form. Holding the title of *Byakutai Gyōja* 白帯行者 (white belt *gyōja*), he will practice for another 200 days until what may be called the turning point of the practice, the *dō-iri*, which is the nine-day period of fasting in the Myōō-do 明王堂 of Mudō-ji.

The figures concerning this extreme ascetic practice are stunning in themselves: nine days without any food, sleep, rest and, more impressively, without a single drop of water. It is only from the fifth day that the *gyōja* is permitted to rinse his mouth with a cup of water once a day. Not a single drop should be swallowed, however, and all the liquid must be spat back into the cup. The *gyōja* should also recite the Fudō Myōō mantra for a total of one million times throughout the nine days, which means practically uninterrupted recitation the entire time. Added to this is the complete recitation of the *Lotus Sutra* once per day.[47] The practitioners say that this is a good exercise for maintaining concentration and staying awake, but it must be an unimaginable effort. Lastly, every day at 2.00am, the *gyōja* is required to perform the *shusui* 取水, the water-taking ritual at the Aka well. This consists of taking a bucket of water from the well and then offering it to the statue of Fudō inside the Myōō-dō. The Aka well is no more than 200 metres from the Myōō-dō, so the trip takes no more than few minutes on the first days. However, as the exhaustion of the *gyōja* grows, the length of time required every day is longer, until it takes up to an hour in the final days.[48] All the practitioners say that during the last part of the *dō-iri*, the sensations of the body are enormously enhanced and they became able to hear the slightest sounds, such as the falling of the ashes from an incense stick located at the other side of the hall.[49]

On the ninth day, when the *gyōja* is literally on the brink of death, the fasting ends and the *gyōja* receives a medicinal herb tea called *hō-no-yū* and an official document of completion from Enryaku-ji. The *dō-iri* is over and the *gyōja* is granted the title of *Tōgyōman Ajari* 当行満阿闍梨: the 'master (Sanskrit, *ācārya*) who fulfilled the practice'. The path of the *gyōja* is not over, however. After his recovery, he starts again his walking route for the sixth year. This time, the course also includes the Sekisan-in 赤山院 at the very base of Mount Hiei and passes along the famous Kirara slope.[50] This causes the route to increase to 60 kilometres per day.

In the seventh year, the *gyōja* faces his other great challenge, second only to the *dō-iri*: the *Kyoto Ōmawari* 京都大回. The entire route, which includes the Hiei course plus the 44-kilometre route around Kyoto, totals 84 kilometres each day.[51] Again, as in the *kirimawari*, the *gyōja* performs a number of worship acts and blesses a remarkably numerous crowd waiting for him on the sides of the road.

In the last phase, almost unexpectedly after such a dramatic climax, the *gyōja* returns on the last 100 days of practice to the 'short' route of the beginning of this practice. The only difference is that he now can bear the title of *Daigyōman Ajari* 大行満阿闍梨 ('great practice-fulfilling master'). Upon the completion of the last 100 days, he is received at the Kyoto imperial palace, where he will celebrate the rite known as *dosoku sandai* 土足参内. As a sign of his high status, he is permitted to keep his *tabi* on while entering the imperial ground,[52] an honour bestowed on nobody else.

From this description, it is clear how the ascetic practice alters the status of the practitioner both within his own religious institution and in regard to the 'outside world'. The *kaihōgyōja*'s progress through the practice runs parallel to his progress as religious professional, with him changing his titles following the accomplishment of certain practices, while at the same time obtaining certain privileges. When a practice is such a long-standing and established tradition as the *kaihōgyō*, these elements are so strong and deeply rooted that they eventually redefine the *identity* of the ascetic practitioner permanently.

Why? Motivation

The choice of the ascetic practitioner

A number of different reasons can push a person to dedicate himself to a period of austerities, and these reasons are generally closely connected to the social and personal elements present in the practitioner's life. Some motivations might be relevant to specific modes of practice. For example, in the case of institutionalized asceticism, the practice or the series of practices are meant to help the ascetic in hierarchical advancement, as in the case of the Tendai priest who is required to perform the 100-day *kaihōgyō* as a requirement to access the rank of *zasu* 座主.

In the case of the Nichiren priests, although undergoing the *daiaragyō* is not a requirement for them, it is something highly pushed by their parishioners, since the *aragyō* bestows power and further skills on the priest.[53] Thus, many priests may feel compelled to fulfil that ascetic routine as a part of their duties. In other cases, such as the *itako* training, the practice must be carried out in order to achieve proper 'professional' status; in this sense, it is not necessarily a 'choice' but a required process. Occasional borrowing of acts during religious celebrations such as *matsuri* also follow this principle, where the ever-present *mizugori* or *takigyō* are meant to be a part of the ritual behaviour at such events and there is no real choice about whether they are performed or not. In these circumstances, however, there can still be exceptions. We have seen in the case of the *harumatsuri* that some of the people clearly *chose* to perform an ascetic feat without being directly involved in the ritual process or in the Iwakuni *kagura*, when an individual chose to be the *gyōja* in a central moment of the event. In other cases, such as the practice of *ontakegyōja*, the practitioner is often a member of a *kō*, and the communal environment, often tinged with long-lasting relationships, can certainly act as a driver for more regular participation.[54] The most striking circumstance, however, is the case of lay participation in highly demanding *shugyō* such as the *akinomine* and the *okugake*. In these cases, there is no compulsion from either the ritual or religious environment; consequently, all of the physical challenges of the practice are undertaken by choice and are accepted quite voluntarily.

The motivation for an ascetic exercise can thus be a choice; a choice which depends greatly on the status of the practitioner and the circumstances of the practice itself. We can then have 'low commitment' and 'high commitment' practices, depending on the level of willingness with which the practitioners offer themselves to the ascetic effort (see Table 3.2).

As I have said, after the occasional acts within *matsuri*, the participation of laypeople in *shugyō* led by religious professionals is possibly the most common ascetic activity in Japan. It is indeed in this situation that 'choice' plays its greatest role, as the practitioners all come to the practice as individuals with quite disparate personal motivations. One thing, however, binds all of these people together. The Hieizan Ajari, the old women at the *hiwatari*, the commoner on a Shugendō trail: all are endeavouring to obtain some form of *benefit*. The character of such benefits is left to the individuals' personal concerns, whether the possible advancement in religious rank, a benefit to the nation or the mere need for a new job. The idea that benefits are produced during and by the practice is commonplace, to the point of being taken for granted. This might be understood as just another side of the performative aspect of bodily practices. Achievement of benefits is considered to be a natural consequence of a properly performed *shugyō*, almost as a properly performed slice with a sharp knife will manage to cut a piece of bread. The proficient combination of a correct performance and adequate tools invariably produces predictable effects. The bodily tool, combined with the ascetic performance, is thus

Table 3.2 Levels of commitment to the ascetic effort

High commitment	*kaihōgyō*
	aragyō
	okugake
	rōhatsu sesshin
	akinomine and *Shugendō shugyō* in general
	itako training
	hawatari
Low commitment	*hiwatari*
	mizugori during *matsuri*

supposed to produce benefits in a way relatively proportional to the effort. This may seem like mere theory, but as with all theories, it is not expounded merely to exist per se but to bring some rationale to actual phenomena. The idea that ascetic performances are efficacious in producing benefits was understood by all practitioners as simple fact, one that practitioners do not seem to feel the need to explain to themselves. The question 'Why?' did not receive a direct answer from any of my informants, but interestingly it was often misunderstood as 'for whom [are you doing the practice]?' 'Why are you doing a *shugyō*?' led to such answers as 'for my family', 'for my business', 'to find a good wife', 'to recover from an illness' and so on.[55]

Even in the most complex and exclusive forms of *ascetic practice*, like the *kaihōgyō*, the aetiology of the ascetic effort concentrates on the effects of the practice and those effects are indeed benefits. We shall now analyze which benefits are sought after by ascetic practitioners in order to delineate a clearer picture of their motivations. Benefits obtained from a *shugyō* can be roughly classified according to their target: the practitioner himself or other people.

Practices for oneself and for others

The division of ascetic practices into practices for *oneself* and for *others* seems to more accurately indicate an 'orientation' in the effort of the practitioner rather than two specific kinds of practices. As we have seen in the examples above, as, for example, in the Spring festival's *hiwatari* and *hawatari*, a number of factors can influence the choice of the practitioner in one or the other direction; in this, no negligible role is played by mere social convention. We can consequently speak more appropriately of 'inwardly oriented' practices and benefits. Examples of inward tendencies in ascetic performances can be identified in almost all practices; in the mentioned activities of the Ontake devotees, in the Ontake *samugyō* or in many water ablutions (*suigyō*) performed on various occasions and for various purposes, from the celebration of a successful graduation to the enhancing of one's possibilities in job-seeking. Practices in established religious environments are no exception here, as the variety of motivations I was able to learn from my interviews with Shugendō practitioners seemed to confirm.

Some occasional practitioners display a certain degree of 'selfish' intentions in performing ascetic deeds. For instance, a consistent number of young people regularly meet in mid-winter in the region of Minami-ashigara 南足柄 (Kanagawa prefecture) to practice *suigyō* in the cold weather in order to 'better their diet and their mood'. After being instructed by a more experienced person on how to perform some simple *kaji* spells, young men and women plunge into the icy pond at the bottom of Sonan waterfall. After a few seconds spent in the water up to their necks, they reach the waterfall where they briefly stand while chanting the *Hannya shingyō*. All this is accompanied by laughter, chatting and a general sense of amusement.[56] It should not surprise us that the person instructing them was the only one with some previous experience of the practice, while the others were complete first-timers. The inward nature of the intentions behind the practice does not invite recurring participation; equally, the absence of a religious institution in the background precludes the possibility of that kind of continuing tie. This is not to say, however, that inward tendencies are a prerogative of this sort of popular, individually oriented and motivated ascetic feat. We may witness similar orientations in more complex settings as well.

Such is the case, for example, of many *ontakegyōja*, who often focus their practice on obtaining benefits for themselves or their families. On one occasion during the winter *samugyō* of the Jiga Daikyōkai, a couple was particularly concerned about their inability to beget a child. They not only earnestly practised each one of the feats required by the *samugyō* but they also added further acts in order to enhance the effects of this *shugyō* to its maximum. Such additional efforts included sweeping the staircase of the various temples and shrines when the practice leaders were approaching, fasting and helping the leaders in their everyday tasks by holding their walking staffs or garments. Their commitment was clearly visible and it was perhaps for this reason that they were the people who interacted least with the other practitioners. For their efforts, they were rewarded with longer addresses by the *kami* during the possession sessions (*kamigakari*). During these sessions, both the couple and the medium wept profusely, while the rest of the group commented on their misfortunes and offered prayers in support. It is clear, then, that the couple joined the practice for their own benefit and did not have any purpose extending beyond the sphere of their family life.[57]

These 'inward tendencies' do not, however, imply selfishness, even in the few cases when the practice is thoroughly solitary, such as Yamada Ryūshin 山田龍真, who was mentioned briefly earlier and now deserves a closer look. Yamada Ryūshin is an acupuncturist and healer as well as an ordained Shingon priest who practised the 1,000-day *daiaragyō* on Mount Kubote from 1983 to 1986. A complete account of his practice is recorded in his book *Aragyō: Tatoe kono inochi, kuchihaterutomo*, which follows the same blueprint outlined earlier as one of the *genres* of 'ascetic literature'. This work depicts the ascetic exercises of Yamada as a very solitary and self-focused practice, taking place in the isolated world of Mount Kubote during the winter season.[58] It may seem that the ascetic finds himself in a double inner-focused situation: first, he does not practice with the aid of an ascetic community, second, although belonging to an established religious environment (here the Shingon school), he is not practising within the infrastructure of that school, as the practice is solitary. The practitioner constitutes in this case both the doctrinal and performative centre of the practice. As a matter of orthodoxy then, he can also be thought to be the master of his own behaviour; in other words, in a solitary practice such as this, the practitioner himself becomes the ultimate religious authority and this authority the practice both justifies and maintains. The 'solitude' of the practice can thus better be understood as the moment of 'desocialization' required for the ascetic to legitimize himself and to become a 'holy person' in extra-ordinary contexts. In this phase, the energy of the ascetic is pointed inwards and the benefits of the practice are accumulated only within himself.

This is just a component of the whole process, however, and not the purpose or final goal of the practice itself. Later on, the *gyōja* will return to the ordinary world and will release the power accumulated for the sake of others. This intention is very clear in Yamada's account and constitutes the backbone of his determination in the practice.[59] People around him are well aware of this and on the few occasions in which he came into contact with other people, the *gyōja* was exhorted to complete the practice for the benefit of all.

Accumulation-and-release process

An even more striking example of this *accumulation-and-release* process is inherent in the very structure of the Tendai *kaihōgyō*. Saying that the *kaihōgyō* is merely continued walking and thus recognizing its basic structure as a form of *iterative asceticism* would be highly reductive vis-à-vis the highly complex and well-defined structure of the whole practice itself. As demonstrated in the scheme above, the nature of the *kaihōgyō* follows what may more correctly be defined as a 'progressive' path. The first three years are apparently still inspired by an iterative model; the *gyōja* conducts a regular, if not 'everyday' life, always undertaking the same acts in the same places and at the same times. The practice is particularly strict, and he cannot wear the *higasa* or the *tabi*. But, unexpectedly, between the 65th and the 75th day of practice, this routine is broken by the *kirimawari*, the route around Kyoto. This is the first sign of what will become a recursive pattern underlying the whole *kaihōgyō* experience. Here we have (for approximately the first two-thirds of this practice) what seems like a period of *purification* and at the same time of *accumulation* of merits and powers, and then at the end of the second third of the practice, a phase of *release* of these merits for the benefit of the community (the *kirimawari*). The structure of this progression is not linear, however, in the sense that it does not end with the phase of *release* as we might expect. Instead, the 100 days ends with the *reprisal* of the ordinary initial phase of *purification/accumulation*. Moreover, a deeper look into the daily practice of the *gyōja* reveals that this basic theme also underlies his basic daily routine. After setting off from Mudō-ji around 1.30am, the *gyōja* walks around the course, incessantly chanting the mantra of Fudō-myōō and worshiping at every sacred place indicated on his *tefuni*. Although for most of the time the concentration of the *gyōja* may be seen as directed 'inwardly' in order to maintain a constant pace and perform the various worship acts correctly, this order is altered on a single occasion. Along the route to Yokawa, there is a place called *gyōkutaisugi* 玉体杉, named after a sacred cedar tree that represents the Emperor (the *gyōkutai*, jewel body, i.e. the body of the Emperor), apparently just another object of worship along the *gyōja*'s course which also offers a beautiful view of the city of Kyoto. What is different here is that beside the cedar there is a stone bench. The *gyōja* is allowed to take his only moment of rest during the entire course on that bench while also reciting a two-minute prayer for the protection of the imperial family (*gyōkutai kaji* 玉体加持).[60] The modalities of this act of worship may be compared to the *kirimawari*. It is, in fact, performed around the end of the second third of the route and represents a complete shift in the focus of the practitioner. He is sitting, the merit-accumulation practice has temporarily stopped and the object of his prayers is not a part of the sacred route he has followed until that moment but something distant, even *external* to the sacred perimeter of both the practice route and the holy mountain. Like the *kirimawari,* the act of praying at the sacred cedar is outwardly oriented; it represents the moment of *release* within the daily practice.

There is consequently a redundant scheme in the whole 1,000-day *kaihōgyō* that apparently stems from this basic threefold feature of *purification/accumulation–release–reprisal*. Moreover, considering the whole practice in its totality, we can discern two important facets in the evolution of the *gyōja*. First, the endeavour itself becomes more and more intense. The number of days of practice during the fourth and fifth year doubles, while in the sixth year the length of the course is increased to 60 kilometres, and in the seventh year, during the *Ōmawari*, reaches the amazing figure of 84 kilometres per day. Following the basic structure proposed above, it is just during the final year that the course is restored to its usual distance and length of time (30 kilometres and 100 days). What marks the turning point here is the practice of the *dō-iri* on the seven-hundredth day. After nine days of complete fasting, the *gyōja* is radically transformed. The general impression that all the *gyōja* report is that everything completely left them; good and bad are now meaningless and their perception of reality is absolutely clear.[61] As a further example, many monks assisting the *gyōja* during the *dō-iri* notice how the water he periodically uses to rinse his mouth appears at first reddish-brown in colour and then, as time passes, it becomes clearer and clearer until it is as clear as pure water.[62] Other symptoms of this perfect purification are the aforementioned enhancement of the sense of hearing, plus occasionally some mystical visions.[63] It is outside of the remit of this chapter to investigate whether these sensations can be considered as mere consequences of a prolonged fast. What is important to note is that this moment marks the highest point in the *gyōja*'s self-oriented practice (for purification and accumulation) and then, at the same time, leads him to a massive shift in his focus. Again, similar to the basic theme of *purification–release–reprisal* that marks every day of the practitioner's life throughout the 1,000 days of practice, at approximately two-thirds of the way along its progression, that is after the *dō-iri*, the focus shifts from an inwardly oriented effort to an outwardly oriented one. The first step that manifests this change is the extension of the route to include the Kirara slope, which means that the walking course is shifted more towards the direction of the city of Kyoto. In doing this, the *gyōja* moves his whole practice (by means of his body) closer to the former capital in order to engage his renewed powers with the people of the city. Again, this phase of *release* reveals a progressive nature. The sixth year of the Sekisan Marathon is followed by the first 100-day term of the seventh year which features the greatest walking effort of all: the 84 kilometre *ōmawari* of the city of Kyoto. Although the present course only covers a part of the city, in the past, when the city was much smaller, it outlined its entire perimeter. Again, it is possible to trace a link between the protective prayers at *gyōkutaisugi*, the *kirimawari* and the *ōmawari*. All are outwardly oriented, all are made for the sake of 'others' and all are apparently the outcome of an initial phase of empowerment. The only difference seems to be the fact that the *ōmawari* is performed walking, as in the ordinary practice. We will return later to this topic in a deeper investigation of the interactions between body and space.

As expected, in the final 100 days of practice, the practitioner returns to the normal route, to 'everyday' life. What I want to point out is that the practice ends as it begins. Again, the basic pattern or scheme is respected – but this is not a mere repetition of individual or sets of practices as in the *iterative* model. Its main characteristic lies instead in the fact that this scheme is recursive and progressive at the same time (see Table 3.3).

As we can see in Table 3.3, the whole 1,000-day practice echoes and magnifies a single day of practice in a fractal form, starting from the basic scheme of *accumulation–release–reprisal*. Moreover, as we have seen, the basic scheme of the fractal is in itself recursive: it ends how it begins but it also ends how the next day of practice is going to begin. This closes the practice in a sort of temporal circle in which every act of the whole 1,000-day course is performed every day and vice-versa. In other words, every day of practice expresses the whole practice. Exerting himself on this solid and highly structured background, the figure of the ascetic practitioner is more ambivalent, more fluid between the two worlds of the secular and the sacred. He takes and gives; he accumulates and releases power not just for himself. His sacred body is meant to act as a bridge between the two worlds; thus the whole practice is not simply aimed at the construction of a highly skilled religious professional.

Ascetic aims

It is then, in all these cases, almost inappropriate to speak of practices benefiting only the practitioner. The possibility that an ascetic practice can benefit the practitioner directly is indeed not a quality of the practice per se but rather a choice that the ascetic makes in orienting his focus while practising. This only confirms the centrality of the figure of the ascetic within the phenomenon of asceticism in general. The power of 'desocializing' and 'resocializing' himself rests only in

Table 3.3 Patterns of practice in the *kaihōgyō*

	Purification/ accumulation	Release	Reprisal
Every day	Walking practice	*gyōkutaisugi* prayers	Walking back to Mudō-ji
100 days term	First 65–70 days	*kirimawari*	Last 30–25 days
1,000 day practice	First 700 days – *dō-iri*	*sekisan kugyō* – Kyoto Ōmawari	Last 100 days

his hand and not in the 'definition' of the practice. Ascetic practices, as we are progressively discovering, are in a sense devoid of definition, as they are not un-relational absolutes. In other words, they can only exist in the presence of a practitioner and in the time and space dimensions in which the practice takes place. Wilful intentions and contextual settings can change or even manipulate the orientation of this tool for the bodily *malleation* that is asceticism. In many cases, and this is often so with popular practices, the vagueness of any doctrinal position explaining what the intention is meant to be and the lack of a coherent context guiding the practice generate a particularly ductile background on which intentions of all sorts can be placed. This is not, however, a fully comprehensive explanation. This ductility in the interpretation of the practice is also present with the asceticism that takes place in institutional and well-recognized religious bodies, such as the Haguro *akinomine*. The *akinomine* should theoretically be undertaken in order to experience the six realms of existence and so eventually achieve buddhahood. In spite of this, it is remarkable to note a variety of intentions among which only a very few seem to adhere to the aforementioned doctrinal tenets. Among the many questions that I posed to my fellow roommates during the *akinomine*, 'why are you here?' was the one which originated the widest spectrum of answers and reactions. Someone was participating only because 'It is a tradition of Haguro, and I belong to this area'; somebody else 'to benefit my family'; 'because this brings me good luck'; 'because this makes me stronger'. A senior practitioner was firmly convinced that his earnestness in the practice was the true reason behind the success of his family-run company. Some had more 'spiritual intentions': the person sleeping right beside me was there to 'find himself, after a life of hard work'.[64] In this sort of restricted environment, it might seem natural to expect a certain uniformity in belief and purpose, but this was clearly not the case. The choice to orient the power of the practice in either an inwardly or outwardly direction appears to rest on the practitioner alone. It can therefore be better understood as just another element inside the performative aetiology of asceticism, namely the one that points the intentionality arrow in either direction. What seems to emerge so far is that the presence of this 'arrow' constitutes an unmistakable characteristic of the ascetic phenomenon. As I have argued in this work, asceticism is not a mere series of acts involving pain or self-harm aimed towards no particular purpose. The presence of a purpose – in this case, an 'orientation' with varying aim – is the retributive element balancing the often uncanny physical exertion that the practice requires; in its absence, asceticism could not be defined as other but sheer madness.

An ascetic practice that seems to refute this idea of the practitioner's role in orienting the aim of his effort is the above-mentioned *rōhatsu sesshin*. In the *sesshin*, the focus of the practice is clearly inwardly oriented as dictated by the very nature of the practice itself and not by the choice of the practitioner. The long hours of meditation and endurance of beating and strict discipline have no other purpose than the enlightenment of the individual practitioner. Because of the single-mindedness of this purpose, we may expect the practitioners to lack the variety of intentions driving the *akinomine* or *samugyō* practitioners. In this respect, it is interesting to underline that even in this case, a variety of purposes still exists and participants employ strategies to diversify their final targets. The goal of the *sesshin* is, as we have mentioned, to obtain *kenshō*, that is the experience of *satori*. Even so, the meaning of what *satori* is, and for which reason it should be obtained, is particular to each individual. The rigid discipline of the practice did not allow me to conduct extensive interviews with the participants; what little free time we did have was better spent in resting than chatting.[65] From what accounts I could collect, however, a familiar picture took shape. Many mentioned their reason for undertaking the *sesshin* as 'problems' generically, often 'personal problems'. At the same time, some claimed that their earlier participation in the practice had helped them in solving those problems. These 'solutions' are, not surprisingly, very practical and effectively this-worldly: some found the will to work again, and to start a family; some managed to recover their own family, from whom they have been long estranged; some got over a critical period and were able to take their life in their hands again. In the midst of the practice, with our bodies weakened by pain, fatigue and lack of sleep, these brief accounts were all exceptionally emotional, with people expressing their deepest feelings without the usual cultural restraint.[66] All of them related their experience and the benefits enjoyed after the practice to somebody else, whether a wife, husband, son or friend. *Satori* was not only meant as a personal ineffable experience but as new way of *being with others*. The strong outburst of feelings in our conversations — and this was true for my part as well — was a reflection of the richness of the relationships the practitioners entertained outside the restricted practice environment on both physical (the temple) and conceptual (the *Sōtō* doctrine) levels.

Gratitude

The last contextual relationship that it is worth noting is the widespread mention of a feeling of 'gratitude' throughout all the practices observed during my fieldwork research, as well as in publications by ascetic practitioners.[67] Gratitude (variably expressed with the terms *ongaeshi* 恩返し or *kansha* 感謝) always implies some kind of debt, which in most cases is extended to all the contextual level of the practice. Ascetic practitioners feel grateful first of all to practice leaders, fellow practitioners, and to those who might have enabled them to undertake the practice. On a broader level they constantly mention of gratitude *kami*, buddhist deities or even to 'nature' in general. In some cases gratitude has not a specific (human or superhuman) subject.[68]

The main reason for such gratitude seems indeed to stem from a widespread feeling (rather than a conceptual idea) of having 'received' something in the course of the practice, what we treated above in terms of 'accumulation'. The harder the practice, the most notable the gains, the stronger the feeling of gratitude is. It is indeed remarkable to see people prostrated by a long and difficult walk, an extended *zazen* session, or returning from a perilous feat on the steep cliff of a mountain, to incessantly thank everybody around them, often in high emotional terms, and often without distinction of rank or seniority.[69] When interviewed they admitted their sense of 'debt' for what they have 'received' even if not always able to express it in intelligible terms. The ascetic effort seems in this case to play a multi-faced role: it is at the same time cause and repayment for the benefit obtained, all in proportional terms with the physical effort involved. The benefits 'felt' through the practitioner's body are ultimately counterbalanced by his or her gratitude, which is later framed inside a pertinent doctrinal framework, but which is first and foremost 'embodied' beyond any conceptualisation. This phenomenon already hints at that level of 'bodily hermeneutic' in ascetic practice that we shall analyze as a fundamental feature of the ascetic experience in the following chapter.

Conclusions

In this chapter, we have analyzed and reconsidered the *modes* of practice outlined in the previous chapter in relation to the actors involved and their motivations. Ascetic practitioners, whether laypeople or religious professional, display a wide range of motivations and purposes for their practice which often coexists within the same group of practitioners (i.e. the same practice can be understood in very different terms by each one of its participants). This makes broad generalisations difficult to construct. However, at least two factors have been outlined as recurring in all the observed phenomena: the idea that ascetic practice produces benefits, and the fact that practitioners can pursue these benefits either for themselves or for other people. It has been noted how the pursuit of benefits for others represents the most widespread attitude, leading us to understand the figure of the ascetic as someone who enjoys a variety of connections and interactions within their social context. In all cases, thus, seemingly self-focused practices are in fact motivated by deeper intentions towards the others, and suggest a very different, more 'permeable', conception of the self.[70] One may indeed wonder if it is at all possible to practice asceticism only for one's sake: the greater the achievements, the greater the efforts required seems to become. All the most extreme examples noted thus far seem to confirm the fact that without the possibility of spreading the powers derived from the practice to other people, the toil of the practitioner outweighs the benefits, or at least equals them. Thus there seems to be a 'conservational balance' in asceticism (analyzed in more detail later on) which allows the power produced during a practice to be passed to others.

4 Ascetic practices in context

Asceticism in Japan, as elsewhere, does not take place in a social and cultural vacuum; the ascetic often builds his identity as 'holy person' in a relational context. The first dimension of this context is the space in which the practices are enacted and the presence in that space of other human beings, both within and outside the practice environment. This is what we shall term 'social context' and the presence of the practitioner's body is pivotal in its definition. Space is not only a physical category; in this sense, the influence of the religious ideas, doctrine and symbols pertaining to the religious environment in which the practice takes place plays an important role in the understanding of the practice and the self-awareness of the ascetic. Buddhist ascetics may see themselves as Buddhas walking a Buddhist 'pure land' for soteriological purposes, while Shinto devotees may want to purify themselves or obtain the favour of the deities. Very often, the religious understanding of a practice is a mixture of various doctrinal positions, which the ascetic feels free to manipulate in order to justify his acts. In the first part of this chapter, we will analyze the spatial dimension of asceticism as well as the interaction occurring between ascetics and society. In the second part, we will employ a comparative example to elucidate the process through which different religious environments interpret similar ascetic practices so as to conform them to their doctrinal tenets.

The spatial and social context

The most widespread case in which ascetic practice is carried out in Japan in close relationship with space is represented by the variety of ascetic practices enacted in relationship to the worship of sacred mountains. The worship of mountains and their role as places for religious practice has often been portrayed as an inherent characteristic of Japanese religiosity, thus often constituting an element in the definition of the Japanese identity itself.[1]

The explicit mention of mountains as places for ascetic practices in Japan is only documented since the late Nara period when the emergence of *hijiri* 聖 (holy persons) who, while undertaking ascetic training in the mountains, often travelled throughout Japan.[2] It is interesting to note the concomitance of the appearance of these first *hijiri* with that of the first Taoist-inspired medical books compiled in Japan, e.g. *Daidō Ruijuhō* 大同類聚方 by Izumo no Hirosada and Abe no Manao or *Setsuyō yōketsu* 攝養要訣 by Monobe no Kōsen, both of which deal primarily with longevity techniques, a practice undertaken by some *hijiri*.[3]

Another explicit mention of the presence of mountain ascetics is connected to the life of Sōō, the founder of the Tendai *kaihōgyō*. In the earliest biography of his life, we are told that Sōō started a long period of practice and austerities in 859 on Mount Hira on the western shore of Lake Biwa.[4] Although the biography does not explicitly mention any reason for the choice of Mount Hira, it does not appear to be a casual one, as the mountain was already known as a place for ascetic practices; its eastern slope in particular had already been used for this purpose in previous times.[5]

The three mountains of Dewa Sanzan, theatre of the *akinomine* practice, have long been considered as sacred by the local population, as they are traditionally thought to be the dwelling place of the spirits of the dead and the abode of various local *kami*.[6] Because of the influence of Buddhism in the formation of the various Shugendō traditions, the sacred mountains came to be regarded as manifestations of Buddhist deities in the terms of the *honji suijaku* 本地垂迹 theory. This theory considers Buddhist deities to be the original manifestation (*honji* 本地) and the sacred mountains as their trace or manifestation (*suijaku* 垂迹). In the case of the Dewa Sanzan, this led to the association of Mount Gassan with Amida Buddha (*Gassan daigongen* 月山大権現); Mount Yudono with Dainichi Nyorai (*Yudonosan Daigongen* 湯殿山大権現) and Mount Haguro with Kannon Bosatsu (*Hagurosan Daigongen* 羽黒山大権現).[7]

On the other hand, the mountain range from Yoshino to Kumano is identified with the dual mandala system of *Kongōkai* 金剛界 (diamond mandala)and *Taizōkai* 胎蔵界 (womb mandala), where Yoshino represents the *Kongōkai* and Kumano *Taizōkai*.[8] Many of the mountain peaks on the route are also considered to be manifestations of various Buddhist deities.[9]

In these last two cases, practitioners seem to demonstrate varying levels of awareness of their presence in a 'sacred space', although most of them are not very familiar with the complex symbolical cosmology of the Dewa Sanzan or the Ōmine-Kumano range. However, it would be wrong to consider the relationship between the ascetic and the sacred space as based purely on doctrinal knowledge. The way in which ascetics organize their relationship with the sacred space is indeed much more complex than a mere spatial theme and involves social and performative themes which contribute to the definition of the 'sacred space' of *ascetic* practice.

A contemporary example of the performance of ascetic feats connected with the worship of sacred mountains is the *shugyō* undertaken as part of the worship of Mount Akakura 赤倉 (Aomori prefecture).[10] Two main events seem to underline the life of Akakura shrine: the Mountain Opening Ceremony held on the first of May, and the *kamado* 竈 cooking pot ceremony performed during the Great Summer Festival. These two pivotal moments in the life of Akakura shrine and the surrounding communities are carefully prepared for by both laypeople and religious professionals by their undertaking a variety of *shugyō*, most of them taking place at Mount Akakura itself. The walking practice, which constitutes the central element of the daily *shugyō*, is similar to some extent to the mountain-walking practices typical of Shugendō environments. It is fundamentally the treading of the sacred geography of the mountain by passing through a number of holy sites, such as the Fudō waterfall (*Fudō taki* 不動滝) and walking alongside the Akakura stream following a series of 33 statues of Kannon 観音.[11] The walking path in Akakura is another example of the high degree of unexplained empiricism that we frequently find in ascetic practices and acts associated with popular religious manifestations. Many points of worship in Akakura are identified as such simply because they were indicated by Kawai Mariko, the founder of Akakura shrine, during her own *shugyō* on the mountain.[12] The empirical emphasis of the ascetic practice seems to make the use of language obsolete. The aim of the practitioner is to get into the closest possible relationship with the mountain which represents the origin of life for the surrounding rural area; the walking practice is a method that aims to achieve such a result. The will to establish a personal relationship with the mountain is also expressed by the fact that when the walk begins, the group breaks up and everybody climbs the mountain as an individual. This mountain *shugyō* is a clear example of *iterative* walking practice, where the mountain is seen in this case as an *absolute sacred*, the practice as the means to encounter that sacred dimension. When we take into account the epistemological function of the bodily practice we can understand why a complex verbal explanation is not requested. In the words of one Akakura practitioner, '[t]he mountain will teach you through your body'.[13] As Schattschneider also points out:

> As she forces her body to conform to the mountain's rocky paths, crevices, inclines, and passageways, she physically and morally internalises important revelatory and cosmological schemes that have been, in effect, handed down from the mountain divinities through elder members of the shrine community.
>
> (Ellen Schattschneider 2003: 158)

Thus, even the simple occasional ascetic acts at Mount Akakura offer the possible fruition of the sacred cosmological dimension of the mountain itself – through the body of the practitioner.

The ascetic in society and space

In Japan, the interaction between the various ascetic practitioners and society or community seems to be particularly rich since the late Nara period. Itinerant *hijiri* travelled across Japan and established an active relationship between themselves and the local populations by performing all sorts of magical and therapeutic acts, from the curing of illnesses to the exorcism of angry spirits.[14] As we will see below, this kind of relationship between ascetics and the local population is still alive today, particularly in rural areas.

The *shugyō* at Mount Akakura displays a variety of connections with the rural life of the local population. During the spring festival, a group of local people perform various *shugyō* on the mountain, culminating in the erection of a great sacred rope (*shimenawa*) across a sacred gorge.[15] They allow themselves only one attempt to properly erect the *shimenawa*, and the result is considered as a prophecy for the results of the crops that year. The erection of the *shimenawa* represents a sort of sexual intercourse between the man of the community and the holy mountain.[16] If it is erected properly and straight, the auspices for the season to come are good, but if the men fail to give it the proper tension and shape, the crops are expected to be meagre.

Three times a year, the head medium of the same Akakura shrine performs the cooking pot ceremony.[17] A quantity of rice is cooked by the medium in a sacred pot and then distributed to the people attending the ceremony. The rice thus prepared is understood as a form of medicine that the local people take for the health and welfare of their family.[18]

The rite is still important in Akakura today, with it bringing virtually all the local community around the Akakura shrine. What is important to note for our study is that the head medium and the committed members of the shrine regularly practice *shugyō* on the sacred mountain in order to be empowered for the performance of these rituals, and for the *kamado* rite in particular. Although all of them also have a 'secular life' within the surrounding community (the head medium being the only exception), their commitment to the practices on the mountain permits to them to shift their social role on those special occasions. They do not withdraw from society, however, but simply occupy a different social slot for the required time. The act of 'social shifting' also works here as an act of 'bridging'; they become a channel for communication between the community and the sacred mountain.[19] These people do not seem to be marginal to their own society but to occupy a respected position carrying considerable importance for the community's practical needs. I would like to point out how the position of the 'holy man' in the community is in many cases so closely linked with the quality of their performance that a bad performance may lead to the loss of such a position. Blacker, for instance, mentions some accounts of the performance of a *miko* in the Hayama festival in Kanazawa village.[20] During the ceremony, a *miko* or another ascetic-trained medium is supposed to be possessed by a deity (usually Hayama Gongen) and then to answer various questions from the audience.[21] These questions generally regard the volumes of the crops for the current season, the quantity of rain and so on. The audience listens closely to the answers of the medium, which are supposed to be as sharp and precise as possible.[22] Blacker witnessed the performance of a *miko* who was apparently not able to provide a good performance, giving only vague answers and also making some obvious mistakes.[23] She was labelled as 'incompetent', although the local community still had to rely on her because she was 'the only *miko* left in the entire area'.[24]

The social role and relevance of ascetic practitioners in Japan therefore appears to be strongly influenced by what kind of public function the practitioner him or herself may have. Powerful mediums may become respected and popular and leave a long-lasting imprint on their community, while unsuccessful ascetics are forgotten on account of their lack of results. We may say that what matters to society is not the theoretical or spiritual value of the practices themselves but what kind of benefits can be obtained from the activities of the 'holy person' that those practices created.

This need for a 'holy person' capable of producing extensive practical results is often translated into a huge pressure on the ascetic practitioner by his religious community. Yamada Ryūshin (see Chapter 3) proudly reports many times about how much the local people near Kubote sustained him in his ascetic effort.[25] In the same vein, it is interesting to note how the parishioners of various Nichiren-shū temples closely monitor the progress of their priests undergoing the 100-day *daiaragyō* training.[26]

Extra-ascetic and intra-ascetic societies

The process of training an ascetic is consequently accompanied by great expectations from his community of non-ascetics, or what we many now define as an *extra-ascetic society.*[27] I would like to use the term *extra-ascetic society* to indicate all those social figures which are in relationship to the figure of the ascetic but are not part of the ascetic training themselves. Please note that this term is not synonymous with 'secular society', as members of the extra-ascetic society can indeed be fully-ordained religious professionals.

The variety of interaction between the *extra-ascetic society* and the ascetics seems to point to the fact that the ascetic is not necessarily a loner or marginal per se. Certainly, he is not what we may call a 'normal' person but to define someone as 'exceptional' (i.e. non-normal) does not necessarily relegate him to a position of marginality. Being marginal means not entertaining any kind of active or meaningful relationship with society,[28] living, as the word suggests, at its margin, having no direct influence or exchange with it and often dwelling in a sort of alternative reality, as in the case of the communes of some new religions, such as Aum Shinrikyō.[29] In the case of the ascetics we have examined so far, these boundaries are much more fluid. The practitioner disappears from time to time into a mountain or a temple for training but, when he comes back, his newly acquired powers allow him to take back his social role as healer, medium, adviser and so forth.[30] The feelings of the society towards him seem therefore to depend mostly on his ability to actively contribute to the social discourse rather than on his mere definition as religious practitioner.[31]

The ascetic thus owes his ambiguity and his ability for 'social re-definition' and 'social shifting' to his capacity to shift back and forth from different worlds, the boundaries of which are defined by the intersection of sacred and actual space. In the examples outlined above, we have inherent spatial themes that play on the dichotomy between the sacred and secular space, and the figure of the ascetic as the person capable of moving between the two.[32] This spatial ambivalence is clearly more physical or 'geographical' in the case of mountain-based practices, such as the Akakura *shugyō* or the Kubote *aragyō*, or rely more subtly on the symbolical component of a consecrated space (like a temple), such as the Nichiren-shū *daiaragyō* period of seclusion. In both situations, however, the ascetic 'enters the sacred' and 'exits into the secular', bringing with him at least a portion of those sacred powers. This way of constructing social interaction patterns through the presence of the ascetics in different dimensions of space(s) also seems to inform the innermost structure of some practices, leading to the creation of what we may call an *intra-ascetic society*.

An example of such an intra-ascetic socio-spatial motif can be seen in the social organization of collective practices such as the Haguro *akinomine* or the Ōmine *okugake*. Particularly in the first case, we can witness the formation of a parallel kind of society within the new sacred spatial dimension of the practice, which first mimics and eventually redefines the original social setting of the practitioners. The *akinomine* practice has already been described in Chapter 2; below I will attempt a second reading of this practice in which I try to magnify its inherent spacial and social motifs. However, first I will discuss some patterns of interaction between ascetics and the *extra-ascetic society*.[33]

Socio-spatial dimensions and extra-ascetic society

The interaction between the ascetic and the surrounding community can take organized forms, particularly when stable institutions are involved. At a non-institutional level, such as with the Agematsu Jiga Daikyōkai, they can also rely on the constant support of a stable number of fellows/practitioners. In this case, however, there is a certain ambiguity between the status of ascetic practitioners and simple supporters, something which also characterizes the status of many members of Ontake confraternities. In these cases, many of the supporters are occasional practitioners, while a group of non-practicing supporters may be formed in order to support certain events (such as the Ontakesan-jinja *harumatsuri*). Here the members move freely between the two statuses, making it difficult to clearly discriminate between practitioners and supporters belonging to the *extra-ascetic society*.

As the institutional strength of the religious environments hosting the practices becomes stronger, the possibility of lay-only support (and of creating lay-only assistance groups) for ascetics becomes more likely. Such is the case, for instance, of the current *kaihōgyōja* residing at Hiei-zan Mudō-ji, Uehara Gyōshō 上原行照, who holds a regular meeting with the both occasional and regular visitors after the *goma* he celebrates daily at the Mudō-ji. The majority of the guests are from the Kansai area but some come over from Tokyo as well. I visited the Mudō-ji on two different occasions, first on New Year's Day, and then on an ordinary weekday in May 2007.[34] The first meeting was held in a more 'formal' way, with the *ajari* and visitors exchanging greetings for the New Year; the time for conversation was limited. During the second meeting, however, it was clear that many of the visitors came to the Mudō-ji under the impetus of specific issues. A young woman, for instance, was uncertain about her decision to switch jobs and move to a different town, while other people had health or family worries.[35] Perhaps surprisingly, the *ajari*'s answers, while certainly pleasant and compassionate, were nothing too different from practical common sense tinged with some traditional Buddhist-flavoured wisdom. Possibly it was the same kind of answer one could receive from one's elder relatives. But here lies a pivotal difference: these words came from a *kahōgyōja*, the *Daigyōman Ajari*, a man who had completed an ascetic practice that brought him to the edge of death; a living Buddha. In other words he was an authority, and in a Nietzschean-fashioned scale for the genealogy of ethical behaviour, he may be considered as standing at the top; namely a source, a living scripture. Authority often needs external legitimization but it is interesting to note how in this case the *ajari* is self-legitimated through the practice of the *kaihōgyō* itself. Self-legitimation through one's practice is a feature that seems to link the ascetic of various places and times. Success in a potentially fatal practice legitimizes the role of the practitioner as 'holy person' without the need for other superior authorities to confirm it.[36] A direct consequence of this perception of authority is the support that the *ajari* receives, also in material form. All the people participating in the meetings left monetary offering, collected at the end by a temple attendant, while some even brought small personal gifts. One person was responsible for collecting all the *goma-ki* for the New Year's *goma* ritual from her area, and was very active in publicising the *ajari* figure among friends and relatives.[37]

The support for the *kaihōgyōja* can manifest itself also in more organized forms, as in the case of the Stopping-Obstacles Confraternity (Sokushō-kō 息障 講) based in Kyoto.[38] The members of the confraternity perform countless tasks for the *gyōja*, such as guiding him through the traffic, while they also:

> walk ahead, asking people to move out of his way so that his brisk step is not slowed down; they direct devotees who wish to receive the *gyōja*'s blessings in the form of *kaji* to kneel on the side of the road; they make the schedule for the practitioner's stops at the homes/businesses of devotees (who are also members of the Kyōto Sokushō kō) on or very near to his circumambulation route; they give constant directions to the devotees following the *gyōja* so that they do not inadvertently disrupt his practice in any way and so that they too are kept well and safe.

(Catherine Ludvik 2006: 121)

Unlike the case of lay participation in ascetic practice outlined in Chapter 3, we have here an organization developing in parallel to the main practices, which displays an internal, complex level of organization. The Sokushō-kō members are placed on a hierarchical scale which identifies the roles of *sendatsu*, *dai sendatsu* and *dai dai sendatsu*, terminology which we have already seen widely employed in Shugendō. Here as well it retains its meaning of 'guide'.[39] Members support the effort of the *gyōja* mainly by following him throughout the streets of Kyoto and by providing him with meals. The duties of the *kō* members are varied: from aiding the *ajari* in his walking practice by holding a lantern at night, carrying his stool, caring for his gear and attire etc., to an around-the-clock attendance during the extreme *dō-iri* practice. In this case, the ascetic practice is centred on the powerful figure of the *kaihōgyōja*; the efforts of the group of lay believers of the Sokushō-kō never assume the characteristics of an ascetic practice per se. As Ludvik points out, '[m]embers often define their attitude as *zuiki* 随喜, a Buddhist term meaning rejoicement in another person's practice of good actions – in this instance, the *gyōja*'s *kaihōgyō* – and also admiration of these good acts'.[40] None of the *kō* members takes a direct part in the practice or tries to emulate the *ajari*'s efforts in any way. They are content to partake of the benefits that the *kaihogyōja* may offer them, for instance, having the *ajari* in their homes to pray for their ancestors. Other motivations, like 'personal challenge, self-discovery, or spiritual advancement… are not considered acceptable approaches in the Sokushō-kō'.[41]

It is interesting to observe how the activity of the confraternity is concentrated in the city during the presence of the *gyōja* during the *Kyoto Ōmawari*, i.e. when the ascetic brings himself closer to the community by extending the space of the practice. From a theoretical point of view, relationship with society may also be seen as relationship with space in general. Many Japanese ascetic practices consist mostly in walking inside the perimeter of a sacred area, often a mountain, like the Tendai *kaihōgyō* or the Shugendō 100-day *aragyō*. The practice thus becomes the result of the interaction between body and physical space; but we must not forget that space is also the *locus* of the social existence.

Sacred space and sacred body

Body, physical space and social space appear to be the three elements that need to be considered together in order to understand the figure of the ascetic practitioner within his socio-spatial context. To this purpose, it is useful to employ a theoretical framework that Michel de Certeau developed in his work *La Fable Mystique* precisely for the purpose of showing the possible levels of interaction between the human body, human society and space at large, as well as how they can be understood as inherent characteristics deriving from the mere ontology of the body itself. De Certeau positions the body as central inside a triangular scheme that represents the possible forms of bodily interactions (see Figure 4.1).[42]

'Social practices' can be further deconstructed into four basic elements: *communication* as the basic content of the social practices, *relationship* (in its general meaning) as its constitutive unit, *sociality* as its function and *place* as its reference.[43] This scheme also contains the basic argument for a discourse of constructive interaction between the body and the physical and social dimensions of space that constitute the *locus* of the ascetic practice. By constructive interaction, I mean that while the body of the ascetic resides in space, in a place, at the same time it defines that same place. In de Certeau's scheme, space is not included in events, which have as their referent time, nor in symbols, having as their referent truth.[44] In other words, in two vertices of the triangle, the body is taken into account as an absolute (it does not need a referent to be understood), but in the third (the social practices) the conceptualization of the body is necessarily

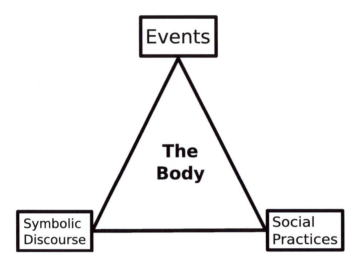

Figure 4.1 de Certeau's scheme of the body

a relative one. Communications, relations and sociality presuppose some kind of interaction between different entities that is true only in the circumstances when they share, even for a moment, a common spatial dimension.

We can employ a triangular scheme similar to de Certeau's in order to interpret the 'sacred space' as a product of the coexistence of three factors:

a   the *sacred body*: the body of the practitioner, sacralised during the ascetic training
b   the *actual space*: the area in which the practice takes place, for instance the mountain area of the Dewa Sanzan or the Yoshino–Kumano route
c   the *symbolic space*: the symbolic understanding of the actual space, such as the mountains as manifestation of Buddhist deities or as the *Kongōkai–Taizōkai* dual mandala.

This interaction can be represented as in Figure 4.2.

As we have said, the body of the ascetic presupposes a relationship with space. The efforts of ascetic practitioners require space in order to be carried out while at the same time they affect space. The performative power of the body of an ascetic consists precisely in this power to extend the locus of the sacred from the sacred body to the surrounding space; this is achieved by its mere physical presence. Through the presence of the sacred body, the extra-ordinary encounters the ordinary and the two dimensions mingle, becoming meaningful to each other.

There is in fact a form of mutual dependence between these holy people and their referential context, and that dependence is an efficacious argument against the traditional position that sees the ascetic as an inherently isolated figure, undertaking something non-essential that eventually will benefit only himself. On

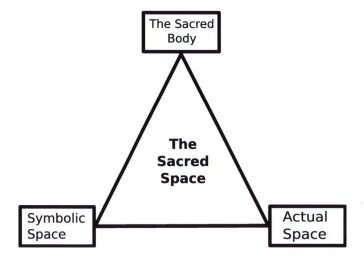

Figure 4.2 The sacred space

the contrary, it appears that the identity of the ascetic is built within a relational context between the secular and the sacred; further, it can be seen to stand as a mediating figure at the point of contact between these two dimensions.

Socio-spatial dimensions and intra-ascetic society

The social dimension of asceticism is not limited to the paradigm sacred versus secular – or ascetic versus non-ascetic – but also involves the social relations which develop within the texture of the ascetic community during its presence in the sacred space. Communally organized practices involving a variety of participants are certainly a favoured case study in this circumstance, many of which we have encountered earlier on in this work. In this section, I would like to re-read a practice already treated as an example of a ascetic activity taking place within a religious institutional body (the Haguro *akinomine*) from a different point of view by trying to magnify its intra-ascetic social structure. This will help to shed further light on the complexity of the interactions between ascetic practitioners and their social context as well as to establish a further hypothesis on the aetiology of asceticism in general.

The initial gathering of the *akinomine* participants is a merry event. On the afternoon of 24 August, the main hall of the Shōzen-in temple in Tōge (Yamagata) fills up quickly with practitioners who come from all over Japan and occasionally from abroad. Many of them are seasoned practitioners who meet no more than once a year (only on this occasion), so their boisterous exchange of greetings is understandable. As the room fills up, everybody has to find a suitable place to store belongings and to unroll their futon at night. As in other kinds of social gatherings, people tend to group. More seasoned practitioners who are already well-acquainted generally choose a space in the hall, sometimes the same space as the previous year, and set up their equipment quickly and confidently. By the same principle, newcomers also tend to stay together, but place their belongings on the ground more or less randomly while nervously looking around, trying to understand what the next step should be.[45]

How people organize themselves inside the main hall of the Shōzen-in is the first step for the construction of the intra-ascetic society that will keep the ascetic group together for the rest of the practice period. Experienced practitioners tend to form age and gender homogeneous groups. Their luggage is abundant and smartly packed in plastic boxes. They generally bring all sorts of amenities with which to fulfil their physical needs during the practice. Wet tissues, crank-charging lamps and mobile phones, full sets of medicines, bandages and first aid in case of minor accidents are just some of the articles included in their boxes. The general feeling is that their stay at Hagurosan can be made more comfortable with a little preparation. The majority already possess a complete *shugenja* outfit that they can neatly put on in a matter of few seconds, and they have lengthy conversations comparing the quality of the fabric, the colour and the circumstances in which their equipment was obtained.[46]

Newcomers, on the other hand, stick together regardless of age and gender and even nationality. The social glue that binds them is the stress of the new experience in the midst of a group of already well-acquainted strangers. Their luggage is sparse, mostly packed in suitcases or backpacks. The items that they bring with them are mainly essentials, collected following the instructions provided by the temple heads a few weeks earlier. For this reason, all newcomers bring with them more or less the same equipment. Their general expectation is that their stay at Hagurosan is not supposed to be comfortable, so nobody packs an extensive set of goods. None of the newcomers possessed a full *shugenja* costume so that they must hire one from the temple instead, with the exception of the few items that had to be bought.

Although the subgroups that comprise the newly formed intra-ascetic society of practitioners form separately, some interaction between them occurs from the very beginning. It seems, in fact, that experienced practitioners think that it is their duty to take care of the newcomers and they generously give advice on practical matters, even if not explicitly asked for it. They are indeed attentive to the needs of others, generous and encouraging. Although the groups are not so prone to mix, the interaction between them is abundant and productive. The heads of the temple seem to be aware of this; in fact, a large share of practical training is entrusted to senior practitioners instead of being performed in an 'official way' by the temple leaders. For example, newcomers are taught by older practitioners how to wear the *shugenja* costume properly, how to hold the *juzu* (the Buddhist rosary) and the meaning of some pieces of the attire. In addition, they are given a number of practical tips about how not to slip on wet ground, what to put in their carrier bags and how to prevent small injuries.[47]

At the end of the first day, the Haguro *akinomine* intra-ascetic society seems to be constituted by at least three different groups. The temple heads and clergy form the first. Most of them are ordained Tendai priests, because of the affiliation of the Hagurosan Kōtaku-ji Shōzen-in to Mount Hiei. In this early phase of the training, they are generally very busy with all the arrangements and so their contact with the other practitioners is necessarily limited.

The people regularly attending the *akinomine* training every year form the second group. They have developed strong ties between each other and also feel confident about the practice and all the formal procedures that will follow. For them, participating in the retreat has become a pleasurable routine, a periodic event that marks this specific period of the year.

Newcomers or occasional practitioners form the last group. They, of course, lack the knowledge and confidence of the more seasoned practitioners but they share the enthusiasm. Feeling like a stranger inside an already well-acquainted group forces people to consider at least two strategies. The first is to isolate them-selves completely, avoiding any form of confrontation that might result in possible threat or loss of face. The second is to fight pressure and isolation by taking as many occasions as possible to engage in a fruitful interaction.[48] One of the easi-est strategies to achieve the latter result in such a context is to ask continuously for information. In the beginning, indeed, the main form of interaction between newcomers and experts is the exchange of various types of information, mostly flowing from the experienced to the novice. Although this facilitates interaction, it also has the side effect of creating a system of implicit vertical relationships. The scheme at this point is thus characterized by a three-group structure bound together by vertical relationships, with strong horizontal relationships present within each group (see Figure 4.3).

The relationship between the temple heads and experienced practitioners is indicated with a double arrow because there is a higher degree of dual interaction between the two groups. Experienced practitioners in many cases help the heads and provide valuable advice, direct activities and organize the work of the other practitioners. During the communal supper at the end of the first day, this three-group scheme is again replicated in the location of people in the main hall. The temple heads have assigned seats in front of the altar, but all other people are free to sit wherever they think is appropriate. Again the newcomers and the experi-enced practitioners group separately, replicating more or less the same subgroups of the initial luggage and bedding arrangement. At this early stage, thus, the *shu-genja* intra-ascetic community is still fragmented, far from being homogeneous, and is bound by horizontal-style relationships. During this communal meal, some time is used for a short self-introduction, then *futons* are distributed to all partici-pants and the hall is set up for the night.

The following day, the attention of all practitioners is focused on the prepara-tions for the Ritual of Conception at the Kogane-dō.[49] Although the *akinomine* itself actually starts the day before with the *Oikaragaki* (the ceremony of 'dec-oration' of the *oi*, the portable altar, where the spirits of the *shugenja* are held),

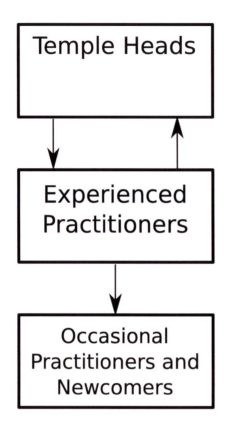

Figure 4.3 Intra-ascetic relations

the rite at Kogane-dō is the one that, from a practical point of view, really marks the start of the practice in powerful spatial terms. This passage into a different dimension creates a palpable, though subtle, state of tension in all practitioners. The newcomers consider the days ahead with some worry, while the seasoned practitioners try to get into the proper state of mind for the efforts that will follow. A visible sign of this concern is the fact that, unlike the previous day, the participants' level of concentration is visibly much higher. Eyes are more attentive, faces more serious, while jokes and laughter disappear from everybody's lips.

After the ritual at the Kogane-dō, the column of *shugenja* in-training passes through the village of Tōge until the precinct of the Dewa Sanzan shrine and during this time the atmosphere loosens up a little bit. Upon entering the precinct of the *jinja*, the atmosphere changes again abruptly – and again this change seems to occur because of a spatial feeling. Entering the precinct of the *jinja* through the main gate (*zuishinmon* 随神門) reveals a stunning view. Centuries-old *sugi* trees (cryptomeria) are everywhere, while enormous fern leaves cover the ground. Broken rays of sun filtering through the leaves illuminate this dreamlike land-scape, while all signs of human civilization suddenly disappear. The sensation of entering a different dimension is indeed powerful and one's senses are lost in this contrasting reality.[50]

Upon arrival at the Kōtaku-ji (the 'First Lodging'), participants are assigned to their 'room' in the temple. Various criteria are used to group the practitioners in their rooms. First of all, one or more rooms are assigned to women, follow-ing different criteria in recent years.[51] Then, two bigger rooms are assigned to the newcomers and the less experienced practitioners. These 'rooms' are actually divisions of the main hall, so there is plenty of possibility for communication between these three groups of practitioners. This division of the main hall also underlines an interesting feature of contemporary Haguro Shugendō: there seems to be almost no form of gender discrimination. Men and women sleep and change their clothes in the same room, share the same toilets and perform the same practices, *sumō* being the only exception. Women themselves seem to be quite conscious of this state of equality. In the words of the eldest female practitioner, and one of the most seasoned practitioners of all: 'Here there is no man or woman. We are all equal, all *shugenja*'.

However, the new arrangement at the Kōtaku-ji upsets the intra-ascetic balance that spontaneously formed at the Shōzen-in. The occupants of the newcomers' room, for example, are exclusively first-timers, and this is irrespective of age.[52] Most of them arrange their belongings against the outer wall, except for some who preferred to place their luggage in the middle of the room. They are conse-quently arranged in a sort of square shape, lying on the floor side-by-side around the perimeter of the room, facing the other people staying in the middle of the room. This means also that when everybody is in his place, there is no way of not looking at another person, except perhaps by staring at the ceiling. In this circum-stance, interaction is unavoidable and one is forced to break the barrier of age, language and social status.[53]

'Where are you from?' is the typical question in these cases. But at Kōtaku-ji, this gains a completely different undertone. Social differences and habitual places of residences are all mitigated by the inescapable sensation of all being strangers in a strange place. The name of Japanese cities like Tokyo and Osaka belong to different realities that seem to be millions of kilometres away. The only factor that seems to break the newcomers group into two smaller sub-entities is the presence in the group of a few fully-ordained Buddhist priests who are new to Hagurosan but not to that kind of practice. They already know all the major sutras and mudras by heart and are familiar with the procedure for rituals. Given their background and experience, it might seem as though the *akinomine* would be less arduous for them, but there is another aspect to consider. Having been sent by their master or religious organization on an official basis, it is expected for them to do every practice to the utmost. In fact, they are always the first to act and the last to rest, working hard until their energies are exhausted, competing among themselves for the best results.[54]

Practitioners participating in the Haguro *akinomine* on a personal basis do not have to deal with such pressure and clear evidence of this may be found in their behaviour. As mentioned before, almost all experienced practitioners came to Haguro with copious amenities for their stay. Despite the fact that everybody is supposed to fast completely during the first three days of practice, drinking just water or green tea, almost all of the older practitioners enact a wide spectrum of little 'cheatings'. Sugar tablets, energy drinks, small candies, *anpan* (buns filled with sweet bean paste) and *dorayaki* (two small pancakes with sweet bean paste between them) are just some of the many snacks that people bring with them to relieve their fast at Kōtaku-ji. These innocent 'cheats' also include perfumed wiping tissues, antiperspirants, inflatable pillows and so on.[55]

As the practice goes on and the weariness of the practitioners increases, all these relationships collapse into a much more uniform division between practitioner and temple leaders. As mentioned earlier, regardless of the importance of the *saitō goma*, most of the people struggled to stay awake, and a few openly fell asleep. The temple leaders still carried on their duties diligently, followed by the small sub-group of ordained priests. The rest of the practitioners became a uniform community of people overwhelmed with exhaustion. This was manifested first by the abandoning of social conventions in speech: after the first days, everyone used a plain, brisk language regardless of their age, status or gender. Behavioural conventions were subsequently discarded and people started to behave following their immediate needs for rest, sleep or water, apparently regardless of the importance of the religious activities being carried out. Identity factors such as nationality or race were perhaps the last to fade away. But eventually even national and linguistic barriers crumbled when foreigners – after the initial period of 'culture shock' – started to practice on the same level as the local participants, even bettering them on some occasions.[56]

A similar process of construction and deconstruction of the intra-ascetic society can be identified in many of the practices we have outlined in the previous chapters, such as the *okugake shugyō* and the *rōhatsu sesshin*, and therefore in very dissimilar cases on both practical and doctrinal levels.[57] This leads us to an important consideration. The process of de-socialization and re-socialization, one of the most prominent characteristics of all ascetics that undoubtedly plays an important part in the acquisition of his supernatural powers, takes place not only by virtue of the spatial dislocation of the ascetic in the 'sacred space' but within the intra-ascetic society as well. The idea of a foetus growing in the womb of the mountain, as used in the *akinomine*, is a most fortunate metaphor in this sense. And, if a communal experience does exist in this sort of practice, it does not necessarily need to be sought by considerations of apparent joint belief or behaviour. The centre of the collective experience is in fact the body, the physical dimension of all practitioners. We shared physical conditions, rather than religious beliefs – and that was the epistemological device defining our intra-ascetic social sense. It is for this reason that the practice is eventually considered to be fulfilled by all in the same way, regardless of the different levels of ability in reading sutras or making mudras.[58] Moreover, as the *akinomine* is a mountain-based practice, its particular spatial emphasis magnifies the interaction between the macroscopic environment of the mountain and the microcosms of our bodies. In a perhaps not too surprising coalescence of bodily epistemology and reductionist ontology, this is well synthesized in the expression *entering the mountain*.[59]

Entering can of course imply *exiting*, and once the older body is disposed of, the individual can be reborn anew from the same substance of the holy place. This sensation of rebirth is vivid and sharp on the last day of the Haguro *akinomine* when, after the final service at the Dewa Sanzan *jinja*, the newborn *shugenja* give a loud cry (the cry of birth) and then rush outside the shrine precinct with the same desperate will for life as a newborn baby. Just as on the day when they entered the precinct, the feeling of now being *out* is equally strong. Ontological themes in the process of *becoming* a holy person are thus not only symbolized by spatial dislocation in actual and symbolical place, but the movement in and through space becomes a 'movement through being' as well.

The liminal place of the ascetic

There seems then to be a certain fluidity between the *intra-* and *extra*-ascetic societies which underlies the paradigm of socialization and desocialization so central to the social definition of the ascetic. This can be understood as one of the subliminal factors from which the 'sense of the ascetic' seems to stem. In the intra-ascetic society, we have the constitution of an inner form of social order, as in the case of the *akinomine*, parallel to ordinary society and to the normal status that the practitioner holds in such society. Beside the aforementioned presence of pain and physical effort, this sense of separation from ordinary society should also be held responsible for the perception of the ascetic state as something extra-ordinary. All ascetics are in this sense inherently de-socialized figures; occasional and popular practices, as well as more doctrinally refined ones, involve moments in which the person of the ascetic is necessarily pulled outside his normal context. Danger, exhaustion, pain or fear should be taken as devices, rather than purposes, through which the ascetic voluntarily alienates himself from his existing context. The 'technical empiricism' of the ascetic acts seems to be justified by this need. In the performance of the ascetic act, the contextual understanding of the ascetic's unity of being is momentarily blanked out and then is readied to be reset. This is a possible translation in ontological terms of the idea of 'discarding' (*suteru*) which many ascetics I have analyzed, through personal encounter or through their writings, tried to express.[60] After one's original contextual identity has been discarded, it is then the moment to choose between remaining a 'body absolute', and therefore not re-socializing in any terms, or re-socializing oneself in a different form of society.[61] It is interesting to note how few are the ascetics who opt for the first choice. If we need to name explicit examples of perfectly solitary ascetics, we may find ourselves in a sudden and unexpected quandary. Even Christian anchorites, Taoist Immortals or Buddhist *pratyekabuddhas* seemed to indulge in a variety of exceptions to their allegedly solitary life (see Chapter 1). In this case, we are also facing an interesting epistemological problem. If the aim of becoming eminently solitary was successful, how can we then know anything about the existence of such ascetics? But this is a paradox in itself because, if perfect isolation was possible and attainable, and if it is an inherent purpose of asceticism, we would have no notion of asceticism as a phenomenon or concept, but just a long record of disappearing persons. We must therefore not confuse the secretive and initiatory nature of many practices with a wilful denial of the environment in which these practices are carried out. None of the cases I have witnessed or had the possibility to participate in seem to produce an absolutely desocialized being. Even the *rōhatsu sesshin*, in which the efforts of the participants seem to be so self-centred, displays recurring themes of interaction with the 'outer world', as discussed in more detail in Chapter 3. We may want here to reconsider the same question: is it possible to practice asceticism exclusively for oneself? Theoretically yes, but this would necessarily involve total seclusion, not just spatial but indeed an *ontological seclusion*, an 'isolation from being [in the world]', and in this case the ascetic will find himself isolated in an epistemic vacuum as well. In other words, if ascetics who practise only for their own benefit in perfect seclusion from the world in fact exist, we could not know anything about them. On the other hand, the very existence of ascetic 'traditions' seems to demonstrate that asceticism is structured and enacted on social terms. What we have tried to undertake here is a reconsideration of the concept of 'ascetic society' and of the interaction between the intra- and extra-ascetic social dimensions. The *locus* of the ascetic practitioner is thus neither exclusively the secular nor the sacred world, but a liminal space between the two.

The religious context

From the discussion thus far, one of the characteristics of ascetic performance in Japan seems to be its trans-sectarian nature, where ascetic acts or practices cannot be identified as a particular feature of one specific religious environment alone. At the same time, however, doctrinal explanations are often provided about a certain practice, which are, to various extents, coherent with the religious orthodoxy of the environment in which the practice takes place. An ascetic practice carried out in a Buddhist environment would, for instance, be described as having 'Buddhist purposes' and employing 'Buddhist means', as, for instance, in the cases of the *akinomine*, the *okugake* and the *rōhatsu sesshin*.[62] Some practices can also become the exclusive of a certain religious group, like the Tendai *kaihōgyō* or the Nichiren *daiaragyō*, however, including many elements vastly employed in other environments, such as the extended walking or the use of the voice.

The coalescence of practice and doctrinal justifications hence seems to be founded upon a fluid relationship in which the two terms are not necessarily the expression of each other. If a certain practice were the expression of specific precise religious values, we could consequently expect that, if the values for some reasons undergo a change, the practice would change as well. This would have given birth to variety of doctrine-specific asceticism(s), which is something that we do not observe. The same ascetic act, as we have seen extensively, can easily be borrowed and exchanged between different religious environments, and the practitioners themselves do not seem to see this as a contradiction.

The presence of this apparent dichotomy between the actual performance of an ascetic act and the doctrinal meanings associated with it does not seem to be caused by a failure in the way in which ascetics conceptualize themselves and their roles. This would be the hypothetical case of ascetics living in an intra-ascetic society secluded to the point of making any interaction with outside society, as well as between different ascetic societies, impossible. This hypothesis is, however, not demonstrated in practice, as ascetics tend to shift easily from one practice to the other and to organize their own 'ascetic schedule' very freely. A number of the people I met and interviewed have a year-round schedule during which they participate in a variety of *shugyō* throughout the country.[63] This often offers one of the most popular topics of conversation during the practice periods; in these conversations, people appear to understand themselves as free to undertake the various practices in ways which seem more convenient for them. For instance, two practitioners I met on the *okugake shugyō* in Yoshino had impressive records of successfully completed practices which they ordered and scheduled according to their own diaries. Each year, they were among the leaders organizing the local festival of their hometown shrine, in which they performed water ablutions (*suigyō*) and fire-crossing practices (*hiwatari*). Later in the spring, they started pilgrimages, from shorter to longer routes, culminating in a Fuji pilgrimage at the beginning of July. After some weeks of rest, they then joined the *okugake shugyō*, which they considered to be the peak of their annual ascetic effort.[64] In their annual schedule, they were thus moving from popular/local non-institutional environments to some eminently Buddhist contexts, such as the *okugake*.

In Japan, this combinatory attitude with regard to religious participation is, of course, not surprising, but a point we may wish to ponder is the fact that all of these different activities were uniformly classed by my informants as *shugyō*, despite the variety of religious contexts.[65] Nor does this view pertain exclusively to 'popular' practitioners. Religious professionals also undergo a variety of ascetic trainings in different religious environments with the precise and conscious purpose of gaining higher benefits from each of them. A benefit highly sought by religious professionals is, as we have seen, the accumulation of powers. The leaders of the Agematsu Jiga Daikyōkai, for instance, engage in regular ascetic training throughout the year with precisely this purpose; further, they organize their schedule around their religious duties, trying to maintain a regular participation in at least five–six *shugyō* per year. In their own words, 'it is not important what we do, but rather the fact that we do something regularly throughout the year in order to preserve our power'.[66] Indeed, they have participated in more than 20 different kinds of ascetic or quasi-ascetic practices in the last 10 years, including Shugendō practices, Zen retreats, Shinto festivals, *kagura* dances, occasional performances such as the ladder of swords climbing (*hawatari*) and so forth. From all of these activities, they attained some degree of 'spiritual energy', which they then put to use in their role as mediums in the Jiga Daikyōkai.[67] The same can be said for Buddhist priests who participate in the *akinomine*, the *okugake* or other Shugendō training, regardless of their sectarian affiliations.[68]

At the same time, none of these people seem to refute the fact that, for instance, the *okugake* is a Buddhist practice or that a certain festival is held for a specific Shinto deity, such as in the case of the *Iwaguni kagura* described in Chapter 2. Some of them may make up their own 'meanings', as we have seen earlier on, but no one thinks that the practice itself has nothing to do with its religious environment. Even sporadic and embryonic ascetic acts, such as the students petitioning for good graduation results in an improvised waterfall ablution (*takigyō*) we described in Chapter 3, involve some degree of religious practice, whether the performance of a few simple mudras or the recitation of some well-known mantras. As I have been told quite a few times, all of these religious acts should be duly performed, otherwise, in the words of Yamada Ryūshin, 'this is just hiking'.[69] How then can we solve this paradoxical lack of continuity between ascetic practice and doctrinal explanations? A category introduced at the beginning of this work may prove to be pivotal in resolving this conflict: the bodily hermeneutic.

Bodily hermeneutic

A greater or lesser degree of doctrinal hermeneutic is clearly present in all the accounts discussed above. People show hermeneutical capacity in their re-elaboration, adaptation and invention of the doctrinal themes associated with a certain practice.[70] At the same time, they show the same capacity for re-elaboration regarding their bodily performance: a certain act can be understood as beneficial to the attainment of a specific religious benefit which varies in relationship to the surrounding environment. To clarify this point, let us examine the ascetic act of 'prolonged walking' more closely.

Bodily hermeneutic of walking practices

During the extensive walking sessions of the *okugake*, the *akinomine*, the *sennichi kaihōgyō*, the Kubote *aragyō* and other forms of walking *shugyō*, some practitioners focus the interpretation of their bodily practice on the exhaustion caused by the incessant walking, the sense of identity loss and the loss of orientation that the practice procures. In their interpretation, extensive walking is destructive of the status quo and 'burns away' some – or even all – of the characteristics and attributes that were particular to the individual in an extra-ascetic environment.[71] The same can be said for some passive ascetic acts as well, such as enduring cold during a winter practice like the Ontake *samugyō* or some of the water practices. A significant portion of my informants reported this sense of loss with a variety of expressions such as: 'I dropped (*suteta* 捨てた) myself'; 'I forgot about myself'; 'I was thinking only about walking and nothing else'; 'It was like I was dead' and so forth.[72] This perception of 'losing' something of oneself does not seem to be a cognitive interpretation of the practice which relies on pre-formulated canonical categories – as in a culturally or religiously sanctioned idea of 'loss' – but rather a way in which practitioners tried to express their physical experience verbally. In this sense, it might be considered as a direct form of a bodily hermeneutic enacted through the performance of the ascetic act by means of one's body, and only later articulated into a more abstract intellectual category.[73]

On the other hand, other practitioners – or the same practitioners mentioned above in different circumstances – remark instead upon the sense of 'gain' that the prolonged walking produces. The sense of an energy surge, sharper concentration, enjoyment and so forth are all understood as phenomena 'produced by the practice' and are again expressed with a variety of expressions which are but another attempt to translate into acceptable language one's bodily sensations.[74] The individual level of physical performance also seems to affect these perceptions. The sense of 'loss' is more frequent among newcomers, inexperienced, physically weak or the occasional participant who openly laments the toll that the practice is taking on them rather than emphasizing the benefits. The second circumstance – a sense of 'gain' – is instead more common among the experienced, the strongly built and the young. Indeed, however inexperienced, and even scared by the practice, young people almost always react with enthusiasm to the bodily solicitations and generally report a 'gain' type of experience.[75]

As my personal experience confirms, a vast range of physical sensations arise in practitioners during the performance of an ascetic practice, and all can certainly challenge the potential of verbal expression. Even the ideas of 'loss' or 'gain' are probably just two broad umbrella categories that can conveniently be associated with the Japanese verbs 'suteru 捨てる' (drop, discard) and 'eru 得る' (receive, obtain) used by my informants to convey their sensations. Circumstantial factors, like physical preparedness, can intervene in shifting the focus of the practitioner in various directions, but the interpretation of one's bodily sensations is more than anything else a matter of interpretation of one's own body: indeed, it is the bodily hermeneutic we introduced earlier. It is only in the second step of this interpretative aetiology that this first-hand bodily hermeneutic is coupled with 'official' meanings pertaining to the various religious environments. Unexpressed bodily interpretations are associated with expressed conceptual meanings, which often happen to be endorsed by the religious orthodoxy of the environment in question. It is at this step in the process of interpretation that 'loss-type' sensations are associated with, for instance, the acquisition of physical purity and purification in a more 'Shinto'-inspired environment or the mitigation of the self, and particularly the idea of 'discarding' of oneself which we have seen as so important in many of the practitioners' accounts, in a Buddhist practice. By the same logic, 'gain-type' sensations are often interpreted as the presence/possession of the deities, the accumulation of magical powers, the awakening of one's Buddha nature and so forth and are always accompanied by a feeling of gratitude.[76] Of course, not all cases are so clearly distinct. Waterfall ablutions (*takigyō*) practitioners, for instance, often report that the practice performs a purificatory function, where they 'discard' their impurity in a way that 'leaves a sensation of lightness in your body', and which is then replenished by the 'heat that the practice awakens in you' few moments after.[77] At the same time, the natural fear awakened by the inherent danger of practices like the *hawatari* or the *uragyōba* is interpreted both as a way to discard one's ego and as empowering focus, concentration and physical strength.

To properly assess the understanding that ascetics have of the religious context in which they carry out their practices, we must take into account this twofold and concurrent hermeneutical process: a bodily hermeneutic on one side and a doctrinal hermeneutic on the other. The relationship between these two hermeneutical forms is, of course, extremely fluid and the two tend to influence each other. As the relationship between the two hermeneutical dimensions is dialogical by nature, it is thus complex to determine which one is influencing the other the most. The ways in which the individual practitioners conceptualize the practices are also very personal, and it would be impossible to trace a complete map of these relations as well as define univocal directions of influence. What is instead clear is that the circulation of ascetic techniques among different ascetic environments does not pose a doctrinal problem, as no ascetic act or practice can be considered to be the exclusive consequence of specific doctrinal tenets. On more practical terms, ultimately a walking practice in the mountain can be interpreted from a 'Shinto' perspective as a way to purify oneself and commune with nature and the *kami*, while from a Buddhist perspective it can be conceptualized as a way to discard one's ego and identify oneself with the mandalized space of the sacred mountain, despite it remaining the same practice at a performative level.

To clarify this theory further, we shall analyze two ascetic practices carried out in the same geographical area which share a very similar legacy and portray very similar sets of ascetic acts, while at the same time are conducted in very different religious environments. One is the *akinomine* practice conducted at the Shōzen-in and Kōtaku-ji I have already discussed, the other is its 'Shinto' equivalent practised at the Dewa Sanzan *jinja* under the name *akinomineiri*.

Akinomine: *Buddhist and Shinto*

The Dewa Sanzan *jinja akinomineiri* begins on 25 August and ends on 1 September, thereby following the same calendar as the *akinomine* practice held at Kōtaku-ji.[78] Both the Buddhist and Shinto versions of the *akinomine* start in a very similar way, with the participants gathering at Shōzen-in temple and Dewa Sanzan *jinja* respectively.[79] Unlike the Buddhist version, however, the participation in the Shinto *akinomine* seems to be planned by the practice leaders in much more detail. On the day before the beginning of the practice, complete *shugenja* attire is distributed to all participants systematically in order to ensure the highest degree of uniformity. The practice leaders seem indeed to consider the external appearance of the *shugenja* very important and no variations or personal modifications to the attire are permitted. Even the use of a personal walking stick is prohibited and all the participants have to use the standard stick provided by the shrine.[80] A very practical reason for this may be the fact that the Shinto *akinomine* enjoys a wider number of participants than its Buddhist counterpart. For example, they numbered more than 160 people in 2006, while the Buddhist version generally gathers between 90 and 100 participants. All of the participants are male, since the shrine organizes a different practice called *miko shugyō* solely for women in September after the *akinomineiri*.[81] Most of the participants were from the Yamagata area and the vast majority of them were 'regular' participants who attend every year.[82] Occasional practitioners were so few in number that it was almost impossible to organize an intra-ascetic group of newcomers, as in the Buddhist case, and most of the new participants blended with the senior practitioners almost seamlessly.

On the first day, the participants gather at Myokō-in 明光院 temple where a brief ceremony of departure is performed, including the same *bonten* ritual used in the ceremony of conception at the Kogane-dō.[83] A portable altar (*oi*), quite similar to the Buddhist one, is also carried throughout the procession of the *shugenja* from Myokō-in to the Dewa Sanzan *jinja*. This initial part of the practice is enacted almost identically to the Buddhist version from a performative point of view, yet a number of differences reside in the doctrinal justification of these acts. The *bonten* ritual, which in the Buddhist *akinomine* represented the conception of the *shugenja*'s foetuses inside the symbolic womb of the *oi*, is now understood as the moment of the beginning of the practice, in which all the impurities of the participants are shaken from their bodies.[84] The ritual thus completely loses its sexual overtones and is reinterpreted in a stricter purificatory fashion. At the same time, this different understanding radically changes the role of the *oi*: the portable altar is carried to the mountain to become the temporary abode of the mountain deities and will be used to bring them the back to the village once the practice is concluded. The womb symbolism of the *oi* is lost, while the symbolic object survives within a different doctrinal narrative, completely transformed in purpose and *essence* but remaining the same in nature.[85]

The route to the Dewa Sanzan *jinja* follows more or less the same path as the Buddhist *akinomine*. The group of participants leaves the civilized world for the sacred world of the mountain, walking the same path – including the long 2,600-step staircase – stopping in the same resting places and enjoying a drink together. Upon arrival at the shrine precinct, a simple ritual is performed at each one of the shrine's buildings. The ritual itself is again a Shinto-revised version of a short Buddhist *gongyō* and involves the communal chanting of the name of the mountain deities as well as a short prayer having purificatory power. The next step of the practice carries the participants to what is going to be their dwelling for the following days: an elongated building set about one kilometre from the shrine, known as the Buchūdō 峰中堂. The Buchūdō is a building approximately 20 metres long and eight metres wide. It has two doors, one on the short side, which is used for entering and exiting the building during everyday activities, and one on the long side called the *naka no kuchi* 中之口 (central door). This latter exit is only used on the final day of the practice, when the *shugenja* leave the building for the last time at the end of the practice. Against the other short side is a wide Shinto altar. The *shugenja* align their bedding along the longer sides, using the shelves provided to store their belongings.[86]

The space of practice

Contrary to the Buddhist practice, there are no 'lodgings', since the Shinto *aki-nomineiri* is not understood as a progressive path.[87] Moreover, the Buchūdō, although performing the same function of the Kōtaku-ji as the dwelling place of the ascetics, is a purpose-built building incorporating a Shinto altar but it is not considered a shrine. Doctrinal motifs seem to inform this difference. In the Buddhist *akinomine*, the emphasis is placed on the transformative power of the practice; in the Shinto version, however, this characteristic is lacking and is reflected in the different understanding that the practitioners have of the notion of 'sacred space'.

Remembering the triangular scheme involving the *sacred*, *actual* and *symbolic* space we developed earlier on (see Figure 4.2), in this immediate, non-trans-formative and immanent idea of sacred space, the importance of the symbolic space element is lessened to the advantage of the actual space, and the notion of sacred space only seems to come into existence as a tension between the *sacred* – here the presence of the deities – and the *actual* space of the mountain. In this case, the symbolic discourse of the identification of the ascetic with the sacred space becomes much less important.[88] This is the consequence of the fact that the Buddhist mandalic symbology of the Dewa Sanzan has been lost and has not been replaced with an alternative symbolic discourse, thus losing the previous doctrinal agenda. This occurs because the modern Shinto theology endorsed by the shrine stresses the ontological immanence of the gods in the actual space rather than its symbolic value. However, despite there being a major shift from the doctrinal positions of the Buddhist tradition of Haguro Shugendō, this does not mean that some of the ascetic acts characterizing the Buddhist tradition could not be renego-tiated using a different hermeneutic, such as one from the twofold hermeneutical system outlined earlier on. Moreover, this is still a dialogical relationship and its influence on the bodily hermeneutic of the practice is clear. In other words, while there is no emphasis on any 'transformative' power of the practice in the accounts of the Shinto practitioners, the interpretations of one's bodily sensations *through* the ideas of 'gain' and 'loss' remain.[89] The disappearance of the progres-sive structure also results in the practice not being as continuous as the Buddhist case. Indeed, the Shinto *akinomineiri* resembles a series of ascetic acts interrupted by long sessions of rest in the Buchūdō rather than one long practice possessing a sophisticated taxonomy and clear final goals, such as the Buddhist 'Practice of the ten realms'. This is not to say that the practice does not display a substan-tial degree of organization. Instead, the awareness of the symbolic position of each practitioner within the practice's symbolic space is much weaker than in its Buddhist counterpart; thus their identity as *shugenja* is less well-defined. This translates into the fact that, for instance, people undertake the practice quite easily, and it is almost impossible to individuate any fracture in the mood of the partici-pants in the various phases of the training, contrary to what clearly happens in the Buddhist *akinomine*. The participants also display a far lower level of expertise in mountaineering and the physical condition of some of them is quite poor and definitely not suited for arduous physical effort. This does not seem to constitute a problem for them. By contrast, in the Buddhist case, the majority of the practitioners tended to be proud of their physical achievements.

Intra-ascetic society in the 'Shinto' akinomineiri

As soon as the participants set up their belongings in the Buchūdō, the *intra-ascetic* society of the *shugenja* consolidates into groups which, contrary to the Buddhist one, are not motivated by the level of expertise or the age of the practitioners, but merely by the proximity of each other's beddings. The groups thus formed engage in long and polite discussions about everyday business, previous experience in the practice and personal interests, all accompanied by the usual jests, infusing the intra-ascetic society with the sense of camaraderie that can be witnessed in many *shugyō*. In this case, however, the ludic component of the practice is particularly paramount, and many people openly admit that they are participating in the practice primarily to enjoy themselves.[90] As in the Buddhist case, their understanding of the religious doctrine behind the practice is varied but generally is much more superficial than that of the Buddhist counterpart. As the conversation goes on, it becomes clear that the doctrine and beliefs connected with the practice constitute only a very minor part of the *shugenja* motivations, and the main motivation for most of the participants is to obtain the *ō-fuda* tablets that will be consecrated during the various rituals in the following days (see Figure 4.4).[91]

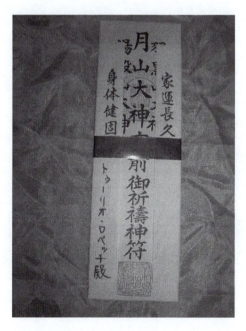

Figure 4.4 Dewa Sanzan *jinja ō-fuda*

For instance, one participant told me that he had participated in the *akinomi-neiri* for more than 10 years, but that it was only in the past year that he started developing the idea that 'these things about the *kami* can be true'.[92] Another participant was considered to be a sort of local healer, and he has participated in many *shugyō* all over Japan in order to empower himself, as we have seen in the case of the Okamoto family. He displayed an above-average knowledge of religious doctrine, although he had a clear-cut awareness of the practice as being 'Shinto', and, because of this, very different from its Buddhist version. Within this group, he was the only person that could be considered close to the figure of a 'religious professional', if we exclude the *sendatsu* and few other shrine priests.

The dinner of the first day is eaten wearing full *yamabushi* gear and it starts quite formally, with all participants receiving their meal diligently sitting with their legs folded under their thighs (*seiza* 正座). The meal itself is very minimal, constituted only by a cup of white rice and a cup of miso soup, but all the participants eat it quickly and attentively. The cups are then cleaned and wrapped in a white cloth, in a particular Buddhist fashion, and collected by the persons in service. The atmosphere is very formal and everyone tries to comply with the rules to the best of his ability. The meal is concluded with a collective chanting of the invocation to the mountain deities and then, almost abruptly, the atmosphere returns to the very casual and relaxed. It is interesting to note how, in the Buddhist counterpart, the meal period is one of the few moments of true relaxation during the practice when the strictness of the training is loosened momentarily. The meal – when eating is permitted – is generally abundant and all the participants sit quite informally while asking continuously for more rice.[93]

The different understanding of one's role in different symbolical landscapes – the two intra-ascetic societies of the Shinto and Buddhist *akinomine* practices – seems to activate different strategies in the construction of their everyday intra-ascetic life. The Shinto *society* privileges the attentive compliance to formal behaviour in all the circumstances in which the *shugenja* acts as a community, while their individual behaviour can be rather relaxed. By contrast, the Buddhist *society* emphasizes individual effort and achievement.

This does not mean that the Shinto practitioners always privilege an 'easier' way of practising. For instance, on the first night of the practice after the main collective ceremony, all the practitioners in the Buchūdō undergo their first *nanban ibushi* experience. As in the Buddhist practice, irritant herbs and spices are burned in braziers inside the sealed building, producing strong coughs and a sense of suffocation.[94] Unlike the Buddhist practice, however, the participants in the Shinto practice chant a hymn to the various deities throughout the *nanban ibushi*, which eventually lasts much longer and in fact proves to be far more distressing than in the Buddhist case.[95] At the end of the *nanban ibushi*, the *shugenja* precipitously rush out of the Buchūdō and perform a ritual offering of water and wood to the *aka no sendatsu* and the *kogi no sendatsu*,[96] an act which is completely identical to the Buddhist practice.[97] In this case, we clearly have a discordant use of the two hermeneutical levels (bodily hermeneutic and doctrinal hermeneutic) in a situation that, solely from the point of view of its series of ascetic acts, could look completely the same as the Buddhist practice. First, the Shinto practitioners understand the *nanban ibushi* through a bodily hermeneutic which privileges physical stress much more than the Buddhist one. In the latter case, the practitioners are permitted to cover their mouth and nose with the sleeves of their robe in order to protect themselves from the fumes, the fumigation time is much shorter, no chanting is performed and the *shugenja* are then allowed to leave the temple hall after having performed the above mentioned ritual offering in rank order. Second, the doctrinal explanation is also completely dissimilar. In the Shinto case, the fumigation ceremony is meant to be another purificatory device, which will 'clean the outside and inside of our bodies' – hence the need to actually breath the fumes. In the Buddhist case it is understood as the experience of the hell realm and of rebirth within the progression of the practice of the 10 realms (*jukkai shugyō*).[98]

Divergent hermeneutics of a segment of a specific practice may also allow for an occasional convergence of specific meanings. The offering of wood and water to the respective *sendatsu* is understood in exactly the same terms in both versions of the *akinomine*, with the same ritual formula employed for the offering. However, the designation *aka no sendatsu*, of probable Sanskrit origin, has clear Buddhist overtones, something which was noticed by some participants in the Shinto practice.[99] This was explained by the Shinto leaders as being a 'reminder' of the previous 'contamination' of the practice by Buddhist influence. One may ponder the reasons why the shrine officials did not go as far as to reform the Buddhist terminology in a stricter Shinto fashion as well.[100] It is not simple to obtain information about this, as the leaders seemed to be somewhat uncomfortable with the issue. They tried to explain the persistence of Buddhist terms in what was otherwise officially defined as a 'pure Shinto' practice as a way of preserving a certain degree of continuity with the historical past and not create too deep a fissure within the history of Haguro Shugendō.[101] Controversial as it may appear, this position suggests that the shrine officials were put in a quandary by their need to reform the activities of the shrine in 'pure Shinto' fashion and at the same time respect the allegiance that the local populace felt, and still feels, towards the traditional Buddhist icons and iconic language. Eliminating the Buddhist statues enshrined in the main hall of the former shrine-temple complex was eventually possible; other Buddhist icons, however, seem to have resisted this challenge and still survive on the very ground of the shrine. One such example is the icon of Fudō myōō located at the eponymous waterfall next to the entrance of the shrine precinct; following a popular protest, its removal was not carried out.[102] The same is true for a small hall enshrining a statue of Jizō; the image still survives but it has been placed outside the shrine boundaries.[103]

These compromises between the Buddhist and Shinto traditions also suggest another approach for the analysis of ascetic practices and their relationship to religious doctrines. Rather than providing a comprehensive and coherent explanation, it seems that doctrine is employed at times in order to supply a specific practice with a particular 'cultural/religious identity' which is often the identity of the religious orthodoxy dominating the cultural landscape in which the practice is carried out. Ascetics are in a sense all potentially heterodox figures, for many of the reasons outlined above (e.g. the capacity for self-legitimization, social shifting and so forth). One way for the religious orthodox elites to cope with these powerful but potentially dangerous individuals is to incorporate them into an aura of accepted doctrine in order to claim them their own, and thus exert a certain degree of control. As in the case of Haguro-jinja, some elements of the Buddhist tradition could simply be abandoned, e.g. the 'practice of the ten realms' and some acts preserved in practice and re-justified within a different heterodox doctrine (the function of the portable altar, the ritual of conception etc.). Yet others had to be tacitly confirmed so as not to create too wide a historical discontinuity, especially when part of the leaders' agenda was to portray the practice's historical continuity. Thus, rather than seeing the Shinto and Buddhist version of the *akinomine* as simply the opposition of two parallel hermeneutics converging on the same set of ascetic acts, we also need to take into account their *inter-ascetic* influences and interactions within their particular religio-cultural context.

Comparison of ascetic routines

On the second day of the *akinomineiri*, the participants are awakened at 5.00am with a gentle call and start to prepare for the day in no particular hurry. This is very different in the Buddhist *akinomine*, where the *shugenja* rise abruptly at the sound of a gong and need to be ready in their full gear in a matter of a few minutes, and there is no fixed timetable, just a general indication of the succession of events. In the shrine version, almost 1.5 hours is given to the *shugenja* to prepare themselves. After the usual frugal breakfast, the participants get ready for their first day of training on the mountain. A roll-call is made outside the Buchūdō and then the practitioners depart for Haguro shrine. Having performed a short ceremony in front of each of the major shrines, the *shugenja* descend the steep slopes of Mount Haguro to reach a small shrine built next to a waterfall which is simply called *Ōtaki-jinja* 御滝神社 (shrine of the waterfall). Here all the practitioners receive a small cup of *sake* and then make their way back to the Buchūdō again by the same path. This process is remarkably quick when compared to other practices, lasting approximately from 7.30am until 12.30pm, and this will remain the main ascetic feat of the day. For the rest of the afternoon, the practitioners are completely free and they enjoy their time in a comradely fashion with tales, conversations, jests and the smuggling of small quantities of 'illicit' food, such as sweets and rice crackers.[104] The *shugenja* therefore remains idle until the evening, when the daily ceremony followed by a *nanban ibushi* is performed, followed by another one around 1.00am.

This daily 'ascetic routine' will remain more or less the same in the days that follow; each one is marked by a different main ascetic feat but underlined by a substantially identical daily routine. The third day is characterized by an extended session of walking in the mountains, with two options available for the participants: climbing Gassan with part of the route covered by bus or, as a more difficult option, the long and somehow more demanding walk from the Buchūdō to the Higashi Fudaraku 東補陀洛. The Higashi Fudaraku is the eastern versant of the Haguro ridge and it is characterized by a high-rising stone pinnacle. This is performed also in the Buddhist version but, here again, we have divergent doctrinal interpretations. For the Buddhist practitioners, a small crack at the pinnacle's base represents the womb; there they 'crawl through a narrow rock cave to venerate Kannon. This is called *tainai kuguri* 胎内潜り, or passing through the womb'.[105] For the Shinto *shugenja*, this is an eminently phallic symbol and is complemented by a rocky formation on the western front (Nishi Fudaraku 西補陀洛) which symbolizes the vagina (although this last site is not part of the Shinto *akinomine* practice route).[106]

The fourth day is billed as a 'day of rest' (*yasumi no hi* 休みの日) and the participants attend the cleaning of the grounds around the Buchūdō, a session of instruction about the meaning of the practice and the preparation of the fire ritual site, which in the Shinto context is known as *hi no matsuri* 火の祭. The fire ritual starts at about 8.00pm and represents the counterpart of the Buddhist *saitō goma*, although the acts and ritual sequences are different. The climax of the event is marked by the opening of the otherwise sealed shrine dedicated to Prince Hachiko 蜂子, the 'opener' of the Dewa Sanzan and thus the founder of Haguro Shugendō.[107] Prince Hachiko is said to have opened the mountain in 593; interestingly, he is venerated in the same role by the Buddhist *shugenja* but under the name Shōken Daibosatsu 照見大菩薩. Despite this difference in name and status, both the Shinto and Buddhist *shugenja* proudly endorse the figure of Hachiko, as he predates the more famous En no Gyōja by almost one century and thus legitimizes Haguro Shugendō as the most longstanding Shugendō tradition in Japan.[108]

The activity of the fourth day therefore portrays a remarkable quantity of discordant doctrinal themes between the Shinto and Buddhist versions of the practice. First of all, we may notice a process of doctrinal reform in the case of the fire ritual: 'purged' of its Buddhist connotations, it is now understood as a Shinto celebration of fire. The practitioners are, of course, well aware of the existence of the Buddhist *goma*, but they consider it to be in essence a pure Japanese ritual which only subsequently has been associated with Buddhist meanings, as explained also by the shrine priests during the day.[109] It is interesting to note how such a-historical understanding of the fire ritual is then coupled with a re-modelled historical setting which emphasizes the historical figure of Prince Hachiko as the original opener of Dewa Sanzan and thus the true founder of Shugendō.[110] In this case, it is clear how the Shugendō lore of Haguro-jinja was tailored to serve the specific political agenda of the Meiji period, which was an extra-ascetic issue. This has been translated into an inter-ascetic competition between the shrine and the temple which eventually affected the intra-ascetic relationships between the bodily and doctrinal hermeneutic of the individual ascetic acts.

The remaining three days of the *akinomineiri* follow the same routine outlined above and are consequently characterized by the performance of ascetic acts similar – or even identical – to the Buddhist *akinomine*, while the doctrinal meanings associated to them are shaped in a clearly 'Shinto' fashion. Within this trend it is possible to note two interesting exceptions. The first is a short practice called *katabako* かたばこ[111] which is performed on the fifth day at 1.00pm. It consists of descending a steep, slippery slope behind the Hachiko shrine in order to reach a sacred stone gushing water and shaped like a vagina. After the stone has been worshipped, the *shugenja* make their way back to the top of the slope and the practice is considered to be concluded. This practice has no equivalent in the Buddhist *akinomine*, and indeed the shrine officials consider the *katabako* location to be utterly secret. Guarding this 'secret' clearly has important identitarian overtones for them and helps in strengthening the understanding of the Shinto *akinomineiri* as something different from the Buddhist practice.[112]

The other exception regards the persistence of a clearly Buddhist doctrinal theme, unchallenged in this Shinto context. On the very last day, when the practice is concluded and the *shugenja* are finally free to leave the Buchūdō, they gather for the last time inside the building wearing their full *shugenja* attire. At the end of the final ceremony, they all abruptly rush out of the Buchūdō using the central door, which has not been used until now. This act is explained as symbolizing birth, in the same way as the 'cry of birth' and the frantic rush outside the Dewa Sanzan shrine represents birth for the Buddhist *shugenja*. The theme of rebirth in and *through* the mountain has thus proven to be resilient to doctrinal reforms and survives even in the complete absence of the Buddhist 'practice of the ten realms'. The leaders of the *akinomineiri* limit their explanation by stating that, having abandoned all of our impurities, we are now reborn as newborn babies[113]

Conclusions

This analysis of the social context of asceticism and its relationship with the spatial dimensions of the ascetic practice has shown how a parallel society can be developed by ascetic practitioners in the course of an ascetic practice or retreat. This is what we have called an *intra-ascetic society* and we have explored the circumstances in which it can overlap with the ordinary *extra-ascetic society*. The capacity of the ascetic to shift between these two social dimensions has also been highlighted as the fundamental reason for his social significance.

In the second part of the chapter, the comparative analysis of practices carried out in two different religious contexts also showed how similar ascetic practices can be easily incorporated into different orthodoxies to serve different agendas. A general conclusion that we can draw from this comparative example is that the interaction between ascetic practice and religious doctrine takes place on a number of concurrent levels which eventually relate in a dialogical manner, influencing one another. Ascetic acts are not necessarily the direct expression of religious doctrine nor are they exclusive to a specific religious environment. They circulate among different religious groups, which appropriate their power for purposes and meanings compatible with their particular orthodoxy. Attaching different, or even competing, religious meanings to an ascetic act does not represent a contradiction nor does it create a conflict regarding the 'true nature' of the act, for this doctrinal hermeneutical process takes place on the cognitive plane, and thus is different from the hermeneutic of the body which is enacted through performance.

5   *Corporis ascensus*

The analysis conducted thus far shows the richness of the Japanese ascetic phenomena, but none seems to have provided a coherent understanding of *what* asceticism (in its broader sense) is and *how* it is supposed to 'function'. If we were asked to offer a definition of 'asceticism' drawing from the previous chapters, it would perhaps sound like 'activities involving a certain degree of bodily pain or exertion, carried out by a variety of people in a variety of contexts following various motivations and purposes generally considered beneficial, while none of these elements is necessarily related to the others' – a rather poor definition indeed.

The vagueness of this definition seems to stem in great part from the variety of the phenomena involved, which do not allow for broad generalizations. Enhancing our analytical approach quantitatively by providing more examples of ascetic practices together with their variety of contexts would certainly make the phenomenon look even richer in its manifestations, but at the same time would not solve the problem of definition. For this reason, this last chapter will take a more inductive approach and re-read once again the ascetic phenomena described in the earlier chapters, in an attempt to theorize the presence of an underlying theme in asceticism that pre-dates specific practices. We will then endeavour to determine the presence of constants among the many variables involved in the phenomena analyzed, and build a theory of asceticism around these constants. Hopefully, this analysis will allow us to identify an underlying theme that can be employed in the analysis of ascetic practices at large, i.e. beyond the specific case studies of this work.

Constants in ascetic practice

The first constant that is evident in ascetic practices is the presence of the human body (see Chapter 1). All of the activities, practices or endeavours we have outlined so far make extensive use of the performative possibilities of human bodies, both in their active and passive forms (see Chapter 2). It might be argued that an 'asceticism of the mind' may exist, but this presupposes a distinction between body and mind that is more metanoetical than ontological, and should not be taken for granted. As discussed in the first chapter this would be a particular stance of the modern period and cultural mind-set.[1]

The second constant we may individuate is the presence of some degree of pain or physical exhaustion. All the ascetic practices we have analyzed thus far are physically demanding, although to different extents. The quantity of 'pain' involved in a certain practice may depend on the structure of the practice itself, as well as on the personal commitment of the practitioner, but nonetheless it should be present for the practice to be effective. It is remarkable to note how experienced ascetic practitioners can gauge their efforts in order to achieve the most proficient balance between their physical abilities and the requirements of the practice. This can be seen when a certain practice starts to become too 'easy' because of the practitioner's experience and increased physical prowess. Then the practitioner tends to re-adjust the practice to make it still 'wisely harder' and thus effective. Ascetic pain is not, as we have seen throughout this work, aimed at mere destruction but is a 'wise pain' through which the ascetic *malleates* his body (see Chapter 2).

This should lead us to reconsider our symptomatic understanding of 'pain' as a disagreeable sensation to be avoided at all costs. This apparently natural understanding of pain as an undesirable physical symptom is in fact a physiological generalization which does not take into account the possibility for human beings to re-interpret their bodily functions or sensations.[2] If this were true, then also the association of sexual arousal with love, the sense of satisfaction in eating, the pleasure in caressing and petting other human beings as a demonstration of inner feelings, and so forth, would all be taken either as physiological absolutes (love is *always* accompanied by arousal, eating *always* generates satisfaction) or as mere cultural coincidences. Human beings seem to be extremely capable of re-interpreting their bodies and the sensations associated with them in a variety of modes beyond their mere physiology. Asceticism is one such case, and the process of understanding and interpreting one's bodily sensation in the presence of pain is exactly what we have earlier on termed a 'bodily hermeneutic'.

Asceticism as an 'ontological progression'

The presence of a body, the willing *production* of a certain degree of pain and the employment of a bodily hermeneutic to interpret the variety of sensations arising from the encounters of body and physical pain seem to constitute the *ascetic constants* we were looking for. Interestingly enough, nothing at this point seems to suggest that asceticism has any specific *religious* connotation to it. It may be posited whether forms of non-religious asceticism(s) exist and if people like athletes can be numbered among the ranks of 'proper' ascetics. Flood's clear-cut affirmation that 'athletes are not ascetics'[3] primarily relies on the idea that asceticism should be understood as the ritualized expression of an internalized *text*, of a specific tradition. Such a definition has been shown to be problematic in the Japanese religious context, where similar practices are shared among different religious groups (see Chapter 4). One explanation of Flood's position is that he identifies the *text* in question with the tradition, scriptural or otherwise, that accompanies a certain practice and is part of the practitioner's cultural identity.[4] In this study, we have proposed instead that the text in question should be identified with the *body* of the practitioner. The ascetic text is in this sense *embodied* because it is produced by the human body, which also becomes its recording medium; analyzing the text thus means to analyze the body itself, its records of sensations and feelings.[5] The bodily hermeneutic provides meanings that, coupled with a further cognitive interpretation, can make this text accessible and communicable to others, eventually creating a 'tradition' in the conventional sense. This 'embodied text' is transversal to specific religious environments, beliefs and social circumstances. It is indeed within this internalized text where we can identify the borderline between ascetics and athletes.

I would like to argue that the theme underlying this ascetic embodied tradition is that the body demonstrates the possibility of being ontologically 'improved': it is a 'perfectible' entity that can ascend from being ordinary matter to something purer and holier. This theme is pre-logical in nature, as it depends solely on a direct bodily hermeneutic; it is the unspeakable set of bodily sensations that many practitioners try to articulate in simple terms like 'loss' and 'gain'. By contrast, athletes are not concerned with ontological issues; the purpose of their practice in this sense is merely quantitative: to make the most of one's bodily performance for performance's sake alone. In more practical terms, athletes train to run faster (or whatever the athletic feat is) because they want to run faster. Ascetics train to run faster because they want to *be* better. This particular assumption of the possibility of an 'ontological progression' can perhaps be considered inherent in all ascetic traditions which do not endorse a clear-cut antagonistic dualism between body and mind/spirit and which tend to explain the body in cosmological terms as well. In this sense, I agree with Flood that 'asceticism occurs *par excellence* in cosmological religion', as far as the body can be considered a reflection of this cosmology.[6] In the case of Japanese ascetic practices, we have seen how the body of the ascetic practitioner is engaged in a variety of cosmological themes: from the 'practice of the ten realms' (the *akinomine* practice) to the 'sacred' spaces of the *okugake* and *kaihōgyō*. It is precisely the presence of this cosmological contextualization that manifests the link between asceticism and religion(s).

As far as our study is concerned, it is this 'ontological progression of the body' that I intend to put forward as the underlying theme of asceticism and which I would like to designate with the term *corporis ascensus*, with an intended pun here on the word *ascensus* with *ascesis* (when in fact the actual meaning of *ascensus* is 'to rise, to ascend').

The concept of *corporis ascensus* carries certain implications. We must first determine the extremes of this progressive process, that is, the starting point of this progression and its ideal end. As this ontological progression is focused on the body, we can expect these two extremes to correspond to two different states of the human body, the lowest being the *non-ascetic* and the highest being the closest thing possible to a theoretically *perfect body*. Within the panorama of Japanese asceticism, I would like to correlate the former condition with bodily impurity and the latter with the perfect body of the self-mummified ascetic briefly mentioned at the beginning of Chapter 1 (and described in detail later in this chapter).

It is between these two extremes that we can identify the various stages of the *corporis ascensus* process by matching the actual ascetic phenomena to specific *ascetic bodies*. We will start our analysis from the *non-ascetic body*, attempting to determine what boundaries constitute the threshold between the non-ascetic and ascetic in actual practice. We will then explore the *ascetic body* and the rationales behind its *malleation* process. This will be followed by the exploration of the *body empowered* where we will consider the association of power with ascetic practice, trying to understand if power must be considered a mere side-effect of proper ascetic practice or as something necessarily inherent to the *corporis ascensus* process. In our final step of *corporis ascensus*, we will touch upon the *perfect body* of the self-mummified Buddhas, who in my opinion are the ascetic figures closest to the ideal *perfect body* constituting the final goal of ascetic practice.

The non-ascetic body: moral themes

As noted, the very concept of *corporis ascensus* presupposes a series of steps in the condition of one's body which leads from a certain minimum state. This minimum state may be conceived of in different ways in various cultural and religious contexts, depending upon how distant the 'normal' bodily condition is from the 'perfect body' ideal. In Christianity, for instance, the condition of the body is sometimes thought to mirror moral behaviour; not surprisingly, two of the seven deadly sins (*gula* – gluttony, and *luxuria* – lust) clearly relate to bodily matters. The bodily state can also be the cause of the manifestation of an internal moral downfall. This is reflected in iconic representations of sinners and demons, who are often depicted as crooked, deformed or with unnatural bodily proportions.[7] In Islam and Judaism, individual morality is only part of this equation. The body can in fact be debased and corrupted not only by sins but also through contact with impure or defiling things, such as blood or excrement, or by the intake of impure food such as pork.[8] In other cases, as with the Indian caste system, a systematization of purity – and at the same time of moral stature – is made on the basis of birth status. Lower caste bodies are innately impure, and this can only be changed in a future life (based upon the meritorious acts of this life). This impurity also affects social behaviour; for example, receiving food or water from a low-caste individual is considered to be polluting, regardless of the origin of the food itself.[9] In all these cases, asceticism is, not surprisingly, seen as a remedy for an improper or too-far-from-perfect body, although the various forms of practice and understanding of it may vary greatly.

In our study of Japanese ascetic practices, it is important to pinpoint which specific attitude towards one's body may coincide with the starting point of the *corporis ascensus*. Moral themes seem to underlie the traditional narrative surrounding at least some notable ascetic figures. The ascetic Tetsumonkai 鉄門海 (d. 1829), whose self-mummified body is venerated at Chūren-ji temple 注連寺 (Yamagata prefecture) and to whose figure we shall return later, clearly enjoyed a less-than-virtuous life before he started his endeavour to become a self-mummified Buddha. We are told that he decided to flee to Chūren-ji and become a monk after a quarrel with two *samurai*, about a prostitute in a pleasure quarter, in which he eventually killed them.[10]

A more recent example – the life of the *kaihōgyōja* Sakai Yūsai 酒井雄哉 – draws on a similar rhetoric of trial and redemption in order to exalt the power and benefit of the practice. Sakai clearly had an uncertain life from an early age. After the Second World War, his family set up a noodle shop which burned down shortly after, leaving the family disgraced. He then married a cousin, who eventually committed suicide. Sakai remembers this part of his life without any self-pity.

> Because I was lazy and had a good-for-nothing life, there was nothing else for me to do. Furthermore, when I was a child at school, I flunked my exams again and again. I completed the *kaihōgyō* once but because I'd needed to do everything else in my life twice, I thought I'd better walk twice if I really wanted to achieve something.
>
> (Video footage from Michael Yorke 1992)

He thus completed the *kaihōgyō* twice, becoming one most revered *kaihōgyōja* in modern times.

In his autobiography, Yamada Ryūshin also states that he started his ascetic endeavour as a way to atone for his lack of filial piety and commitment towards his ailing mother. He deeply regrets not having been at her side in the final stages of her fatal disease and presents this as the main reason that drove him towards his ascetic path.[11] Similarly, one of the practitioners I had the occasion to meet during my fieldwork among Japanese ascetics started his ascetic endeavours after an admittedly reckless life as a member of the *yakuza* (Japanese criminal fraternity) as well as the extended illness of his mother.[12]

A much greater number of ascetics, however, led more linear lives not shaped by such a pattern of fall and rise. Most of the great ascetics of the past lived an exemplary existence and their ascetic achievements were clearly not a way to atone for their sins. Rather, they were more a natural step for their progression in their religious practice. Of the famous Sōō, the founder of the *kaihōgyō* practice, for instance, we are told that the desire for enlightenment was aroused in him after reading the chapter about the Bodhisattva Never Disparaging from the *Lotus Sutra*. Sōō is a clear example of virtue and humility: gathering flowers every day for the main hall of Enryaku-ji and refusing his ordination in 854 to recommend another monk instead.[13] The life of Sōō as an ascetic monk starts when, longing for a more austere and solitary practice, he founded the Mudō-ji in 856, still the centre of the *kaihōgyō* practice, on the southern part of Mount Hiei, where he resided for three years. Then, in 859, Sōō started a new and deeper period of practice and austerities on Mount Hira on the western shore of Lake Biwa. As recorded in the *Katsuragawa Engi*, it was during this retreat on Mount Hira that Sōō started his practice with the precise aim to see a living Fudō Myōō before his very eyes. For this purpose, he started purifying himself for long periods under a waterfall; after more days of practice, Fudō Myōō himself appeared in the waterfall.[14] Unable to restrain himself, 'Sōō jumped in the waterfall to embrace the deity. But what he embraced was not Fudō but a log of the *katsura* tree. Pulling the log out of the water, Sōō enshrined it and continued his practices.[15]

The lives of many of the self-mummified Buddhas are no less commendable. Honmyōkai 本明海, whose self-mummification dates back to 1683, was a former retainer of a feudal lord of Tsuruoka. We are told that he left his family to pursue an ascetic path of life at the Chūren-ji temple in order to pray for the recovery of his lord from some serious illness. Another self-mummified ascetic, Chūkai 忠海, who was Honmyōkai's nephew, had a firm veneration for his uncle and eventually resolved to follow his steps as an ascetic. He was buried alive in 1755 after leading an exemplary life.[16]

Present-day ascetics frequently display a similar degree of virtue. The biographies of some contemporary *kaihōgyō* practitioners, such as Uehara Gyōshō, are very different from Sakai's trial and redemption model. They depict the lives of dedicated and well-intentioned religious professionals and seem to be more concerned with the benefit they can provide to others and their religious institution, and more generally to the future of Japanese religion and culture, than with their personal sense of guilt.[17] The same can be said for the vast majority of lay practitioners participating in the numerous *shugyō* we have mentioned throughout the course of this work. Most of them are respectable people dedicated to their family and business; in many cases, as we have seen, this is one of the reasons prompting their participation in the practices, rather than a desire to atone for their sins.

Non-ascetic bodies and impurity

In the case of Japanese ascetics, it is thus difficult to identify the starting point of the *corporis ascensus* progression purely in moral terms. However, the non-ascetic body seems to be characterized by the presence of an equally distinctive mark: impurity. On many occasions, the Japanese ascetics' behaviour implicitly acknowledges the inherent impurity of the human body as the threshold on which the dichotomy between the non-ascetic and the ascetic is resolved. Examples from the *modes* of practice outlined in Chapter 2 appear to confirm this consideration, regardless of how different the doctrinal conception underlying the doctrinal hermeneutic of the practice may be.

In the case of the occasional borrowing of ascetic acts, an obvious emphasis is put on the purifying effect of cold-water ablutions. This is the case of festival preparation, as in the documented *Iwaguni kagura*. The pure/impure dichotomy in this case suggests only two statuses of the practitioner's body: the participants are considered pure enough to perform their duties in the festival or to enter the *kagura* sacred stage only *after* their performance of *mizugori*, *takigyō* or other form of water ablution practice. In other cases, this difference in purity and status is more subtle, such as in the *hiwatari* and *hawatari* ascetic acts. In these cases, however, the underpinning conception of the non-ascetic body is marked by some form of purity. In the *hiwatari* case, the practitioner is requested to step on a heap of salt and to pass inside a circle formed by a sacred *shimenawa* rope. Bodily purity in this case overlaps both with traditional and spatial themes. The impure body exists outside the ritual symbolic space, yet after its passage onto the salt and inside the circle of sacred rope, it is re-defined as a pure body, ready to undertake the next step in the practice: the passage over the bed of *goma* embers which will imbue it with power. This is true for the *hawatari* as well, where the practitioners should be in a clear state of mind and must not be inebriated before their attempt on the ladder of swords. Here the concern for purity is treated as a necessary pre-condition rather than an integral part of the practice itself.

As the structure of the practice became more complex and concrete, as with organized practices taking place outside institutional religious bodies, the bound-ary between the non-ascetic and ascetic also seems to consolidate into more determined forms. In the case of the Ontake *samugyō* practice, we can see a clearer definition of the purity requirements in the extra-ascetic environment, as all the practitioners are required to abstain from meat and alcohol for three days prior to the practice. Further purificatory practice is then included in the first seg-ment of the *samugyō*, by means of cold-water ablutions under a waterfall. This remains an underlying theme throughout the practice, and one is reminded of the continuous presence and benefit of the cold: 'You see, this cold cleanses you, can you feel it?'[18] The case of *itako* and other non-institutional practitioners is not dis-similar: the first steps of their ascetic endeavour (water ablutions, endurance of cold, abstentions) are clearly focused on the attainment of bodily purity, both as a prerequisite for the ascetic practice and as an integral part of it.[19] Religious profes-sionals appear to be even more aware of this boundary separating the non-ascetic from the ascetic; they can make use of a remarkable variety of doctrinal herme-neutics in order to re-negotiate their self-awareness. As we have seen in Shugendō practices, the pure/impure dichotomy often overlaps with spatial themes and influ-ences the behaviour of individual participants. On a more personal basis, some of the participants in the *akinomine* sometimes abstain from alcohol or meat before starting the practice, even if they are not explicitly advised to do so by the practice leaders, while others pay continuous attention to the maintenance and cleanliness of their attire, before and during the practice.[20]

The dichotomy of pure/impure thus seems to be the most widespread motif establishing the threshold between the ascetic and non-ascetic bodies in Japanese ascetic practice, and hence may be considered the initial step of our *corporis ascensus* aetiology. Consequently, we will next examine what agents cause the transition from the non-ascetic to the ascetic, and the mechanism of such a transition.

The ascetic body: sacred pain and effort

As a first step in the *corporis ascensus* aetiology, we have identified the acknowl-edgement of the existence of the non-ascetic body, which in our case study corresponds to the body-impure. As we have seen, various strategies of practice are enacted as a 'remedy' to this condition, having as their common result the attainment of the body-pure via practices from water ablutions to the abstention from some kinds of food.[21] It would be a mistake, however, to understand the body-pure as synonymous with the *ascetic body*. The difference is perhaps conceptually subtle yet radical. The body-pure does not denote a precise being; rather, it connotes a lack of an attribute which we have stated as being 'normal' for a certain being (i.e. the body-pure is a body lacking impurity). The body-pure is therefore better expressed in a negational form as the non-body-impure, which, however, still does not provide a definition of what the body-pure is. The difficulty in pinpointing such a definition is because the pure/impure dichotomy is a rather blurred theme in respect of the body, weaving between the ontological understanding of specific bodily attributes as specific bodily properties (or *epistemes*) and their moral themes characterized as mere external attributes.[22] The removal of one of such attribute, impurity, is not enough per se to justify an ontological transition in the body itself, while the removal of a bodily *episteme* will negate the nature of the body as we know it, thus creating a new body for the ascetic out of a lack of that property, which is an ontological absurdity. In other words, it is not purity that realizes the transition between the non-ascetic and ascetic body (since it is an *attribute* rather than a *property*) but something even more radically connected with the nature of the body itself: the capacity to perform. A body can indeed lack impurity, and for this reason can be deemed pure, but in no circumstances can it lack performance, for, as we have seen, the mere physical presence of a body already performs a variety of functions.

Translating Flood's affirmation 'the ascetic self is performed' to suit our analysis, we may want, then, to state that 'the ascetic body is performed'.[23] In so doing, we establish and identify between the performance of ascetic acts or practices and the ascetic body as a being. This is well expressed in the *kaihōgyōja's* self-determinatory statement, 'while I am doing this, I am a Buddha', which puts into words this exact correspondence between being and performing. Still, we need to determine why not all performances of the body can qualify as ascetic performances and why only those involving a certain amount of pain and effort seem to act as such.

An analogical theory of ascetic performance and its limitations

As we anticipated in the introduction, the role of pain in ascetic practice is connected with its *malleating* power. This reasoning is clearly drawn from analogies with other forms of physical *malleation*; sculpting, carving, polishing and so forth are all actions with the power to alter the object under attention and reshape it in a new form. *Malleation* also 'rationalizes' the object: a naturally and irrationally shaped log can became a plank, a rough block of stone a statue or a building block, an incoherent mound of clay a vase or another object of utility. If the same analogy is applied to the human body, if the wish of the ascetic is to reshape the body and rationalize it to put it to better purpose, we may, at least in part, perceive a coherent rationale behind the need for pain in asceticism.

Many of the ascetic practitioners we have encountered in this study appear to conceptualize their efforts in this sense. As mentioned earlier, some of the participants of the *okugake shugyō* told me that they increased the amount of effort they put into the practice when they felt that the long hours of walking in the mountains were not causing the same level of strain for them anymore. Some were doing so by walking faster; in fact, the ambition of one of them was even to 'make it all running, one day'.[24] The practice leader was also particularly keen to explain the need for the practitioner to wear the incredibly uncomfortable *jikatabi* shoes for the duration of the practice in similar terms:

> Walking in the mountain should affect you in some way. Here you step over a sharp stone and you feel the pain, there you feel logs, bumps and pebbles under your sole. In this way, the nature (*daishizen* 大自然) of the mountain makes its way in your body through your feet.[25]

This strategy of continuously trimming of one's bodily pain is also present in practices where the participants may look less bodily proficient. In the *akinomine* case, despite the fact that many of the senior practitioners try to make their presence in the mountain temple as comfortable as possible (as mentioned in Chapter 4), those same practitioners can be also be seen to be personally engaging in demanding ascetic feats, which they often see as a progression from their previous year's experience. For instance, some of them try to walk a longer and harder route while others endeavour to actually give up food altogether in the allotted period of fasting. One instance in which I witnessed this attitude at work was during the long performance of prostrations after the third day of practice. After this ascetic feat was concluded, people discussed their performance and compared it with the previous year's one. Some of them acknowledged their improvements: 'Last year I fainted halfway through; this year I was able to reach the end of it!'[26]

Even the participants to a practice which does not seem as centred on active ascetic acts, the *rōhatsu sesshin* treated in Chapter 2, display similar patterns of behaviour and self-understanding. This was particularly so for those struggling to achieve the experience of enlightenment, having participated in the *sesshin* for many years without result. These individuals were practising harder and were actively encouraged by elder practitioners to do so.[27] They put more energy into the continuous repetition of the *kōan* '*mu*' by literally screaming it at the top of their lungs for long hours, and by dedicating a good portion of their sleeping and resting time to sitting in meditation. In this case, too, a higher level of result is associated with an increased amount of bodily performance, a fact that apparently confirms our analogical hypothesis.

Limits of the analogical theory

Although it certainly explains part of the phenomenon, the analogical theory seems to have at least one significant point of weakness. We have so far established that the ascetic body is a body-performed, and that performance can be understood by analogy with similar phenomena in the reshaping of other physical entities. We have affirmed that these entities are 'rationalized' in order to put them to a more efficacious use. But why can a body in pain or under physical strain be considered

a 'rationalized body'? As extensively discussed in Chapter 1, asceticism seems
to discipline a variety of uncontrolled bodily cravings inherent to human beings.
However, other forms of discipline exist in this respect, starting from societal
conventions, which discipline sexual, dietary and temperamental issues as well,
but which are not necessarily considered ascetic.[28] In this sense, it is difficult
to distinguish the ascetic practitioner from the dedicated member of the secular
community by the term 'discipline' alone, even if he is attentive to his duties to
the point of self-sacrifice.[29] An answer may come once again from a closer observation of the practices themselves and of the condition of the body-performed in
each practice's circumstance. Complex practices are characterized by a deliberate
taxonomy aimed at putting the practitioner in a condition proximate to death. But
simple ascetic acts can also display a certain degree of danger, whether environmental (cold water or weather, dangerous locations), volitional (extended
walking, extended chanting, fasting etc.) or inherent in contextual objects (ladders
of swords, path of embers). As Blacker points out, this ceaseless effort seems to
be made *ad hoc* to bring the practitioner to the extreme edge of physical and psychological resistance.[30] The deliberate purpose of ascetic performance thus seems
to be to 'manage death', to be able to put oneself in a near-death condition while
still preserving a degree of control of oneself. The subject of death is of course not
the self but the body, and in this light, asceticism rationalizes the most irrational
property of a living body: its inherent necessity to die. It is true that numerous
ways to cope with the event of death are also developed in extra-ascetic environments, such as funerary rituals and eschatological ideas, but they are all developed
to rationalize the dead body, not the living one. For the non-ascetic living body,
death remains an unpredictable, radically transforming event, the presence of
which will negate the living body as a whole. The ascetic body realizes this paradox; it experiences death-in-life, thus gaining power over it and rationalizing its
extreme transformative power.

On a more practical level, the ascetic performance is the controlled performance of acts that, if uncontrolled, would certainly lead to death, and ascetics
themselves are very well aware of this. During the *okugake*, for instance, some of
the older practitioners remarked, in an apparently off-hand way, the fact that the
Sanjogatake-*nabiki* practice could be potentially fatal.[31] In this sense, I agree with
Flood's argument that asceticism is fundamentally a reversal of the 'flow of the
body' and this flow-reversal may be taken as the underpinning theme in the *corporis ascensus* theory.[32] In addition to Flood, however, I would like to point out
that the efficacy of this reversal seems to depend on quantitative factors as well.
On a number of occasions, we have seen how practitioners distinguish between
more and less difficult practices. This level of difficulty is naturally directly
proportional to the level of pain and effort that the practice requires, while everybody agrees on the fact that the benefits obtained from the practices are similarly
proportioned.[33]

This progression necessarily implies at least the theoretical existence of an
ideal ascetic body, in which the reversal of the body flow is completed and death
completely rationalized. The *corporis ascensus* can therefore better be conceived

as the quest for the perfect body, while the ascetic body involved in this quest is the *body-performed*.

This process can be understood in even more general terms as the tension that exists between the ontic and ontological dimensions of existence. As we have seen, the body of the ascetic is still a 'body in context' of which a higher degree of existence consists in *becoming*, or as we have defined it, a *bodily relative*. The path of progression of the *corporis ascensus* seems directed towards the ontological ideal of the perfect body, while the practice is nothing but the ontic manifestation of it. This may, in fact, be the common theme connecting the puzzling expression of many high-level ascetics, such as the *kaihōgyōja*'s 'when doing this, I am a Buddha' or the idea of selfless (*mushin* 無心) walk in a demanding Shugendō practice like the *okugake*, with simpler ascetic acts, like the *hawatari* or the *hiwatari*. They are not the expression of different 'ascetic theories' but rather a different enactment of the *corporis ascensus* principle, of which all variations should be taken as being quantitative rather than qualitative.

The body empowered: powers produced during the ascetic practice

Almost all the ascetic practices we have used as case studies here have as underlying motivation the attainment of some degree of benefits or powers. From the highly internalized achievement of the *rōhatsu sesshin* to the very practical *ō-fuda* consecration of the Shinto *akinomine*, the ascetic performance invariably produces some degree of benefit that can be enjoyed by both the practitioner and other people. Regardless of substantial doctrinal differences, the performance of ascetic deeds is accompanied by the attainment of some degree of power or supernatural manifestations in non-Japanese traditions as well. The achievement of powers is an integral part of the life of Taoist and Brahamanic ascetics alike, and it is inherent in Christian asceticism as well. Catherine of Siena was famous for her unnaturally long fasts[34] and Teresa of Avila for her mystic visions, while a variety of miracles are attributed to the Desert Fathers and other remarkable ascetics like Anthony.[35] It is therefore of pivotal importance to understand the relationship of the ascetic body to these powers as well as the extent to which the attainment of powers and benefits can be understood as another step in the *corporis ascensus* aetiology.

Introversive and extroversive powers

The different kind of powers produced during ascetic practice may be understood under two rubrics, *introversive* and *extroversive*.[36] In the first case, the power attained is channelled towards the practitioner, who enjoys the benefits produced, while in the second the power is directed outwardly, producing benefits for others. Representative of the first category are practices such as the *itako* training and the *rōhatsu sesshin*, which are enacted with the primary purpose of empowering or transforming the practitioner. The second case is represented by practices conducted for the benefit of the community, such as the Akakura *shugyō*. It is important to note how the introversive and extroversive kinds of powers do not necessarily correspond to the 'practice for oneself' and 'practice for the others' categories we employed in Chapter 3. For instance, the case of Yamada Ryūshin is a clear example of an introversive practice enacted for the benefit of others, as the practitioner is using the powers accumulated in himself to benefit the public through his deeds as a healer. A similar circumstance that has been analyzed in detail is the *kaihōgyō* practice, where there is a series of phases in the accumulation and release of introversive powers in the course of the practice itself.

However, some of the ascetic practices examined in this study do appear to be characterized by the potential for producing both introversive and extroversive powers. Such is the case of the simple ascetic acts enacted by Ontake devotees during the Spring festival or during the *samugyō* practice. Some of the participants considered the practice beneficial for themselves, while others thought that their relatives were enjoying the result of their efforts. More complex practices, such as the *akinomine* and the *okugake shugyō*, are marked by the coexistence of both powers. During the *okugake*, for instance, one of my informants openly declared that her practice had positively affected the life of her family for the past 10 years, yet did not mention any benefit for herself as 'this was not her purpose'.[37] On the other hand, another informant at the same practice attributed to his regular attendance of the practice his exceptional vigour, in spite of his elderly age. Pressed by my questions, he straightforwardly admitted that 'all the power was in himself' and that he had no other benefits to mention.[38] It is also interesting to note how, in certain circumstances, some of these powers are produced during an ascetic practice, but not necessarily by performing specifically ascetic deeds. In the case of the Shinto *akinomine*, for instance, a good deal of the benefits that the practitioners enjoy is on account of their consecration of the *ō-fuda* tablets, which are not exclusive to this ascetic practice and are regularly consecrated in shrines in non-ascetic circumstances.[39] In a similar way, the *kaihōgyōja* uses his powers to serve the wider community by burning an enormous quantity of *goma* sticks during the New Year's *goma* ritual, which again is not a particularly ascetic activity.[40]

Power-yield as an inherent property of the ascetic body

I will define this production of power as *power-yield* and the relative practices and activities as *power-yielding*. If it is taken for granted that ascetic practice produces powers, less obvious is the relationship between these powers and the body of the practitioner. We need to ask two fundamental questions: *who* is the powers' producer, and *how* are the powers produced? The *who* will help us to determine the function of the ascetic body as the agent of the *corporis ascensus* while the *how* will help us in determining if the powers produced can be considered an inherent quality of the ascetic body or if they are no more than a side-effect. I shall try to illustrate this complex proposition by beginning with a simple example. In the 'Buddhist' *akinomine* practice, participants are instructed to rub the beads of their rosary in the classic Buddhist fashion in order to produce some kind of power.

The longer, more intense and noisy the rubbing is, the more power is produced. After rubbing, the practitioner needs to discharge that power somehow and this can be done in two directions. By quickly rubbing the beads one last time towards oneself, the power is released inside the body of the practitioner, becoming thus an introversive kind of power. However, if the last action of rubbing is released away from the body of the practitioner, an extroversive kind of power is produced, which can be offered to other practitioners for their benefit or to a deity as a gesture of praise.[41]

The agent of this performance obviously appears to be 'the ascetic practitioner', but the presence of the ascetic implies the existence of the ascetic body. Because the ascetic body is 'a body-performed', it follows that all the deeds enacted by such a body are necessarily ascetic as well. The simple act of rubbing, which is not ascetic per se, generates a particular amount of power because of its agent, rather than its ascetic nature. This possibly explains why both non-ascetic and ascetic deeds can produce powers if the agent is an ascetic.

Considering that the ascetic body is the *power-yielding* agent and that asceticism is always accompanied by the manifestation of some degree of power, we may assume that *power-yield* is one of the properties of the ascetic body. To explain this property, we must return to one of our most basic considerations in respect of asceticism: *asceticism is the reversal of the flow of the body*.[42] At the ontological level, ascetic practices seems to be structured so as to place the practitioner in a rationalized position in regard to death. At the epistemological level, asceticism rationalizes the most irrational activity of the body. Having said this, it follows that the performance of ascetic practices also constitutes the reversal of the non-ascetic performance. Thus, in ordinary practice power is used in order to produce performance, whereas in the case of the ascetic it necessarily follows that performance produces power. Everything in the ascetic body works with a reversed economy: pain does not debilitate but strengthens, death is in life, activity does not consume power resources but produces them, or at least produces more power than it expends. An ascetic body not manifesting any form of *power-yielding* properties is either inactive or power-consuming. Both of these propositions are unacceptable, as the ascetic body is necessarily performed and reversed vis-à-vis the non-ascetic.

This is of course mere philosophical theory, or better a metalanguage through which I am trying to translate performance and experience in verbal terms,[43] and it would be inappropriate to assume that similar thoughts actually inform the mind and self-awareness of the ascetic practitioners we have examined here. However, their attitude towards the practice seems to demonstrate an unconceptualized awareness of the existence of a virtuous economy between their efforts and the benefit and power obtained. This awareness is expressed in a variety of ways and is influenced by contingent factors and by the religious environment in which the practice is carried out. In a sense, the analogical theory we dismissed earlier in this chapter as inappropriate for justifying a phenomenon involving activities naturally thought to be detrimental to the body, can be reconsidered if we take into account that the performance of the ascetic body works on a *reversed* analogy.

Affirmations such as 'I was feeling close to death and then I suddenly felt a burst of new energy', or the sense of 'gain and loss' where gain is greater than loss, imply a paradox because they reverse the analogy between the *malleation* of an object where more energy is depleted than produced and the *malleation* of the ascetic body where more energy is produced than depleted. *Power-yield*, then, is the result of a reverse *malleation* analogy which is inherent in the reversal of the flow of the body that characterizes asceticism.

Even so, the fact that *power-yield* is an inherent property of the ascetic body does not imply that the production of power is a step forward in the ontological progression of the body – the *corporis ascensus*. This power is better understood as a manifestation of this progression, 'a symptom of holiness, not its cause'.[44] *Power-yield* accompanies every stage of the *corporis ascensus*, from the simplest practices to the more refined ones, but it is not the cause of it.

The body as perfect body: self-mummification

The concepts of non-ascetic body, rationalization of death and *power-yield* can help us to understand which characteristics the 'perfect body', the final goal of the ascetic progression, should possess. Such a 'perfect body' should display a complete bodily reversal: absence of the characteristics of the non-ascetic body, complete rationalization of death, effortless *power-yield*. Let us analyze these characteristics in detail.

1   In the Japanese contexts, where we have distinguished the non-ascetic as the non-pure, the perfect body should then be inherently pure with no possibility of gathering further impurity. In cultural environments where the non-ascetic is connected with moral themes, this essentially means the absence of sin. In the Christian tradition, the sinless body of the saint does not decay after death but emanates the fragrant 'odour of sanctity'. This can be seen as another variant on the 'body reversal' theme, as the body of ordinary people instead putrefies and reeks after death.

2   Complete rationalization of death implies the conquest of death, an immortal body. The idea of immortality in this case should not be understood merely as an indefinitely extended life span but rather as a condition transcending death by making the distinction between life and death meaningless. In this sense, the Taoist Immortals achieve only a partial result, as they avoid death rather than conquering it. The Indian *aghorīs* come much closer to this result by mingling death in their daily life to the point that the separation between the two becomes meaningless. In the Japanese case, the inherent association of death with pollution would make the idea of death-in-life almost paradoxi- cal vis-à-vis the necessity for the perfect body to be utterly pure. The perfect ascetic body must then transcend death to the point of not being considered impure even in death.

3   Effortless *power-yield* implies that the perfect body should produce power without any activity, thus completely reversing the natural performative

physiology of the body in which greater performance is the consequence of greater labour. The perfect body must instead 'perform without performing' so that it does not contradict the ascetic reversal of bodily flow principle but expresses it to its maximum.

It is clear from these premises that the perfect body is no less than a paradox. It is dead without death and pollution, it is performing without performance. It is a body completely 'reversed' and, for this reason, on the borderline of our epistemological possibilities. And yet it is possible to find an actual example of such a perfect body inside the Japanese religious context in the figure of some peculiar ascetics known as self-mummified Buddhas, or sometimes as *miira* ミイラ (mummies). To describe them with the term 'mummy' is not appropriate. They are not merely preserved corpses but *sokushinbutsu*, 'Buddhas in their very bodies', and in this sense they are still alive, resting in a perfect state between life and death, untouched by impurity and producing power and benefit from their perfect stillness. They can then be understood as representative of the *corporis ascensus*' final stage, that is, the closest example to the 'perfect body' ideal that we can find in the Japanese religious tradition.

Sokushinbutsu *in Japan*

The area of Japan in which *sokushinbutsu* can be found is mainly the northern part of Honshū (the central and largest of the Japanese islands). A total of 21 mummies have been found there, most of whom are still preserved in the original place where they 'entered deep meditation' (*nyūjō* 入定). To these we may add another nine figures whose names have been preserved in literature but of whom no actual physical remains are extant.[45] Six interrelated figures are concentrated around the mountain area of the Dewa Sanzan (Yamagata prefecture), the same area where Haguro Shugendō is practised. I will concentrate my analysis on the *sokushinbutsu* preserved in this particular area as it is where I have conducted my observations; additionally, we possess a number of detailed accounts regarding the life of the ascetics in this area, both before they 'entered the ground' and after.

The first and oldest *sokushinbutsu* that we can find in the Dewa Sanzan area is Honmyōkai 本明海, whose *nyūjō* dates back to 1683. A former retainer of a feudal lord of Tsuruoka, we are told that he left his family to pursue the ascetic path of life at the Chūren-ji temple in order to pray for the recovery of his lord from some serious illness. He followed a strict ascetic regime in Senninzawa 仙人沢 (lit. 'Swamp of Wizards'), an uninhabited portion of land that lies between Chūren-ji and Yudonosan where people seeking magical and supernatural powers traditionally used to train (see Figures 5.1 and 5.2).[46]

The practices he underwent at Senninzawa are generally known as *mokujiki* 木喰 (lit. 'wood-eating'), a term that indicates the total abstention from the consumption of the six kinds of cereals, while maintaining a diet consisting of pine needles, tree bark, pinecones, chestnuts and occasionally stones and crystals. This diet closely resembles the diet prescribed to those seeking immortality in

Figure 5.1 Senninzawa, the Swamp of the Wizards (Dewa Sanzan, Yamagata prefecture)

Figure 5.2 Honmyōkai, preserved in Honmyō-ji temple (Higashi Iwamoto, Asahi Mura, Yamagata prefecture)

Taoist scriptures, such as the Lingbao texts (see Chapter 1).[47] After 10 years of this alimentary regime, Honmyōkai is said to have entered a small stone chamber set in the ground where he entered 'perpetual *samādhi*' while chanting the *nenbutsu*. His body was then almost immediately exhumed, dried by incense and charcoal fumes and then put to rest for another three years. After this period, the body was completely mummified and then set on an altar at Honmyō-ji 本明寺 (the temple founded by Honmyōkai himself) and venerated as a living relic.[48]

The next *sokushinbutsu*, chronologically, was Chūkai, whom I also mentioned earlier in this chapter. He was buried alive in a wooden coffin in 1755 at the age of 58 after a period of ascetic training identical to the one described above for Honmyōkai.[49] The next *sokushinbutsu* has a somehow more complex and less straightforwardly apologetic story than the ones outlined so far. Shinnyōkai 真如海 was a simple farmer born in the late seventeenth century who accidentally killed a samurai after an argument (see Figure 5.3).

He then fled to the Dainichi-bō 大日坊, a group of ascetics settled near Yudonosan. There he was protected by the principle of extraterritoriality granted to temples during the Edo period. He resolved to become a *sokushinbutsu*, following the same training path as his predecessors at Senninzawa. He finally entered the ground in a wooden coffin in 1783 at the age of 96.[50] The episode that was the

Figure 5.3 Shinnyōkai, preserved in Dainichibo temple (Yamagata prefecture)

turning point in the life of Shinnyōkai – the killing of the samurai – belongs to a tradition of tales called *bushigoroshi* 武士殺し (samurai-killing), in which the protagonist kills a samurai, often following false accusation or misbehaviour by the latter, and is then forced to escape from the punishment awaiting him.[51] This framework is a powerful rhetorical device used to tell stories of moral redemption and exemplary loyalty; it is used for this purpose as well in the clearly apologetic accounts of the lives of some *sokushinbutsu*.

Two interesting, and contradictory, *bushigoroshi* tales also frame the life of the next self-mummified ascetic, Tetsumonkai, who was briefly mentioned at the beginning of this chapter. The first story tells us how the future Tetsumonkai, at the time still named Sada Tetsu, harshly rebuked two drunken samurai for neglecting their duties as guards at the banks of a river close to flooding. To defend himself from their rage, he was eventually forced to kill them and then fled to Chūren-ji.[52] However, another version of the story gives us a less virtuous impression of the deeds of Sada Tetsu. He started quarrelling with two samurai about a prostitute in a pleasure quarter, eventually killing them. He then fled to Chūren-ji where he engaged in ascetic practice and subsequently wandered throughout northern Japan, benefiting people through the use of his supernatural powers and knowledge of herbs. On one occasion, when he was visiting Edo, he came to know that an eye epidemic was spreading through the population. In order to halt the spread of the disease, he took out one of his eyes and offered it to the Yudono deities. On another occasion, back at Chūren-ji, Tetsumonkai was visited by his former lover. She implored him to return to her and, as a response, he cut off his penis and offered it to the woman. She preserved the mutilated organ as a relic and we are told that because of that, her business prospered.[53] The mutilated organ of Tetsumonkai is actually still kept at Nangaku-ji 南岳寺 in Tsuruoka.[54] Tetsumonkai entered his final meditation in the year 1829 at the age of 61, following the pattern outlined above; his body was then enshrined at Chūren-ji where it is still visible today. Tetsumonkai is probably the best-known *sokushinbutsu* in Japan, to the point of becoming, in some cases, a sort of pop icon.[55]

The last two *sokushinbutsu* of the Dewa Sanzan area were both inspired by the strong figure of Tetsumonkai and closely followed his steps. Enmyōkai 円明海 entered his final *samādhi* in 1822, thus prior to Tetsumonkai, and is remembered for his various meritorious deeds, while Tetsuryūkai, chronologically the last *sokushinbutsu* of the Dewa Sanzan, can be remembered as the only known case in which the process of mummification was completed by artificial means after his exhumation. He was buried alive in 1868, but when his body was exhumed three years later, the process of mummification was not yet complete. His disciples then removed his internal organs, filling the cavity with clay and then dried the body with candle smoke and incense.[56]

The last *sokushinbutsu* we know of entered his tomb in 1903 under the name of Bukkai 仏海 in the city of Murakami (Niigata prefecture). His fate was, however, quite different from that of his predecessors. In 1903, the Meiji government, in its pursuit of a total modernization of the country and restoration of imperial rule, banned all forms of 'superstitious and popular belief' including the veneration of the self-mummified ascetics. Following this, and a new edict prohibiting the opening of tombs, the body of Bukkai was never retrieved and it had to wait more than 50 years before it was finally rescued by the same group of researchers who conducted an extensive survey of the mummies in the Dewa Sanzan area.[57] The body of Bukkai was well preserved and, after the investigation, was finally enshrined at the Kanzeondera in Murakami.[58]

A far greater number of people are missing from this necessarily brief list of self-mummified ascetics in the Dewa Sanzan area than those mentioned. They are those people who tried the same pattern of self-mummification, and endured the same harsh austerities in Senninzawa, but eventually failed to preserve their bodies from decay. Their names and their deeds are now forgotten and their remains probably lie around Senninzawa, hastily buried by their followers to pacify a potentially dangerous wandering spirit.[59] They were considered merely 'dead' – while the successful practitioners became 'Buddhas in their own bodies'.

Self-mummified Buddhas as perfect bodies

As with other ascetic practices, the process of self-mummification did not happen in a doctrinal vacuum. Two important precedents were understood as the ideal models for the aspiring *sokushinbutsu*. The oldest of these precedents is also the most mythical in content. The *Miroku geshōkyō* 彌勒下生經 (*Sutra of Maitreya's Descent*) is a 'prophetic' sutra foretelling the deeds of Maitreya, the Buddha of the future. In this sutra, we learn that in order to properly greet the future Buddha, Śākyamuni Buddha asked his disciple Mahākāśyapa not to enter nirvāna immediately (thus reaching complete 'extinction' and abandoning forever the cycle of death and rebirth) but to wait for the coming of the future Buddha so as to offer him a robe as a sign of praise. When Maitreya comes to this world, the sutra tells us, he will crack open Vulture Peak, revealing Mahākāśyapa still in deep meditation in its depths. Mahākāśyapa will subsequently be awakened by Brahmā and will then fulfil his duty, offering to the new Buddha the robe entrusted to him by Śākyamuni.[60]

Centuries later, in 835, the life of Japan's greatest esoteric master, Kūkai, was nearing the end. We are told that, perhaps inspired by the figure Mahākāśyapa, he stopped eating and drinking, and on the twenty-first day of the third month, he entered 'eternal *samādhi*'. Following this belief, his body was not cremated as usual but put in a cave in the eastern peak of Mount Kōya.[61] The legend of his immortality is testified in numerous sources. From the *Konjaku monogatari* 今昔 物語 (*Tales of Times Now Past*, compiled *c.* 1120) to the *Heike monogatari* 平家 物語 (*Tales of the Taira Family*, compiled in 1371), we have numerous examples of both priests and laypeople visiting Kūkai's last abode and tonsuring his hair, changing his robe, repairing his rosary or simply marvelling at the perfect state of preservation of his body.[62]

It can be argued that Kūkai constituted the original example for the *sokushinbutsu* of the Dewa Sanzan; this is attested to by the fact that the character *kai* 海 of Kūkai is utilized in all their names: Honmyōkai, Chūkai, Shinnyōkai, Tetsumonkai, Enmyōkai, Tetsuryūkai and Bukkai.[63] Together with the legend and teachings of Kūkai, we can assume, then, that all the practitioners who succeeded in pursuing the *sokushinbutsu* path were aware of the doctrinal and theoretical background elaborated by Kūkai himself. This suggests that the path of the *sokush-inbutsu* towards immortality was considered a refined exercise of high ascesis and the living incarnation of some of the most powerful Buddhist teachings. The incorruptibility of their bodies was an unequivocal sign of their spiritual achievements, becoming a 'living' incarnation of the non-duality of Buddhahood.

The self-mummified ascetics reflect all the paradoxical characteristics of the perfect body that we outlined at the beginning of this section.

1   The *sokushinbutsu* are inherently pure and incorruptible, as their body neither decays nor accumulates impurity. In more precise terms, the body of a *sokushinbutsu* does not allow for any increase or decrease of its attributes. It cannot become more or less pure, older or younger, as quantitative attributes lose meaning vis-à-vis its perfect stasis.
2   Dead but yet alive, the body of the *sokushinbutsu* has completely rationalized death in a non-dualistic manner. Death is always present, not avoided, alongside life.
3   The body of the *sokushinbutsu* produces power and benefits by its mere presence, without the need for activity. They are objects of veneration, dispensers of gifts, refuges in time of calamity. Like living Buddhist saints, they spread the Dharma throughout the world by their mere physical presence.[64]

The *sokushinbutsu* thus completed the process of *corporis ascensus* to its utmost, transforming their bodies into perfect bodies through a radical process of reversal of the body flow. They represent one of the highest manifestations of the Japanese ascetic tradition, and certainly one of the most refined and demanding forms of ascesis in general.

Conclusions

In this chapter, I have offered a theoretical answer to our initial questions: what asceticism is and how it is supposed to function. From the arguments offered in this chapter we can reconsider our understanding of asceticism in the broadest sense as 'a structured and defined process of reversal of the flow of the body, resulting in the ontological progression of the body of the practitioner, and having as a consequence the production of power'. The presence of the ideal of the 'perfect body' contributes to this progression by defining its final theoretical goal. Of course, achieving a 'perfect body' is not necessarily the goal of all Japanese ascetics, or of ascetics more generally. What I have attempted to demonstrate is that all kinds of ascetic achievements can be considered as quantitative variations of this same theme rather than being understood as qualitatively different practices. I hope to have shown the centrality of the body and performance in ascetic practice. Asceticism is an 'embodied tradition' and its underlying themes should thus be understood in bodily terms as well.

Notes

Introduction

1 Video footage from *The Marathon Monks of Mt Hiei*. Directed by Michael Yorke (Channel Four Productions, 1992).
2 The autobiography of Wazaki Nobuya, *Ajari tanjō. Hieizan sennichi kaihōgyō: Aru gyōja no hansei*, published in 1979, sold over half a million copies throughout Japan. Source: Kodansha 2004.
3 Yamada Ryūshin 1988; Shima Kazuharu 1983.
4 Massimo Raveri 1992.
5 Works representative of this *genre* are: Wazaki Nobuya 1979; Shima Kazuharu 1983; Yamada Ryūshin 1988; John Stevens 1988; Masaki Akira,Yamaori Tetsuo and Nagasawa Tetsu 1992.
6 Representative of this *genre* are works like Hiramatsu Chōkū 1982; Matsumoto Akira 1985; Kawamura Kunimitsu 1991; Naitō Masatoshi 1999; Ellen Schattschneider 2003; Janine Anderson Sawada 2004; Ian Reader and Tony Walter 1993; Ian Reader 2005.
7 Representative of this *genre* are: Hori Ichiro 1953; Hori Ichiro 1968; Namihira Emiko 1979; Inoue Nobutaka 1988; Janet Goodwin 1994; Ikegami Yoshimasa 1999; Carmen Blacker 1999 (1975); Miyake Hitoshi 2001; Miyake Hitoshi 2002; Miyake Hitoshi 1989; Shinno Toshikazu 1991; Miyake Hitoshi 1992; Miyake Hitoshi 2000a; Miyake Hitoshi 2000b; Clark Chilson and Peter Knecht 2003.
8 Stephen Covell 2004.
9 Ibid.: 257–8.
10 The most representative are: Ishida Hidemi 2000; Yuasa Yasuo 1977; Michael Pye 1997; Leonore Friedman and Susan Moon 1997.
11 For example, Ikegami Koichi 1991.
12 Immanuel Kant and Mary Gregor 1991; Friedrich Wilhelm Nietzsche *et al.* 1998: 79–80.
13 Pivotal in this sense is Weber's distinction between religious 'other-worldly' asceticism and lay 'this-worldly' asceticism. See Max Weber 2001, also quoted in Oliver Freiberger 2006: 3.
14 Charles Riley 1998.
15 Johannes Bronkhorst 2001: 374.
16 The term 'nonverbal' is here borrowed from linguistics, where it indicates all the differences in pitch, stress and facial expression that constitute that part of language still carrying meaning, but going beyond words. See Kenneth Lee Pike 1971: 50.
17 Max Scheler in Stuart Spicker 1970. Maurice Merleau-Ponty 1970. See also Max Scheler 1961; Jean-Paul Sartre 1957.
18 Maurice Merleau-Ponty 1970: 259.
19 Michael D. Jackson 2005.

20 Maurice Merleau-Ponty 1970: 241 and ff.
21 Geoffrey Madell 1988: 116–17.
22 It is interesting to notice the similitude with the Gramscian concept of hermeneutic, inspired by his idea of unity of though and action. See Antonio Gramsci and Valentino Gerratana 1975: 519–22.

1 Translating fundamental categories: the human body and asceticism

1 Gavin Flood (2004) starts his study of the 'ascetic self' from very similar premises to make a claim for 'some degree of universalism'(2004: 3) of ascetic phenomena. The purpose of my work is certainly less ambitious, but an adequate evaluation of the categories involved is nonetheless felt as necessary.
2 Consider, for example, the now-abandoned theory of Malinowski (1944). For a critical argument see Tamara Hareven (2000: 9).
3 The etymology of 'translate' implies indeed 'to remove from one place to another' (from the Latin *translatus*, 'carried over'). See Ernest Weekley (1967) *ad vocem* 'translate'.
4 Sherry Simon 1999: 58.
5 Mary Louise Pratt 1992: 6.
6 Maria Tymoczko 1999: 24–6. The orientalistic conception of 'the East' has been subject to a vast critical deconstruction, which perhaps found its more famous incarnation in Said's *Orientalism*. The same is however not always true for the equally essentialized notion of 'the West', a problem that emerges often in the critique of Said and other anti-orientalists (see, among the others, James G. Carrier 1995; and Philip Mellor 2004: 99–112).
7 Paul Ricoeur 2006: 26.
8 Ibid.: 13.
9 Kenneth G. Henshall 1988: 33.
10 Hensan inkai 編纂委員会, eds. *Gyakubiki bukkyōgo jiten*, 逆引き佛教語辞典 1995.
11 Even the widespread term *shugyō* is in fact not universally employed in all cases of bodily practices, as we shall see later.
12 Wazaki Nobuya 1979: 80–2.
13 For instance, in regard to the Tendai *kaihōgyō*, the same biography of Sōō (the founder of the practice) mentions that his only apparent reason for undertaking the mountain practice was his personal desire to see a living Fudō Myōō. Before that, he used austerities as a means to obtain powers for his thaumaturgical activities, like other ascetics of his time. He apparently did not look for other doctrinal justification inside Tendai doctrine. See Hiramatsu Chōkū 1982: 192.
14 Here 'holy' is mostly to be understood as 'possessing some form of sacred powers' rather than an ethical trait. Far from being 'imaginary' or merely symbolic persons, ascetics are often believed to incarnate and be able to manage a variety of powers; cf. Richard Valantasis 1995: 798.
15 Clark Chilson and Peter Knecht 2003: 11.
16 The chanting of the *nenbutsu* (name of Amida Buddha) while rhythmically dancing around a statue of Amida Buddha (or also in a square or park), usually understood as a folk practice. Often associated with the figure of the medieval monk Ippen (1239–1289), the practice was already present in Tendai environments during the earlier Heian period as a form of walking meditation (*jōgyō zanmai* 常行三昧). See Ippen and Dennis Hirota 1986: 46; also Richard Bowring 2005: 202.
17 Sitting meditation, central to both the Rinzai and Sōtō Zen schools.
18 The idea of bodily '*malleation*' is introduced by William LaFleur in Mark C. Taylor 1998: 39.

19 Ariel Glucklich 2001: 16–18.
20 Ibid.
21 Ibid.: 32–3.
22 Alphonso Lingis 1994: vii.
23 Michel Feher *et al*. 1989. See also Shigehisa Kuriyama 1999: 13.
24 With the term 'man' I refer, of course, to neutral understanding of the 'human being' regardless of gender, as in the Latin 'homo'.
25 Roy Porter 2003: 168–9.
26 Thomas Hobbes 1675: Chapters II, IV, V; Geoffrey Madell 1988: 126–8.
27 Thomas Hobbes 1675: Chapter XII.
28 Michel Foucault 1973: 128.
29 Roy Porter 2003: 33
30 Mary G. Winkler and Letha B. Cole 1994: 11–13.
31 Mary Midgley 1997: 56–7.
32 Mark Morford 2002: 7, 206.
33 Leif Vaage and Vincent Wimbush 1999: 97–8.
34 Leviticus 13. All the quotations from the Bible are from the King James version.
35 Peter Brown 1988: 36.
36 Leviticus 13 and 14.
37 Numbers 19:13 'Whoever touches a dead person, the body of any man who has died, and does not cleanse himself, defiles the tabernacle of the Lord, and that person shall be cut off from Israel; because the water for impurity was not thrown upon him, he shall be unclean; his uncleanness is still on him.'
38 Psalms 16:9 'Therefore my heart is glad, and my soul rejoices; my body also dwells secure.' Psalms 31:9 'Be gracious to me, o Lord, for I am in distress; my eye is wasted from grief, my soul and my body also.' Proverbs 16:24 'Pleasant words are like a honeycomb, sweetness to the soul and health to the body.'
39 Carr indeed reminds us how even the concept of 'spirit' (*nephesh*) had rather physical implications in biblical texts: 'Although this word *nephesh*, is often translated as "soul," it refers just as much to a person's bodily vitality and intellect, their life force.' See David Carr 2003: 30.
40 Genesis 17:11 'You shall be circumcised in the flesh of your foreskins, and it shall be a sign of the covenant between me and you.'
41 Philippians 3:21.
42 Romans 7:24.
43 1 Corinthians 6:19 'Do you not know that your body is a temple of the Holy Spirit within you, which you have from God? You are not your own.' Cf. Kallistos Ware 1997: 91.
44 Even in the case of desert-dwelling ascetic (the Desert Fathers who we shall analyse in more detail later), the amount of ascetic effort was moderate, as '[t]he monks were aware of the complex relationship between the body and the mind and knew better than to attribute the source of all their problems to their bodies', Douglas Burton-Christie 1993: 193–4.
45 Kurt Rudolph and R. Wilson 1987: 60.
46 Valentinus was a Gnostic theologian active in the second century CE. He was born in Phrebonis in upper Egypt about 100 AD and educated in nearby Alexandria. There he became a disciple of the Christian teacher, Theudas, who had been a disciple of Saint Paul. Valentinus claimed that Theudas initiated him to the secret wisdom that Paul had taught privately to his inner circle. His esoteric theology and soteriology became particularly popular in Egypt and Syria. In 136 AD, he moved to Rome where he quickly rose to prominence and became famous, particularly, for his eloquence. He probably died in Rome around 155 AD. Thereafter, his disciples developed his ideas further, spreading them throughout the Roman Empire. See Kurt Rudolph and R. Wilson 1987: 317–20.

47   Peter Brown 1988: 108.
48   For the 'soul journey', see Kurt Rudolph and R. Wilson1987: 58.
49   Ibid.: 171.
50   Ibid.
51   Henri Crouze 1989: 13–14.
52   See Douglas Burton-Christie 1993; Derwas Chitty 1995.
53   It is well-known that the historicity of *The Life of Anthony* is highly disputed. However, in hagiographic works, the idealized models portrayed in the narrative often prove to be more influential and durable than the actual historical figures. See David Brakke 1995: 210–14.
54   Douglas Burton-Christie 1993: 291.
55   Anthony, Letter 1: 5; also quoted in Peter Brown 1988: 224.
56   Peter Brown 1988: 306.
57   Ibid.: 220. See also Athanasius of Alexandria 2003.
58   This clearly refers to the biblical episode in Genesis 3.
59   Peter Brown 1988: 223.
60   Michel Foucault 1973: 3.
61   Irvine Loudon 1997: 86. See also Michel Foucault 1973: 33–4.
62   Michel Foucault 1973: 32–3.
63   This paradigm shift also affected the understanding of 'religion' in a more general sense. Hanegraaff aptly describes this process in terms of 'psychologization of religion' and 'sacralization of psychology', namely the fact that, in the modern idea of religion, the mind becomes the main means for religious practice, and the same time the main object of religious concern. See Wouter Hanegraaff 1996: 224–8.
64   Roy Porter 2003: 242–4.
65   The *aghorīs* are a group of Indian ascetics noted for their extreme behaviour, including necrophagia, self-cannibalism and necrophilia. See Massimo Raveri 1992: 184–9.
66   J. Moussaieff Masson 1976: 611–25.
67   Roy Porter 2003: 45ff.
68   Similar concerns are also put forward by Flood: 'The enterprise of comparing asceticism is an exercise in comparative religion, yet an exercise that wishes to acknowledge the problematic nature of the enterprise in the first instance and to offer some new ways forward' (Gavin Flood 2004: 20). Inspiring as a 'way forward' in this sense is Kuriyama's comparative exercise (1999).
69   The fundamental rules of monastic discipline, contained in the *Suttavibhanga*, the first book of the *Vinaya Piṭaka*.
70   John Kieschnick 1997: 19.
71   All quotations from the *Patimokkha* are from the translation from the Pâli by T. W. Rhys Davids and Hermann Oldenberg 1881.
72   A Bhikkhu who is not sick may take one meal at a public rest-house. Should he take more than that — that is a Pākittiya (Pākittiya 31).
      There is Pākittiya in going in a body to receive a meal, except on the right occasion. Herein the right occasion is this: (to wit), when there is sickness, when robes are being given, when robes are being made, when on a journey (on foot), when on board a boat, when (the influx of Bhikkhus) is great, when a general invitation is given to Samanas. This is right occasion in this passage (Pākittiya 32).
      Should any Bhikkhu chew or consume staple or non-staple food at the wrong time, it is to be confessed (Pākittiya 37).
      Whatsoever Bhikkhu shall take or eat any food, whether hard or soft, at the wrong time – that is a Pākittiya (Pākittiya 38).
      Whatsoever Bhikkhu, when he is not sick, shall request, for his own use, and shall partake of delicacies – to wit, ghee, butter, oil, honey, molasses, fish, flesh, milk, curds – that is a Pākittiya (Pākittiya 39).

Whatsoever Bhikkhu shall place, as food, within the door of his mouth, anything not given to him, save only water and a tooth-cleaner – that is a Pākittiya (Pākittiya 40). Whatsoever Bhikkhu shall take a seat, in secret, with a woman, in a concealed place – that is a Pākittiya (Pākittiya 44).

Whatsoever Bhikkhu shall take a seat, in secret, with a woman, one man with one woman – that is a Pākittiya (Pākittiya 45).

Whatsoever Bhikkhu, who has been invited (to a house), and has been (thus already) provided with a meal, shall, without having previously spoken about it to a Bhikkhu, if there is one there, go on his (begging) rounds among the families, either before meal-time or after meal-time, except on the right occasion – that is a Pākittiya (Pākittiya 46). There is Pākittiya in the drinking of fermented liquors, or strong drinks (Pākittiya 51). Whatsoever Bhikkhu shall bathe at intervals of less than half a month, except on the proper occasion – that is a Pākittiya (Pākittiya 57).

73 *Vinaya* 1, 10.
74 Ibid.
75 Steven Collins 1997: 202–3.
76 Ibid.: 188.
77 All the quotations are from Burton Watson, *The Vimalakirti Sutra* 1997.
78 *Vimalakīrti Nirdesa*, 1.
79 *Vimalakīrti Nirdesa*, 2.
80 The doctrine of the three Buddha bodies – *dharmakāya*, *sambhogakāya* and *nirmānakāya* – represent, respectively, the Buddha nature that dwells in itself, the Buddha in his soteriological action (preaching the Dharma) and the Buddha manifested through his acts. The three bodies are distinct but at the same time are completely identified in each other.
81 Leon Hurvitz 1976: 295.
82 John Kieschnick 1997: 12.
83 Ibid.: 46 and 124.
84 Steven Collins 1997: 188. It must be stressed, however, that this does not imply that Theravāda Buddhism is *ontologically* dualistic.
85 The Buddha-body in its absolute aspect.
86 Yoshitake Inage 1965: I, 512. See also Kūkai and Yoshito S. Hakeda 1972: 90.
87 Yoshitake Inage 1965: III, 402.
88 Gestures of the hands, usually performed in conjunction with the utterance of dhāran☐īs (utterances) or the recitation of Sūtras.
89 Yamada Ryūshin 1988: 64–7; Wazaki Nobuya 1979: 97.
90 Sutta Nipāta 3,1, also quoted in John E. Cort 1999: 88.
91 Paul Ricoeur 2006: 26.
92 Ibid.: 27.
93 This is of course no more than a veiled reference to Heideggerian idea of *Geworfenheit*. We are not attempting an ontological argument in this section, but we shall return on it in the final chapter. See Martin Heidegger 1962: 174.
94 Peter Brown 1988.
95 Seeing footprints or a felled tree gives us a hint that somebody was walking there or that someone cut down that tree. However, these 'signs' also result from an act.
96 Gavin D. Flood 2004: 216.
97 Clifford Kirkpatrick 1955: 4ff.
98 Peter Brown 1988: 94–5.
99 Douglas Burton-Christie 1993: 197.
100 Derwas J. Chitty 1995: 218.
101 Peter Brown 1988: 306.
102 Ibid.: 323–5.
103 Ibid.: 260–5.

104   Athanasius *et al.* 1904: 62–3. Also quoted in Susanna Elm 1994: 231.
105   Peter Brown 1988: 260.
106   See, for instance, the accounts of the life of Thecla in *Vita Theclae* (collected in Patricia Cox Miller 2005).
107   Clifford Kirkpatrick 1955: 47ff.
108   Peter Brown 1988: 260.
109   *Vita Theclae* 16. Also quoted in Peter Brown 1988: 5.
110   Peter Brown 1988: 86–7.
111   *Majjhima Nikāya* (III.254). Also in Martin Wiltshire 1990: 3.
112   Martin Wiltshire 1990: 196.
113   Ryokai Shiraishi 1996: 163–4.
114   Martin Wiltshire 1990: 85–8.
115   Ibid.: xxvii.
116   'I arrive all alone, I sit all alone. I do not regret that the present-day men do not know me' (Lu-tsou tche – Tao-tsang n.1484 – 4, 12a quoted in Kristofer Marinus Schipper 1982: 211).
117   'Thereupon [Zhang Min] abandoned his wife and children, left his family and received the Tao. He ate vegetarian food and engaged in a perpetual retreat … He did away with food for over twenty days' (*Sandong zhunang* 5/8a-b, quoted in Stephen Eskildsen 1998: 41).
118   Kristofer Marinus Schipper 1982: 138ff.
119   Yamada Toshiaki 1989: 99ff.
120   Stephen Eskildsen 1998: 40.
121   See Yamada Toshiaki 1989: 104; and Stephen Eskildsen 1998: 22.
122   Eskildsen 1998: 60 and Kristofer Marinus Schipper 1982: 219–20.
123   'In the distant mountains of Kou-ye dwell divine beings. Their skin is fresh as the fallen snow, they are delicate and soft like virgins. They do not eat cereals [e.g. ordinary food], but inhale the wind and drink the dew' (*Tchouang-tseu*, 1:28, quoted in Schipper 1982: 216).
124   Ibid.: 213.
125   Shigehisa Kuriyama 1999: 9.
126   Ibid.
127   Besides their specific value for a certain area of knowledge, the broader purpose of works such as Kuriyama (1999) and the present study is to undermine two facile epistemological prejudices on apparently 'obvious' categories and entities. Kuriyama's concluding words are enlightening in this sense: 'I have tried to suggest how comparative inquiry onto the history of the body invites us, and indeed compels us, ceaselessly to reassess our own habits of perceiving and feeling, and to imagine alternative possibilities of being – to experience the world afresh' 1999: 272.

2 Modes of ascetic practice

1   This is the case, for instance, of cold water ablutions, which can be seen indiscriminately practised by *kagura* dancers, festivals participants, local healers or Nichiren and Tendai priests alike.
2   See Chris Knight *et al.* 2000: Chapter 1.
3   Shinno Toshikazu has dedicated considerable attention to the problem of definition of *minzoku shūkyō* and its relationship with the broader field of the Study or Religions. See Shinno Toshikazu 1991, and 1993: 187–206.
4   See Hori Ichiro 1968; Francesco Dentoni 1980: 112; Miyake Hitoshi 2002: 49 ff.
5   Ian Reader 2005: 84–5.
6   Water ablutions are often accompanied by other austerities such as abstention from

certain foods, sexual intercourse, alcohol etc. Plutschow considers such purificatory acts and austerities as a necessary preliminary part for any *matsuri*, rather than mere accessory events. This consideration reinforces the understanding of such acts as being 'borrowed' by other practices or religious activities. See Herbert Plutschow 1996: 41–2 and 118–19. A similar function of the purificatory phase is also highlighted by Sonoda Minoru as a part of the 'paradigm of action' in a *matsuri*. See Sonoda Minoru 1975: 108.

7   TL 090407 PFI#1. See also Herbert Plutschow 1996: 155.

8   TL 090407 PFI#1.

9   The production of 'ascetic' heat during the Kagura dance itself is also documented by Averbauch, who also remarks on its cathartic properties: '[...] it is the dances themselves that produce this power, endowing their performers with an energy that promotes inner heat. It is a cathartic, cleansing experience'. See Irit Averbuch 1995: 70.

10 TL 090407 PFI#1. The Kagura dancers never meant their kagura performance as a *shugyō*, and it was clear that this particular ascetic held a peculiar role in virtue of his specific training. Averbuch argues that kagura in the past 'served as a method of *shugyō* for its practitioners, and that the ability to perform it meant the achievement of special powers' but confirms the fact that nowadays this understanding is generally lost, with the exception of Kagura master Oguni Seikichi of Dake. See: Irit Averbuch 1995: 67 and ff.

11 Flood indeed finds in pain a common denominator for ascetic traditions in general: 'Pain, willingly accepted becomes the method for the body's transcendence. This is a common feature of ascetic traditions' (Gavin Flood 2004: 6). The issue of pain will remain central also in this study, although we shall reconsider the idea of 'body's transcendence' in regard to a different understanding of the human body.

12 Ikoma Kanshich 1988: 7–9.

13 Carmen Blacker 1999: 287. See also: Mark Teeuwen *et al.* 2003: 176–7: Akaike Noriaki 1981: 51–82.

14 Ikoma Kanshichi 1988: 23–40.

15 TL 100407 PFN#1.

16 TL 100407 PFN#1

17 An interesting semiotic analysis of the purificatory and apotropaic meanings of this 'moment of danger' in a *matsuri* has been put forward by Maurice Coyaud 1977: 95–6.

18 TL 100407 PFN#1.

19 I performed the *hiwatari* on the Ontake *matsuri* held on 10 October in Ontakesanjinja. This *matsuri* is somewhat less solemn than the one held in April, and the *hawatari* is absent. The circumstances and mode of the *hiwatari* are, however, identical.

20 TL 100407 PFN#1.

21 An almost identical experience is described by Blacker, although she was not apparently instructed in such practical 'ascetic technique' and remained 'sceptical of explanations that the usual purifying libation of salt scattered over the embers will reduce their heat, that the Japanese sole is tougher than the western one or that a collected mind is required if one is to walk across unburnt'. See Carmen Blacker 1999: 251.

22 TL 101006 PFN#1. Two lay ascetic practitioners I met in a different circumstance (the *okugake shugyō* which will be treated later on) were used to organize a *hiwatari* festival for their local Shrine in Niigata. Interviewed, they expressed this same feeling of empowerment: the *hiwatari* was for them a good way to regularly 'receive strength from the fire' and ensure good health (TL 150706 PFN#1).

23 Amy Hollywood 2002: 93–115.

24   A theory which Turner put forward in regard of ritual performance, but that later has been efficaciously deconstructed by Bell. See Victor Witter Turner 1967: 19 and Catherine Bell 1992: 184. Some interesting considerations on the balance between symbolism and performance in *matsuri* can be found in Jan van Bremen and D. P. Martinez 1995: 161–2.

25   Shinno Toshikazu 1993: 12.

26   Miyake Hitoshi 1971: Chapter 2.

27   Carmen Blacker 1999: 249.

28   Tamotsu Aoki 1985: 203.

29   TL 100407 PFN#1.

30   TL 100407 PFN#1.

31   Cf. Ariel Glucklich 2001: 127–8, who instead sees self-inflicted torture as a way to 'displace the soul from its habitual center of consciousness' and that again seems to exclude any rational force behind the ascetic effort. His insistence on re-conducting asceticism to pathological models is perhaps appropriate for its more self-nihilistic forms, but certainly cannot justify the lucid pursuit of well-being that characterises so many of the practices treated in this study.

32   The Okamoto brothers, leaders of the Jiga Daikyōkai, an Ontake group based in Agematsu village (Nagano prefecture), who we shall encounter again when dealing with the *samugyō* practice.

33   TL 100407 PFN#1.

34   TL 100407 PFN#1. Akaike Noriaki mentions the proficiency in performing protective spell through the use of the *kuji* syllables as one of the characteristics of Ontake devotees leaders. In the case of the Ontakesan-jinja *harumatsuri*, the leading roles are perhaps less clearly identifiable, but this remains a task for the eldest and more experienced nonetheless. Akaike Noriaki 1981: 57.

35   TL 100407 PFN#1.

36   TL 100407 PFN#1.

37   TL 100407 PFN#1.

38   The usual pronunciation of ascetic practices taking place in the cold is *kangyō* (see Anne Bouchy 1992: 235. It is interesting that the Jiga Daikyōkai seems to claim some sort of 'trademark' for the practice through the use of a different pronunciation. Participants are not unaware of this; they pointed out to me on several occasions how the *samugyō* differs from 'ordinary' *kangyō* – despite being practically the same thing.

39   TL 220207 I#1.

40   Anne Bouchy 1992: Chapter 3.

41   Their role as leaders as a matter of fact incorporate the function of an Ontake-*kō sendatsu*, as described by Akaike Noriaki 1981: 56–7. Differently from Akaike's case studies however, the Okamotos consider themselves and the Jiga Daikyōkai as something peculiar amongst the Ontake-kō phenomenon, and when interviewed they were very keen to affirm their identity as professional *gyōja* (TL 220207 I#1).

42   TL 220107 PFN#1.

43   TL 220107 PFN#1.

44   This is not to say, of course, that pilgrimages do not include ascetic elements. Particularly those people who act as *sendatsu* are indeed often supposed to have undergone some kind of ascetic training (see Ian Reader 2005: 171 and ff). What I wish to point out here is that, in this case, the ascetic character of the practice overwhelms its pilgrimage-like aspect and leads the participants to understand it above all as *shugyō*.

45   This kind of abstinence is not uncommon also before or during pilgrimages (Reader 2005: 215). Interestingly, the practice leaders continuously invited the participants to take advantage of the food and drink available 'because this is a *shugyō* and you'll need the strenghth' (TL 220107 PFN#1).

46 TL 220107 PFN#1. My personal experience of the *takigyō* on a different – and slightly warmer – occasion confirms this impression (TL 260806 PFN#1). See also the similarity with declarations of the people involved in the Iwakuni *kagura* and Anne Bouchy 1992: 101. A colourful depiction of a 'collective' *taki gyō* at Ontake-san can also be found in Kitamura Minao's documentary, *Nihon no meizan* (vol. 6), min. 55 and ff.

47 The necessity to make one's body acceptable to the *kami* is a fundamental preliminary phase of any *kamigakari*, as implied by Bouchy (1992: 86–8) and Blacker (Carmen Blacker 1999: 273–4). Averbuch also points out how some *kagura* dances may have held a similar purificatory power (Irit Averbuch 1998: 303).

48 All the messages from the *kami* were duly transcribed during the possession and then a printed copy was sent to each participant some weeks after the end of the practice (included in TL 220107 PFN#1). They ranged from general advice to very personal and heartfelt considerations about of their life conduct and expectations. All messages were very personal and directed to individuals, rather than a community, as sometimes is the case with *miko* or during Shamanic *kagura* (cf. Carmen Blacker 1999: 272–3.). As a curiosity, the message I received from the *kami* was to divulge the circumstances and meaning of this practice 'to the West in English' and to work less for the sake of my health and happiness.

49 TL 220107 PFN#1.

50 While one fellow practitioner was pointing out to me 'you see, this cold cleanses you, can you feel it?', two other acquaintances were merrily discussing the fact that 'it's cold, it's cold, isn't it?' 'Yes it is! But the colder the better!', and then all burst into a laughter that hinted at a sort of unexpressed mutual understanding (TL 220107 PFN#1).

51 Those defining themselves as *junreisha* (pilgrims) meant that they were habitual Ontake pilgrims, visiting Mt Ontake's various shrines regularly during the year. In this circumstance they thought about themselves as being Ontake pilgrims undergoing a *shugyō* but not as *gyōja*. Cf. Ian Reader 2005: Chapter 3.

52 These devotees may have receive their certificate from other *kō* or inherited the title from family members. Cf. Akaike Noriaki 1981: 55.

53 I was unable to find mentions of this place of worship in the available literature. This account is drawn from my personal notes and from the information contained in the pamphlets available at the shrine (TL 280606 OFN#1).

54 TL 280606 OFN#1.

55 TL 280606 OFN#1.

56 TL 280606 OFN#1.

57 TL 280606 OFN#1.

58 Miyake Hitoshi and Gaynor Sekimori 2005: 90–2.

59 In 2004 the practice was documented in its entirety by director Kitamura Minao in the ethnographic film *Shugen – Hagurosan akinomine*. A version with English subtitles and commentary was released in 2009.

60 TL 240805 PFN#1. See also Miyake Hitoshi and Gaynor Sekimori 2005: 92

61 The term *sendatsu* originally indicated *yamabushi* 山伏 acting as local guides for pilgrims. In practices such as the *akinomine*, it is used as a title for the practice leaders. See Miyake Hitoshi and Gaynor Sekimori 2005: 54–6 and Paul Swanson 1981: 62–3.

62 TL 240805 PFN#1. See also Miyake Hitoshi and Gaynor Sekimori 2005: 104.

63 TL 240805 PFN#1.

64 Miyake Hitoshi and Gaynor Sekimori 2005: 131–2.

65 See video footage from Kitamura Minao, *Shugen: The Autumn Peak of Haguro Shugendō*, min. 44 and ff.

66 TL 240805 PFN#1.

67 Cf. Carmen Blacker 1999: 146.
68 Masaki Akira, Yamaori Tetsuo and Nagasawa Tetsu 1992: 20 and ff. See also Shinno Toshikazu 1991: 5–6.
69 This also leads to an overlap between the doctrinal meanings and the ways in which they are performed, in Hollywood's words, '[a]n efficacious performative … constitutes that to which it refers' (Amy Hollywood 2002: 95, note).
70 Miyake Hitoshi 2000a: Chapter 8.
71 All practitioners are certainly proud of their efforts, but also invariably grateful for having the possibility to join the practice year after year (see video footage from Kitamura Minao, *Shugen*, min. 111 and ff.). A longstanding presence in the practice is interpreted at the same time as a consequence of their ascetic effort and as a manifestation of the received benefits. As one participant told me when interviewed, 'I am in good health because I participate every year, and I participate every year because I am in good health' (TL 240805 PFN#1).
72 Daiun Sogaku Harada Rōshi (13 October 1871–12 December 1961) was a Sōtō Zen monk remarkable for including also Rinzai teachings in his *zazen* practice, like the use of Kōan. He has also been the subject of some controversy for his support of Japanese militarism during the Second World War. See Brian Daizen Victoria 2006: 135–6.
73 From the records preserved at Tōshō-ji temple (TL 010407 PFN#1).
74 See also Ian Reader 1991: 82–3.
75 TL 010407 PFN#1.
76 TL 010407 PFN#1.
77 TL 010407 PFN#1.
78 Interviewing participants during the practice was not possible because of the strict discipline, and also because all wished to take advantage of the few moments of rest. However, I interviewed four participants a few days after the end of the practice, two of which were new to the *sesshin* (but not to *zazen*) while the other two had been participating regularly in the *sesshin* for the past three years, albeit without achieving *kenshō*. In spite of their different levels of experience, all reported similar feelings of near-breakdown and utter exhaustion, particularly in regard to the incessant *kyōsaku* beating and mantra chanting. Contrary to other examples, then, in this case there seems to be no significant difference between new and experienced practitioners, the only important factor being the achievement of *kenshō* (TL 130407 I#1).
79 TL 010407 PFN#1.
80 Cf. Janine Anderson Sawada 2004:124–7.
81 TL 010407 PFN#1.
82 For example, none of my informants considered him/herself a *gyōja* or *shugyōsha*, displaying at the same time a certain unfamiliarity with the terms (TL 130407 I#1).
83 Carmen Blacker 1999: 145–6.
84 See similar positions from Wazaki Nobuya 1979: 177.

3   The ascetic practitioner: identity and motivation

1 Lawrence E. Sullivan 1986: 23.
2 As Reader aptly points out, such 'seemingly "folk" religious phenomena' are in fact 'central and critical within normative religious structures, of equal value and import as, for example, text and doctrine [...]' (Ian Reader 2006: 66–7).
3 Social factors, such as the depopulation of the area surrounding certain practices, can also play a role in the variation of the participants' numbers. The situation seems, however, to be more variable than a simple decline (cf. Carmen Blacker 1999: 162). For example, the numbers of some practices have been sensibly increased after the Second World War by admitting a broader female participation, like Omine-area

Shugendō (Gaynor Sekimori 2002: 216), while the male-only *akinomine* retreat at Dewa-sanzan *jinja* has been operating on a full-house basis for at least the past 20 years (see Chapter 4).

4 See Ian Reader 2005: 29–31.

5 Cf. Shinno Toshikazu 2002: 457.

6 Rather than controlled interviews in a separate setting, I preferred to conduct my investigations through a a series of simple questions in the form of small talk during the festival and asked to the widest possible sample of participants. This proved to be the only possible way to approach an adequate number of people in such a lively and rather chaotic event as this *matsuri*, and led to a number of open-ended discussions and spontaneous declarations. For similar considerations see also Scott Schnell 2006: 388–9.

7 Regular attendance at local festivals is, however, by no means an exception in Japan. See Herbert Plutschow 1996: 31.

8 TL 100407 PFN#1. Cf. Ian Reader and George Joji Tanabe 1998: 72.

9 Interestingly, none seemed to be concerned with the clearly materialistic nature of their wishes and purposes. As Reader and Tanabe puts it, this might be in fact a form of spirituality 'not of an otherworldly kind: it is necessarily limited to the cares and concerns of everyday living' (Ian Reader and George Joji Tanabe 1998: 124).

10 I excluded from this account, of course, the Okamoto brothers, since their understanding is closer to that of a religious professional than a layperson.

11 TL 100407 PFN#1. Although there are many 'self-centred' this-worldly benefits to be attained by women as well, most of them are concerned with marriage or beauty (see Reader and Tanabe 1998: 178–9), none of the women interviewed mentioned any of them, perhaps because they are more usually associated with other deities and places of worship such as Izumo Taisha or Yasaka Shrine.

12 For some further elaboration on this slightly Marxist argument see Anthony Synnott 1993: 22–6.

13 'Gratitude' was one of the feelings most mentioned by all practitioners I had the occasion to interview in the course of my fieldwork. It will be analyzed in more details in Chapter 4.

14 We may be tempted to consider the simpler forms of asceticism as a performative approach to everyday experiences and issues, in other words re-enacting the problems and their solutions in a ritualized form as a measure of control (see Amy Hollywood 2002: 112–13). This approach appears problematic, however, if we consider the fact that we have the same practices enacted in different religious environments, each time charged with different meanings or sets of meanings belonging the performers' belief or religious orthodoxy. This suggests to us that, in fact, the embodied 'ascetic tradition' may have a life of its own, and circulates amongst a variety of religious settings independently of the specific circumstances. This theme will be developed in detail in Chapter 4.

15 For details about this famous pilgrimage route, see D. Max Moerman 2005.

16 In a 1981 article, Paul Swanson provides a detailed description of the practice organized by the Shōgo-in temple, which is, in many respects, similar to the Tōnan-in version I took part in during July 2006 (TL 150706 PFN#1). See Paul L. Swanson 1981: 55–84. Other descriptions may be found in Miyake Hitoshi 1971: 65–86 and Gorai Shigeru 1991: 153–221.

17 Gorai Shigeru 1991: 154–65.

18 Although the Kinpusen-ji was in close relationship with the Tendai sect of Buddhism before the Meiji period, since 1948 the temple complex is an independent Shugendō sect known as Kinpusen Shugen Honshū 金峯修験本宗. However, in Yoshino town (where Kinpusen-ji is located), there are numerous Shugendō temples, variously affiliated, performing mountain entry rituals including the *okugake*. These

include Sakuramotobō 桜本坊 (Kinpusen Shugen Honshū), Kizo-in 喜蔵院 (Honzan Shugenshū) and Tōnan-in (Kinpusen Shugen Honshū). See Miyake Hitoshi 1992: 126.

19 *Jikatabi* is a kind of Japanese outdoor footwear characterized by having a very thin sole. They are often worn together with *geta* 下駄 or *zōri* 草履 clogs, but during the *okugake* practice, they must be worn alone.

20 The total number of 'official' *nabiki* is 75. Please refer to Paul L. Swanson 1981: 73–8, for a complete list.

21 Only men are allowed in the inner precinct of Ōmine-san, while women will return to Dorogawa village and rejoin the group on the following day (cf. Swanson 1981: 65). Suzuki Masataka has treated the subject of prohibition of women from the Ōmine sacred precinct in detail in Suzuki Masataka 2002: 28 and ff. See also video footage from Abela and McGuire 2010, mins. 68–9.

22 See video footage from Abela and McGuire 2010, min. 76 and ff.

23 Cf. Paul L. Swanson 1981: 72.

24 Although no complete documentary film exists about this practice, it is possible to get a glimpse of the ascetic effort of the participants from Kitamura Minao's documentary *Nihon no meizan* (vol. 9), min. 32 and ff. The 'Lotus ascent' portrayed in Abela and McGuire's documentary *Shugendō Now*, min. 67 and ff. is substantially similar to the first day of practice (the ascension to Mt Ōmine).

25 Paul L. Swanson 1981: 62.

26 TL 150706 PFN#1.

27 On this 'economy' between ascetic effort and power or benefits in various forms see Carmen Blacker 1999: 85; Ian Reader and George Joji Tanabe 1998: 179.

28 Two fellow practitioners at the *okugake shugyō* were a sort of '*shugyō* aficionados', used to practicing various feats throughout Japan and even organizing their own *hiwatari* in Niigata. In their opinion, the *okugake* was 'the most difficult *shugyō* in all Japan', and they were worried about their chances to actually complete it (TL 150706 PFN#1).

29 TL 150706 PFN#1. Compare the different awareness of *samugyō* practitioners as detailed in the second chapter. The importance of *hijiri*-type ascetics in the creation of pilgrimage routes since the Nara period, however, must not be forgotten. See Shinno Toshikazu 1991: 68–81.

30 As Bell points out, 'possession of this sense of ritual does not mean that members of a community always agree on how to do a ritual or what to make of it' (Catherine Bell 1992: 80). It is not my intention to necessarily assimilate asceticism to ritual – and to explain it merely through ritual theory – but it is important to stress how this similar theoretical interpretation probably came from the fact that both ritual and ascetic practice are bodily-based, performance-oriented religious activities. Cf. Catherine Bell 1992: 38–9 and Amy Hollywood 2002: 103.

31 In Flood's words: 'asceticism is always performed' Gavin D. Flood 2004: 7.

32 We still need, however, to address the question of the cultural significance of the body, so aptly posed by Coakley: 'if we can no longer count on a universal "grand narrative", then does not the "body", too, become subject to infinitely variable social constructions?' (Sarah Coakley 1997: 3), which resonates of Lingis' words we used to introduce this same problem in Chapter 1 (Alphonso Lingis 1994: vii). We shall, indeed, try to answer this issue in the following chapter, where we will propose an explanation of bodily performance in hermeneutical terms.

33 Ikoma Kanshichi 1988: 232–3.

34 Kawamura Kunimitsu 1991: Chapter 4.

35 I was not able to witness the *itako* training personally. Thus, for this analysis, I draw my considerations from a number of relevant studies on Japanese blind mediums by scholars such as Tokutarō Sakurai 1974, and Kawamura Kunimitsu 1991: 88ff. See also Carmen Blacker 1999: 142; Anne Bouchy 1992: 86–91.

36 Carmen Blacker 1999: 143.

37 Ibid.: 147–8; Clark Chilson and Peter Knecht 2003: 17–20.

38 The 100-day *daiaragyō* practice takes place every winter at the Hokekyō-ji in Chiba prefecture from the beginning of November until the following February. The training is very harsh and includes cold water *mizugori* seven times per day. The participants eat only two meals a day, consisting only of some rice gruel and miso soup. Only four hours of sleep per night are allowed and shaving and cutting one's hair are prohibited. Most of the participants' time is used chanting the *Lotus Sutra* and practising the use of the *bokken* 木剣 (magic castanets employed during *kitō* 祈祷 rituals). See Ōmori Tatari 1993: 80ff.

39 It must be noted, however, that there is a variety of patterns through which lay-people entertain relationships with the *kaihōgyō* ascetics. During the practice, in fact, numerous people alternate in around-the-clock shifts to aid the ascetic by holding a stool for him to rest during brief pauses, push him up the steeper slopes, help in cooking his meals etc. Also, the current Mudō-ji Ajari (Uehara Gyōshō, the *kaihōgyō*ja now resident at Mudō-ji temple) is regularly offering 'one-day-*kaihōgyō*' (*ichinichi-kaihōgyō*) experiences open to all. We shall return to this in the section below dedicated to the social dimension of asceticism.

40 John Stevens 1988: 59; Robert F. Rhodes 1987: 193.

41 TL 170507 I#1.

42 See Wazaki Nobuya 1979: 19–20.

43 Video footage from Tabata Keiichi 1982.

44 John Stevens 1988: 63.

45 Video footage from Michael Yorke 1992.

46 John Stevens 1988: 67.

47 Ibid.: 75.

48 The practitioner, however, is not alone in his effort. During the entire nine days he is helped by numerous assistants, which help him to stay awake and to carry the bucket to and from the well. See the video footage from Tabata Keiichi 1982 and Michael Yorke 1992.

49 Wazaki Nobuya 1979: 189.

50 This slope is famous because it was used by the Tendai warrior monks to reach the city of Kyoto quickly.

51 Again, the practitioner is not left alone. A number of assistants follow the *gyōja* while he walks across the city, and some of them literally push the *gyōja* by means of a T-shaped stick. See the video footage from Tabata Keiichi 1982.

52 John Stevens 1988: 83.

53 Nakao Takashi 1973. The Nichiren *daiaragyō* has also been documented in a 2001 documentary produced by NHK (Japanese, colour, 30 mins.). In a sequence it is possible to see how the parishioners visiting the priests during the practice period are indeed very concerned with their performance and progress.

54 Akaike Noriaki 1981: 76–7. See also Shinno Toshikazu 1993: 201.

55 TL 240805 PFN#1; TL 220107 PFN#1; TL 100407 PFN#1.

56 This activity was reported to me during an interview (TL 220207 I#1). The group also uploaded some videos of their waterfall practice on YouTube: www.youtube.com/watch?v=hPCU6nWgrHg [last accessed 21 Jun 2010] and www.youtube.com/watch?v=by-MkeWoih0 [last accessed 21 Jun 2010].

57 TL 220107 PFN#1. Many of the practitioners I interviewed in other practices, such as the *akinomine* and the *okugake shugyō* manifested similar intentions. They were practising for the success of their business, of their marriage etc. See video footage from Kitamura Minao 2004, min. 113.

58 Yamada Ryūshin 1988: 132 and ff.

59 Ibid.: 126–7.

60 Robert F. Rhodes 1987: 195.

61 Wazaki Nobuya 1979: 190–2.
62 John Stevens 1988: 75–6.
63 Hiramatsu Chōkū 1982: 132.
64 TL 240805 PFN#2.
65 TL 010407 PFN#1 some interviews were, however, conducted some days after the end of the *sesshin*.
66 TL 010407 PFN#1.
67 As a matter of fact, almost all my interviewees mentioned 'gratitude' as one of the most overwhelming feelings arising during and after their ascetic experiences (see also Chapter 2 and Chapter 4). 'Gratitude' features prominently in works like Yamada Ryūshin 1988; Wazaki Nobuya 1979; Shima Kazuharu 1983; and Masaki Akira, Yamaori Tetsuo and Nagasawa Tetsu 1992. The current Mudō-ji *ajari*, Uehara Gyōshō, also mentioned his gratitude to the nature of Hiei mountain during an inter-view, and the fact that such gratitude was an 'unchanging everyday feeling', even if much time elapsed after the completion of the practice (TL 170507 I#1). On the account of gratitude towards nature, see also Ian Reader 1991: 127.
68 This can be witnessed also during pilgrimages, again another form of bodily-based religious practice. See Ian Reader 2005: 90.
69 TL 010407 PFN#1 and TL 150706 PFN#1. For instance, during the Ontake *samugyō*, practitioners wept profusely while thanking the mediums of the *kamigakari* and, at the same time, the leaders of the Jiga Daikyōkai offered their thanks to Ontake Daijin in equally heartfelt terms. The same happened also during the *akinomine* and the *okugake shugyō*, where deeply moved leaders thanked the participants at the end of their efforts.
70 The ambiguous nature of the ascetic's individuality is addressed by Flood also in regard to tradition (as representative of the 'cultural other'): 'On the one hand the ascetic entails the assertion of the individual will [...] yet on the other it wishes to wholly form itself in the shape of tradition and in terms of the tradition's goals' (Flood 2004: 4).

4 Ascetic practices in context

1 Miyake Hitoshi 2002: 37. In my opinion, there is no substantial evidence of continuity in the worship of mountains from prehistoric times until the earliest documented his-tory. The theory that the *kofun* 古墳 (tumuli) could be considered a sort of 'miniature mountain' and thus prove the long-standing presence of a mountain-based religious culture seems to be at odds with archaeological theories about the significance of the tumuli in pre-historic or protohistoric periods, where they are thought to mark the development of social differences and the consolidation of ruling classes. See Imamura Keiji 1996: 14–15.
2 As Hori points out, there were two types of *hijiri*: some of them, particularly in the earliest phase, were mountain dwelling ascetics, avoiding any contact with other human beings and dedicating themselves single-mindedly to ascetic fasting, similar to the one undertaken by Taoist Immortals, and to the recitation of a particular sutra (often the *Lotus Sutra*). The other type incessantly wandered across towns and vil-lages performing magical-religious services for the common people. See Hori Ichiro 1953: Chapter 1.
3 See Livia Kohn and Yoshinobu Sakade 1989: 2.
4 *Tendai nanzan Mudō-ji konryū oshō den* 天台南山無動寺建立和尚伝 (Biography of Sōō oshō, founder of the Mudō-ji of the Southern Mountain), collected in the fourth chapter of the *Gunsho Ruijū* 群書類従. See Hiramatsu Chōkū 1982: 13–25; and Robert Rhodes 1987: 186.
5 Robert Rhodes 1987: 188.

6   Michiaki Iwahana 1996: 11–15.
7   Miyake Hitoshi 1999: 387–90. See also Janet Goodwin 1994: 50.
8   Paul Swanson 1981: 59.
9   This symbology is also widely employed in pilgrimage spaces. See Ian Reader 2005: 50–3; and Allan Grapard 1982: 195–221.
10 I use as reference the complete account of Akakura practice by Ellen Schattschneider (2003).
11 Ibid.: 50–1.
12 Ibid.: 66.
13 Ibid.: 158.
14 In the Kamakura period, *hijiri* were the driving force behind fund-raising (*kanjin*) campaigns, which became major occasions during which common people came into contact with elements of Buddhist doctrine (Janet Goodwin 1994: 27 and ff.). See also Carmen Blacker 1999: 165.
15 Ellen Schattschneider 2003: 96.
16 Ibid.: 99–100.
17 Ibid.: 89ff.
18 Ibid.: 90. Also note the similarity with the *kamado* ritual performed during the Ontakesan-jinja *harumatsuri* of Honjō treated in Chapter 2.
19 Ibid.: 47–51.
20 Carmen Blacker 1999: 256–64.
21 The medium generally undergoes a number of days of fasting followed by water ablutions and a final goma ceremony. This pattern may vary locally and from one person to another. See Kawamura Kunimitsu 1991: 60ff.
22 Carmen Blacker 1999: 261.
23 Ibid.: 262–3.
24 Ibid.: 263.
25 Yamada Ryūshin 1988:158–9.
26 Ōmori Tatari 1993: 83.
27 For the terminology 'intra-ascetic', 'inter-ascetic' and 'extra-ascetic', I am indebted to Oliver Freiberger and his excellent work (2006: 10–15).
28 Marginality is also accompanied by a clear sensation of separation from the dominating culture: 'The marginal person is faced with the dominance of the host culture in cultural issues such as language, custom, mores, habits of thought, religion – all of which he encounters as a stranger' (Adam Weisberger 1992: 425–46).
29 Most committed members of Aum Shinrikyō used to live in rigidly controlled communes where they performed all sorts of ascetical disciplines. These communes were like isolated 'micro worlds' totally impermeable to external society where the members lived in a sort of alternative reality. See Ian Reader 2000: 123–4.
30 As Goodwin reminds us, rather than remaining on the margins, '[h]ijiri, who traveled freely, both in actual space and from one segment of society to another, were the nodes and channels of a communications network that helped to integrate the whole nation' (Janet Goodwin 1994: 27).
31 Interestingly, a Shugendō practitioner I interviewed about this topic did not share this point of view. For her, such figures as *miko, itako, gomiso* etc. are indeed to be considered marginal because they cannot find a proper place within the ordinary texture of society. They are, in her words, 'feared, but also perceived as inferior'. It is natural, however, to attempt to downplay the things we fear the most, and fearing something is a clear way of acknowledging its power over us. My feeling is that she was interpreting the word 'marginal' as 'not-normal'.
32 This 'mobility' was also one of the more evident characteristics of *hijiri* since the Heian period, and, as Goodwin observes, one of the reasons allowing them to promote 'a type of Buddhism that answered the mundane needs of ordinary people as

well as their spiritual aims', thus enjoying an active role within a society where 'they were often of practical use to their followers' (Janet Goodwin 1994: 30).

33   It seems to me that that the association of space to society as an important element in the sociology of certain religious phenomena is surprisingly overlooked in existing literature, such as Malcolm Hamilton (2001) and even Max Weber (1964).

34   TL 010107 I#1; TL 170507 I#1.

35   TL 170507 I#1.

36   Davis outlines a similar argument in regard to the process of legitimization of a religious founder through suffering, and of leadership in general: 'Part of the moral legitimation of leadership in Japan is the idea that the founder of an institution suffered in order to bring it into existence. The sacred ancestors of the family, industrial entrepreneurs and emperors alike, are thought to have suffered in order to bestow upon the people the "blessings" they now enjoy' (Winston Davis 1992: 198).

37   When the *ajari* left the room at the end of the meeting, I had the opportunity to ask a few question to the participants. Besides providing information about their relationship with the *ajari*, all were very eager to express their gratitude for the benefits they received (TL 010107 I#1; TL 170507 I#).

38   The activities of this confraternity is covered in an excellent article by Catherine Ludvik (2006: 115–42).

39   Ibid.: 126.

40   Ibid.: 136.

41   Ibid.

42   Michel de Certeau 1982: 101.

43   Ibid.

44   Ibid.: 102.

45   TL 240805 PFN#1.

46   Miyake Hitoshi and Gaynor Sekimori 2005: 97–9.

47   TL 240805 PFN#1.

48   A similar problem has been observed in the case of the relationships between senior and new students in college environments. See James Ponzetti Jr. 1990: 336–40.

49   Miyake Hitoshi and Gaynor Sekimori 2005: 104–5.

50   Blacker's account of her experience in Hagurosan seems to be inspired by this same sense of wonder (1999: 221).

51   In 2005, new and junior women were at one end of the main hall, and senior women either upstairs or in one of the rooms in the living quarters section – divided from the men only by the wooden runners on the tatami. Today, all the women are located in the two back rooms and senior men in the front two – but there are no doors between them. Thanks to Gaynor Sekimori for this clarification (from personal correspondence).

52   TL 240805 PFN#1.

53   Breaking the barrier with strangers *through* language is also a fundamental protective mechanism, in that it may allow one to distinguish friends from foes. Though beyond the purpose of this study, it is interesting to note how, in this kind of situation, people tend to become very talkative and speak extensively about themselves, their inner feelings and fears. This is not that common in Japan in 'ordinary society' and might be taken as further proof that the spatial dislocation in this kind of ascetic setting also corresponds to the more subtle dislocation from the societal convention in which one has to 'redefine' oneself in new terms. This is a recurring theme in cognitive psychology; see Marc Bornstein and Jerome Bruner 1989: Chapter 3.

54   They also constituted a sort of 'second level' religious professionals' group, parallel to the temple leaders. Although they did not have any official leadership in the group, they interacted greatly with the upper echelon of the intra-ascetic society and were always very supportive of the other practitioners, regardless their experience level. TL 240805 PFN#1.

55 Discipline has, however, become more strict in recent years (Gaynor Sekimori, from personal correspondence).
56 The sumo tournament in 2005 was in fact won by a non-Japanese practitioner who happened to be a *jujitsu* master. TL 240805 PFN#1.
57 In the case of the *rōhatsu sesshin* in particular, it is interesting to note the same patterns of behaviour and progressive desocialization, despite the fact that the retreat was conducted in an urban temple set in the metropolitan area of Tokyo. TL 010407 PFN#1.
58 Completion certificates are issued to all practitioners on the last day of practice. They certify the fulfilment of the practice and officially state the *shugenja* rank. Newcomers are officially authorized to use their new *shugenja* names as a proof of their achievement. See Miyake Hitoshi and Gaynor Sekimori 2005: 108.
59 See also Massimo Raveri 1984: 144–5.
60 TL 150706 PFN#1; TL 010407 PFN#1. See also, for instance Masaki Akira, Yamaori Tetsuo and Nagasawa Tetsu 1992: 8–12.
61 Michel de Certeau 1982: 101–3.
62 Doctrinal explanations are often provided by practice leaders in the course of the practice. These views may also be collected in written documents or in books which may later on become a sort of 'reference text' for practitioners. See for instance Asada Masahiro (2000) which deals mostly with Ōmine Shugendō.
63 TL 240805 PFN#1; TL 101006 PFN#1.
64 TL 150706 PFN#1.
65 The case of pilgrimages is more ambiguous. Some practitioners, such as the *okugake* devotees we analyzed in Chapter 3, proudly make a distinction between themselves and 'mere' pilgrims. Others, like the above-mentioned informants and some of the participants in the Shinto version of the *akinomine*, also tended to consider their pilgrimages as *shugyō*. Cf. Ian Reader 2005: 202–3.
66 TL 220207 I#1.
67 TL 220207 I#1.
68 See Chapter 2 and also Miyake Hitoshi 1992: 213ff.
69 TL 150706 PFN#1. Also, Yamada Ryūshin 1988: 132–3.
70 See for instance the *hiwatari* and *hawatari* practices described in Chapter 2.
71 Wazaki Nobuya 1979: 33–4; Yamada Ryūshin 1988: 117. This also matches my personal observations in the *okugake* and *akinomine* practices (TL 240805 PFN#1; TL 150706 PFN#1).
72 TL 240805 PFN#1; TL 150706 PFN#1; TL 250806 PFN#1; TL 220207 I#1. See also Masaki Akira, Yamaori Tetsuo and Nagasawa Tetsu 1992: 185–6.
73 Cf. Ariel Glucklich 2001: 126, who, however, privileges psychological explanations. I consider it particularly inappropriate to apply psychological methodologies developed in the West, in regard to 'western minds', to people belonging to different cultures who may well have different psyches.
74 The term *chikara* 力 is a favourite in this circumstance, as it preserves a certain ambiguity between the physical '*strength*' and the more abstract '*force*'. Many also describe the surge of energy in emotional terms, such as joy or peacefulness. A few even become euphoric and start weeping uncontrollably for the bliss that the practice procured them and express strong feelings of gratitude. TL 240805 PFN#1; TL 010407 PFN#1.
75 TL 150706 PFN#1.
76 See Chapter 3. See also Ian Reader 2005: 145.
77 TL 220107 PFN#1; TL 220207 I#1. See also Wazaki Nobuya 1979: 121.
78 In the early twentieth century, the Hagurosan shrine-temple complex was heavily reformed to restore it to a 'pure Shinto' style. This represented a major cultural disaster for the institution, as a number of precious Buddhist statues, artefacts and scriptures

were removed from the various halls and discarded or destroyed. Most of the surviving materials are now kept at the Kogane-dō temple in Tōge, including the tree, the original object of worship (*honzon*), which also is the *honji* (true nature) of the three mountains once enshrined in the main hall: Kannon (Haguro), Amida (Gassan) and Yakushi nyorai (Yudono). See Miyake Hitoshi 2000a: Chapter 7.

79   The terms 'Shinto' and 'Buddhist' versions are employed here for the sake of brevity. A more accurate definition would be: *akinomine* practice as conducted by the Dewa Sanzan-jinja and by the Kōtaku-ji temple. The Buddhist practice has been described in other sections of this work. I have not discussed the Shinto practice before, so I will describe it in detail here based on my personal participation in the practice.

80   TL 250806 PFN#1.

81   See Gaynor Sekimori 1994.

82   A complete list of all participants, including their place of origin, is provided by the shrine priests at the beginning of the practice (TL 250806 PFN#1).

83   See Chapter 2. It is interesting to notice how a practice portraying itself as eminently 'Shinto' may instead start from a Buddhist temple/shrine. The reasons here are of an extra-ascetic nature, as the Myokō-in is a temple attached to a pilgrim lodging (*shukubō* 宿坊) which is closely associated to the shrine.

84   TL 250806 PFN#1.

85   Cf. Miyake Hitoshi and H. Byron Earhart 2001: 81; and Miyake Hitoshi and Gaynor Sekimori 2005: 104–5.

86   TL 250806 PFN#1.

87   Cf. Miyake Hitoshi and Gaynor Sekimori 2005: 105.

88   Massimo Raveri 1992: 128–9.

89   TL 250806 PFN#1.

90   TL 250806 PFN#1.

91   *Ō-fuda* tablets are purchased by all the participants for a variety of this-worldly benefits, from business success to family health. As these *ō-fuda* are produced during a *shugyō*, they are considered to be particularly powerful and a sufficient reason in themselves to participate to the *akinomineiri*. *Ō-fuda* also constitute visible evidence of one's participation in the practice. Cf. Ian Reader 2005: 20–1.

92   TL 250806 PFN#1.

93   TL 240805 PFN#1; Miyake Hitoshi and H. Byron Earhart 2001: 89.

94   Miyake Hitoshi and H. Byron Earhart 2001: 89–91.

95   As breathing and chanting becomes more and more painful, many people visibly start to choke or cough convulsively. The senses of sight and balance are altered and a few persons stumble on the *tatami* when leaving the Buchūdō. Despite all this, the vast majority of the participants chant the hymn stoically for the entire period of fumigation, which can last from 20 to 40 minutes, depending on the day (TL 250806 PFN#1).

96   The *aka no sendatsu* 閼伽の先達 and the *kogi no sendatsu* 小木の先達 are the authorities (guides) responsible for water (*aka*) and ritual functions concerning wood (*kogi*). See Miyake Hitoshi 1971: 71.

97   The *shugenja* line up outside the Buchūdō; once their turn comes, they petition the *aka no sendatsu* and the *kogi no sendatsu* with the formula: '*Aka/kogi no sendatsu, annai annai o mosu!*' (Water/wood guide, please guide us!). A dipper-full of water and a stick of wood is then offered to the *aka* and *kogi-no-sendatsu* respectively (TL 240805 PFN#1; TL 250806 PFN#1). See video footage from Kitamura Minao 2009, min. 46 and ff.

98   TL 240805 PFN#1; Miyake Hitoshi 1999: 118; Miyake Hitoshi and Gaynor Sekimori 2005: 105.

99   The prefix 'aka' seems to derive from the Sanskrit *ambhas*, meaning 'water'. See Miyake Hitoshi 1986.

100 In the *Sanyama tebumi* (*Guide to the three mountains*, compiled in *c.* 1885) there was such an effort and alternate designations were formulated, like: *sōchō* 総長 (substituting *dōshi* 導師), *fukusōchō* 副総長 (*kogi no sendatsu* 小木の先達), *kanji* 幹事 (*aka no sendatsu* 閼伽の先達). Thanks to Gaynor Sekimori for these highlights (from personal correspondence).

101 TL 240805 PFN#1; TL 250806 PFN#1. For an extensive study of the phenomenon of separation of Kami and Buddha in Haguro Shugendō see Gaynor Sekimori 2005: 197–234.

102 TL 240805 PFN#2.

103 TL 250806 PFN#1.

104 We have already encountered similar behaviour in the Buddhist practice. In this case, however, the circulation of 'forbidden' food is open and explicit and definitely overlooked by the practice's leaders.

105 Narration from Kitamura Minao's film (2005); script courtesy of Gaynor Sekimori.

106 Iwahana Michiaki 1996: 86; TL 250806 PFN#1.

107 Prince Hachiko is also known as Nojo Taishi, the third son of Emperor Sushun 崇峻天皇 (d.592). He is said to have founded the first temple on Mount Haguro in 593, thus 'opening' the mountain for ascetic practice. See Miyake Hitoshi 1999: 495.

108 En no Gyōja 役行者 (also known as En no Ozunu 役小角 and En no Shoukaku 役小角) is a mythical ascetic traditionally held to be the founder of Shugendō. He was allegedly active in the Nara period, opening various mountains to the Shugendō practice, particularly in the Ōmine–Kumano area. See Miyake Hitoshi 2000b.

109 TL 250806 PFN#1.

110 Gaynor Sekimori 2005: 208.

111 My informants could not clarify if there is any relationship between the name of this practice and the scriptures box traditionally carried by *yamabushi* which is also called *katabako* 肩箱 (TL 250806 PFN#1).

112 TL 250806 PFN#1.

113 TL 250806 PFN#1.

5 *Corporis ascensus*

1 It is perhaps for this reason that the idea of an 'asceticism of the mind' is not developed in ascetic literature, also in the western context. As Brakke points out, even in the *Life of Anthony*, where Athanasius explains that bodily temptations and heretical ideas are caused by the same demons, no significant effort is made to establish any form of 'intellectual asceticism', while the traditional bodily practice is understood as the most efficacious means of fighting both kinds of negative influences. See David Brakke 2001: 19–48.

2 Cf. Ariel Glucklich 2001: 11.

3 Gavin Flood 2004: 216.

4 Ibid.: 216–17.

5 Cf. Ibid.: 218–19.

6 Ibid.: 10.

7 Ibid.: 40; and Anthony Synnott 1993: 88.

8 Ze'ev Maghen 2005: 161–2.

9 Robert Lewis Gross 1992: 73–7.

10 Naitō Masatoshi 1999: 230–4.

11 Yamada Ryūshin 1988: 53.

12 TL 240805 PFN#1.

13 Details about Sōō's life may be found mainly in the *Tendai nanzan mudō-ji konryū oshō den* 天台南山無動寺建立和尚伝 (Biography of Osho, Founder of Mudō-ji of

the Tendai Southern Mountain) contained in the fourth chapter of the *Gunsho ruijū* 群書類従, and also in the *Katsuragawa engi* 葛川縁起. Cf. Robert Rhodes 1987: 14–18.

14 Hiramatsu Chōkū 1982: 192.
15 Robert F. Rhodes 1987: 189.
16 Nihon-miira-kenkyū-gurupu 1969: 56–8.
17 Michael Yorke 1992; TL 170507 I#1.
18 TL 220107 PFN#1.
19 Kawamura Kunimitsu 1991: 26–30.
20 TL 240805 PFN#1; TL 150706 PFN#1.
21 See Carmen Blacker 1999: 92.
22 If the attributes of the body are treated as *epistemes*, they are prerequisite to the existence of the body as such. We can thus say, for instance, that a human body is specific to a human being and that it is characterized by possessing four limbs. This, however, would imply that a person born without limbs is not a human being. This paradox may resolved by considering the limbs attributes of the body, so that a human body can still be considered as such even without limbs. This implicitly creates an ambiguity between the reality of *being* and our interpretation of it. A similar argument is developed by Foucault in more historical terms (1973: Chapter 5).
23 Gavin Flood 2004: 213.
24 TL 150706 PFN#1.
25 TL 150706 PFN#1.
26 TL 240805 PFN#1.
27 TL 010407 PFN#1.
28 This argument has been notoriously developed by Weber in his famous work *The Protestant Ethic and the Spirit of Capitalism*, in which interestingly he describes capitalism as the rationalization of the pursuit of economic wealth (2001: 33–9).
29 Ibid.: 180.
30 Carmen Blacker 1999: 146.
31 'Be careful. If you misplace your feet, you'll die!' But they then added: 'See, now you have nothing else to think about. You have no other concerns in the world, as you might be about to die' (TL 150706 PFN#1). See also Paul Swanson 1981: 70–2.
32 Gavin Flood 2004: 4–6.
33 TL 240805 PFN#2; TL 220107 PFN#1; TL 220207 I#1; TL 010407 PFN#1.
34 Rudolph Bell 1985: Chapter 2.
35 Douglas Burton-Christie 1993: 170–1.
36 These terms are employed here using their literal meanings with no particular emphasis on their physiological implications: introversive is the act of directing one's interest inward or to things within the self; extroversive is the act of directing one's interest outward or to things outside the self. See Roger Pease 2006.
37 TL 240805 PFN#2.
38 TL 150706 PFN#1.
39 It is possible to purchase the same *ō-fuda* from Dewa Sanzan shrine without the need to participate in the *akinomine*. However, all the participants agree that the ones consecrated during the practice are 'far more powerful' (TL 250806 PFN#1).
40 Wazaki Nobuya 1979: 138. See also video footage from *Yomigaeru Tōtō* (NHK, 1979).
41 I personally benefitted from the latter kind of performance on the occasion of a small injury, when some fellow practitioners released their power onto my injured leg using exactly this technique (TL 240805 PFN#1).
42 Cf. Gavin Flood 2004: 3–7.

43 A critical evaluation of the concept of 'experience' in religious studies is offered by Robert Sharf (1998: Chapter 5). Sharf's somewhat drastic conclusions generated numerous counter-arguments, particularly notable among which is Brian Bocking (2006).
44 Peter Brown 1988: 224.
45 Matsumoto Akira 1985: 287.
46 Carmen Blacker 1999: 87.
47 A detailed exposition is available in Stephen Eskildsen 1998: 95ff.
48 Nihon-miira-kenkyū-gurupu 1969: 34–9.
49 Ibid.: 56–8.
50 Ibid.: 59–61.
51 Naitō Masatoshi 1999: 222–4.
52 Hori Ichiro 1962: 225.
53 Naitō Masatoshi 1999: 230–4.
54 Nihon-miira-kenkyū-gurupu 1969: 125.
55 Pictures of Tetsumonkai appear for instance on phone cards sold in Tsuruoka. He is also featured in some *anime* and as the 'final boss' in the video game *Ninja Spirit*.
56 Ibid.: 69–76.
57 Matsumoto Akira 1985: 39–44.
58 Nihon-miira-kenkyū-gurupu 1969: 77–82.
59 Carmen Blacker 1999: 89.
60 Supporting this as an historical fact, Faxian, in 399, testifies to having seen Mahākāśyapa in deep meditation in Mount Kukkuttapādagiri in India. See Helen Hardacre and Alan Sponberg 1988: 225.
61 Kūkai and Yoshito S. Hakeda 1972: 59–60. Cf. Massimo Raveri 1992: 20.
62 *Konjaku Monogatarishū*: 11, 25, quoted in Raveri 1992: 21–2. *Heike Monogatari*: 10, 9. See Helen Craig McCullough 1988: 344.
63 Cf. Massimo Raveri 1992: 25.
64 Cf. Ibid.: 38.

Bibliography

Akahori Akira. 'Drug Taking and Immortality'. In Livia Kohn and Sakade Yoshinobu (eds), *Taoist Meditation and Longevity Techniques*. Ann Arbor, MI: Center for Chinese Studies, University of Michigan, 1989: 73–98.

Akaike Noriaki. 'Festival and Neighborhood Association: A Case Study of the Kamimachi Neighborhood in Chichibu'. *Japanese Journal of Religious Studies* 3, no. 2–3 (1976): 127–74.

——. 'The Ontake Cult Associations and Local Society: The Case of the Owari-Mikawa Region in Central Japan'. *Japanese Journal of Religious Studies* 8, no. 1–2 (1981): 51–82.

Ambros, Barbara. *Emplacing a Pilgrimage: The Ōyama Cult and Regional Religion in Early Modern Japan*. Cambridge, MA: Harvard University Asia Center; Harvard University Press, 2008.

Aoki Tamotsu 青木保. *Ontake junrei: Gendai no kami to hito* 御岳巡礼—現代の神と人. Shohan edn. Tokyo: Chikuma Shobō, 1985.

Asada Masahiro 浅田正博. *Bukkyō kara mita shugen no sekai: Shugendō kyōgi nyūmon: 'shugen sanjūsan tsūki' o yomu* 仏教からみた修験の世界: 修験道教義入門:「修験三十三通記」を読む. Tokyo: Kokusho Kankōkai, 2000.

Athanasius of Alexandria. *The Life of Antony: The Coptic Life and the Greek Life*. Kalamazoo, MI: Cistercian Publications, 2003.

Athanasius of Alexandria, Wilhelm Riedel and W. E. Crum. *The Canons of Athanasius of Alexandria*. London: Published for the Text and Translation Society by Williams and Norgate, 1904.

Averbuch, Irit. *The Gods Come Dancing: A Study of the Japanese Ritual Dance of Yamabushi Kagura*. Ithaca, NY: East Asia Program, Cornell University, 1995.

——. 'Shamanic Dance in Japan: The Choreography of Possession in Kagura Performance'. *Asian Folklore Studies* 57, no. 2 (1998): 293–329.

Bachnik, Jane M. 'Orchestrated Reciprocity'. In Jan van Bremen and Dolores P. Martinez (eds), *Ceremony and Ritual in Japan: Religious Practices in an Industrialized Society*. London; New York: Routledge, 1995: 108–45.

Banks, Caroline Giles. '"There is No Fat in Heaven": Religious Asceticism and the Meaning of Anorexia Nervosa'. *Ethos* 24, no. 1 (1996): 107–35.

Bassnett, Susan and Harish Trivedi (eds). *Post-Colonial Translation: Theory and Practice*. London; New York: Routledge, 1999.

Bell, Catherine. *Ritual Theory, Ritual Practice*. New York; Oxford: Oxford University Press, 1992.

Bell, Rudolph M. *Holy Anorexia*. Chicago: University of Chicago Press, 1985.

Bhagat, M. G. *Ancient Indian Asceticism*. New Delhi: Munshiram Manoharlal Publishers, 1976.

Blacker, Carmen. *The Catalpa Bow: A Study in Shamanistic Practices in Japan*. Richmond, Surrey: Japan Library, 1999 (Curzon Press, 1975).

Bocking, Brian. 'Mysticism: No Experience Necessary?' *Diskus* 7 (2006), www.basr.ac.uk/diskus/diskus7/bocking.htm.

Bornstein, Marc H. and Jerome S. Bruner (eds). *Interaction in Human Development*. Hillsdale, NJ: L. Erlbaum Associates, 1989.

Bouchy, Anne. *Les oracles de shirataka, ou, la sibylle d'Ôsaka: Vie d'une femme spécialiste de la possession dans le Japon du XXe siècle*. Arles: Editions P. Picquier: Diffusion, Harmonia Mundi, 1992.

Bowring, Richard John. *The Religious Traditions of Japan, 500–1600*. Cambridge, UK; New York: Cambridge University Press, 2005.

Brakke, David. *Athanasius and the Politics of Asceticism*. Oxford: Clarendon Press, 1995.

——. 'The Making of Monastic Demonology: Three Ascetic Teachers on Withdrawal and Resistance'. *Church History* 70, no. 1 (2001): 19–48.

Breen, John and Mark Teeuwen. *Shintō in History: Ways of the Kami*. Curzon studies in Asian religion, Richmond: Curzon, 2000.

Bremen, Jan van and Dolores P. Martinez (eds). *Ceremony and Ritual in Japan: Religious Practices in an Industrialized Society*. London; New York: Routledge, 1995.

Brock, S. P. 'Early Syrian Asceticism'. *Numen* 20, no. 1 (1973): 1–19.

Bronkhorst, Johannes. 'Asceticism, Religion and Biological Evolution'. *Method and Theory in the Study of Religion* 13, 2001: 374–418.

Brown, Peter Robert Lamont. *The Body and Society: Men, Women and Sexual Renunciation in Early Christianity*. New York: Columbia University Press, 1988.

Burghart, Richard. 'Wandering Ascetics of the Ramanandi Sect'. *History of Religions* 22, no. 4 (1983): 361–80.

Burton-Christie, Douglas. *The Word in the Desert: Scripture and the Quest for Holiness in Early Christian Monasticism*. New York: Oxford University Press, 1993.

Butler, Judith. *Bodies That Matter: On the Discursive Limits of Sex*. New York: Routledge, 1993.

Carr, David M. *The Erotic Word: Sexuality, Spirituality and the Bible*. New York: Oxford University Press, 2003.

Carrier, James G. *Occidentalism: Images of the West*. Oxford: New York: Clarendon Press, Oxford University Press, 1995.

Carrithers, Michael. 'The Modern Ascetics of Lanka and the Pattern of Change in Buddhism'. *Man* 14, no. 2 (1979): 294–310.

——. 'Naked Ascetics in Southern Digambar Jainism'. *Man* 24, no. 2 (1989): 219–35.

Certeau, Michel de. *La Fable Mystique: XVIe-XVIIe Siècle*. Bibliothèque des histoires, Paris: Gallimard, 1982.

Chackraborti, Haripada. *Asceticism in Ancient India in Brahmanical, Buddhist, Jaina and Ajivica Societies*. Calcutta: Punthi Pustak, 1973.

Chilson, Clark and Peter Knecht (eds). *Shamans in Asia*. London; New York: Routledge Curzon, 2003.

Chitty, Derwas J. *The Desert a City: An Introduction to the Study of Egyptian and Palestinian Monasticism Under the Christian Empire*. Crestwood, NY: St Vladimir's Seminary Press, 1995.

Clark, Elizabeth A. 'New Perspectives on the Originist Controversy: Human Embodiment and Ascetic Strategies'. *Church History* 59, no. 2 (1990): 145–62.

——. *Reading Renunciation: Asceticism and Scripture in Early Christianity*. Princeton, NJ: Princeton University Press, 1999.

Coakley, Sarah (ed.). *Religion and the Body*. Cambridge ; New York: Cambridge University Press, 1997.

Collins, Steven. 'The Body in Theravada Buddhist Monasticism'. In Sarah Coakley (ed.), *Religion and the Body*. Cambridge: Cambridge University Press, 1997: 185–204.

Cort, John E. 'The Gift of Food to a Wandering Cow: Lay–Mendicant Interaction Among the Jains'. In K. Ishwaran (ed.), *Ascetic Culture: Renunciation and Worldly Engagement*. Boston: Brill, 1999: 87–109.

Coyaud, Maurice. 'Fêtes japonaises: Un essai d'analyse sémiotique'. *L'Homme* XVII, no. 4 (1977): 91–105.

Crouzel, Henri. *Origen*. Edinburgh: T.&T. Clark, 1989.

Crystal, David (ed.). *The Cambridge Encyclopedia*. Cambridge: Cambridge University Press, 1990.

Davis, Winston. *Japanese Religion and Society: Paradigms of Structure and Change*. Albany: State University of New York Press, 1992.

Deems, Mervin Monroe. 'The Place of Asceticism in the Stabilization of the Church'. *The Journal of Religion* 10, no. 4 (1930): 563–77.

Dentoni, Francesco. *Feste e Stagioni in Giappone: Una Ricerca Storico-Religiosa*. Roma: Borla, 1980.

Doniger, Wendy. *Siva, the Erotic Ascetic*. New York: Oxford University Press, 1981.

Dreyfus, Hubert L. and Paul Rabinow. *Michel Foucault: Beyond Structuralism and Hermeneutics*. Brighton: Harvester, 1982.

Eliade, Mircea. *Yoga: Immortality and Freedom*. Princeton, NJ: Princeton University Press [for Bollingen Foundation, New York], 1969.

——. *Le Chamanisme et les Techniques Archaïques de l'extase*. 2 édn, Revue et augm. Paris: Payot, 1974.

Elm, Susanna. *Virgins of God: The Making of Asceticism in Late Antiquity*. Oxford classical monographs, Oxford; New York: Oxford University Press, 1994.

Eskildsen, Stephen. *Asceticism in Early Taoist Religion*. Suny series in Chinese philosophy and culture, Albany: State University of New York Press, 1998.

Faure, Bernard. *Chan Insights and Oversights: An Epistemological Critique of the Chan Tradition*. Princeton, NJ: Princeton University Press, 1993.

——. *The Rhetoric of Immediacy: A Cultural Critique of Chan/Zen Buddhism*. Princeton, NJ: Princeton University Press, 1994.

Feher, Michel, Ramona Naddaff and Nadia Tazi (eds). *Fragments for a History of the Human Body*. New York: Urzone, Inc, 1989.

Flood, Gavin D. *The Ascetic Self: Subjectivity, Memory, and Tradition*. Cambridge; New York: Cambridge University Press, 2004.

Foucault, Michel. *The Birth of the Clinic: An Archaeology of Medical Perception*. London: Tavistock, 1973.

——. *The Order of Things: An Archaeology of the Human Sciences*. New York: Vintage Books, 1973.

Freiberger, Oliver (ed.). *Asceticism and Its Critics: Historical Accounts and Comparative Perspectives*. Oxford; New York: Oxford University Press, 2006.

Friedman, Lenore and Susan Ichi Su Moon (eds). *Being Bodies: Buddhist Women on the Paradox of Embodiment*. Boston: Shambhala, 1997.

Glucklich, Ariel. *Sacred Pain: Hurting the Body for the Sake of the Soul*. Oxford; New York: Oxford University Press, 2001.

Goodwin, Janet R. *Alms and Vagabonds: Buddhist Temples and Popular Patronage in Medieval Japan*. Honolulu: University of Hawai'i Press, 1994.

——. 'Building Bridges and Saving Souls. The Fruits of Evangelism in Medieval Japan'. *Monumenta Nipponica* 44, no. 2 (1989): 137–49.

Gorai Shigeru 五来重. 'Shugendō Lore'. *Japanese Journal of Religious Studies* 16, no. 2–3 (1989): 117–42.

——. *Yama no shūkyō: Shugendō kōgi* 山の宗教: 修験道講義. Tokyo: Kadokawa Shoten, 1991.

Gramsci, Antonio and Valentino Gerratana. *Quaderni Del Carcere*. Torino: G. Einaudi, 1975.

Grapard, Allan. 'Flying Mountains and Walkers of Emptiness: Toward a Definition of Sacred Space in Japanese Religions'. *History of Religions* 21, no. 2 (1982): 195–221.

Groner, Paul. *Saichō: The Establishment of the Japanese Tendai School*. Honolulu: University of Hawai'i Press, 2000.

Gross, Robert Lewis. *The Sādhus of India: A Study of Hindu Asceticism*. Jaipur: Rawat Publications, 1992.

Hamilton, Malcolm. *The Sociology of Religion: Theoretical and Comparative Perspectives*. London; New York: Routledge, 2001.

Hanegraaff, Wouter J. *New Age Religion and Western Culture: Esotericism in the Mirror of Secular Thought*. Leiden; New York: E. J. Brill, 1996.

Hardacre, Helen and Alan Sponberg (eds). *Maitreya, the Future Buddha*. Cambridge: Cambridge University Press, 1988.

Hareven, Tamara K. *Families, History and Social Change: Life Course and Cross-Cultural Perspectives*. Boulder, CO: Westview Press, 2000.

Hasebe Hachiro. 'Le gyōja et le Bouddhisme japonais: Le monde du Bouddhisme ascétique'. *Shūkyō kenkyū* 76 (1939).

Hayes, Dawn Marie. *Body and Sacred Place in Medieval Europe, 1100–1389*. New York: Routledge, 2003.

Heidegger, Martin. *Being and Time*. London: SCM Press, 1962.

Hensan inkai 編纂委員会, eds. *Gyakubiki bukkyōgo jiten*. 逆引き佛教語辞典. Tokyo: Kashiwa Shobō, 1995.

Henshall, Kenneth G. *A Guide to Remembering Japanese Characters*. Rutland, VT: C. E. Tuttle, 1988.

Hiramatsu Chōkū 平松澄空. *Hieizan kaihōgyō no kenkyū* 比叡山回峰行の研究. Tokyo: Miosha, 1982.

Hobbes, Thomas. *Leviathan. Or the Matter, Form and Power of a Common-Wealth Ecclesiastical and Civil*. London: Printed for Andrew Crooke, 1675.

Hollywood, Amy. 'Performativity, Citationality, Ritualization'. *History of Religions* 42, no. 2 (2002): 93–115.

Hori Ichiro 堀一郎. *Waga kuni minkan shinkōshi no kenkyū* 我が國民間信仰史の研究. Tokyo: Sōgensha, 1953.

——. 'Self-Mummified Buddhas in Japan. An Aspect of the Shugen-Dô ("Mountain Asceticism") Sect'. *History of Religions* 1, no. 2 (1962): 222–42.

——. *Folk Religion in Japan: Continuity and Change*. Haskell lectures on history of religions, no. 1, Chicago: University of Chicago Press, 1968.

Hurvitz, Leon. *Scripture of the Lotus Blossom of the Fine Dharma*. New York: Columbia University Press, 1976.

Ikegami Kōichi 池上 幸一. *Nihon no mizu to nōgyō* 日本の水と農業. Tokyo: Gakuyo Shobō, 1991.

Ikegami Yoshimasa 池上良正. *Minkan fusha shinkō no kenkyū* 民間巫者信仰の研究. Tokyo: Miraisha, 1999.

Ikoma Kanshichi 生駒勘七. *Ontake no shinkō to tozan no rekishi* 御嶽の信仰と登山の歴史. Tokyo: Daiichi Hōki, 1988.

Imamura Keiji 今村 啓爾. *Prehistoric Japan: New Perspectives on Insular East Asia.* London: UCL Press, 1996.

Inoue Nobutaka 井上順孝 (ed.). *Matsuri: Festival Ad Rite in Japanese Life.* Tokyo: Institute for Japanese Culture and Classics, Kokugakuin University, 1988.

Ippen and Dennis Hirota. *No Abode: The Record of Ippen.* Kyoto, Japan; San Francisco, California: Ryūkoku University (Distributed by Buddhist Bookstore), 1986.

Ishida Hidemi 石田秀実. 'Body and Mind: The Chinese Perspective'. In Livia Kohn and Sakade Yoshinobu (eds), *Taoist Meditation and Longevity Techniques.* Ann Arbor, MI: Center for Chinese Studies, University of Michigan, 1989: 41–72.

—— (ed.). *Higashi ajia no shintai gihō* 東アジアの身体技法. Tokyo: Bensei Shuppan, 2000.

Ishwaran, K. (ed.). *Ascetic Culture: Renunciation and Worldly Engagement.* International studies in sociology and social anthropology, Vol. 72, Leiden: Brill, 1999.

Iwahana Michiaki 岩鼻通明. *Dewa sanzan no bunka to minzoku* 出羽三山の文化と民俗. Tokyo: Iwata Shoin, 1996.

Jackson, Michael D. *Existential Anthropology: Events, Exigencies and Events.* New York; Oxford: Berghahn, 2005.

Jacobs, Andrew S. 'Writing Demetrias: Ascetic Logic in Ancient Christianity'. *Church History* 69, no. 4 (2000): 719–48.

Kant, Immanuel and Mary J. Gregor. *The Metaphysics of Morals.* Cambridge: Cambridge University Press, 1991.

Kawamura Kunimitsu 川村邦光. *Miko no minzokugaku: 'onna no chikara' no kindai* 巫女の民俗学:「女の力」の近代. Tokyo: Seikyūsha, 1991.

Kelsey, W. Michael. *Konjaku Monogatari-Shū.* Boston: Twayne Publishers, 1982.

Kieschnick, John. *The Eminent Monk: Buddhist Ideals in Medieval Chinese Hagiography.* Honolulu: University of Hawai'i Press, 1997.

Kirkpatrick, Clifford. *The Family as Process and Institution.* New York: Ronald Press Co., 1955.

Knight, Chris, Michael Studdert-Kennedy and James R. Hurford (eds). *The Evolutionary Emergence of Language: Social Function and the Origins of Linguistic Form.* Cambridge, UK; New York: Cambridge University Press, 2000.

Kodera Bun'ei 小寺文穎. 'Hieizan *kaihōgyō* no shiteki tenkai 比叡山回峰行の史的展開'. *Nihon bukkyō gakkai nenpō* 45, (1979): 273–86.

Kohn, Livia. *Laughing at the Tao: Debates Among Buddhists and Taoists in Medieval China.* Princeton, NJ: Princeton University Press, 1995.

——. *Monastic Life in Medieval Daoism: A Cross-Cultural Perspective.* Honolulu: University of Hawai'i Press, 2003.

Kohn, Livia and Yoshinobu Sakade (eds). *Taoist Meditation and Longevity Techniques.* Ann Arbor, MI: Center for Chinese Studies, University of Michigan, 1989.

Kroll, Jerome and Bernard S. Bachrach. *The Mystic Mind: The Psychology of Medieval Mystics and Ascetics.* London; New York: Routledge, 2005.

Krueger, Derek. 'Hagiography as an Ascetic Practice in the Early Christian East'. *The Journal of Religion* 79, no. 2 (1999): 216–32.

Kūkai and Yoshito S. Hakeda (ed.). *Kūkai: Major Works.* New York: Columbia University Press, 1972.

Kuriyama, Shigehisa. *The Expressiveness of the Body and the Divergence of Greek and Chinese Medicine*. New York: Zone Books, 1999.

——. *The Imagination of the Body and the History of Bodily Experience*. Kyoto: International Research Center for Japanese Studies, 2001.

Law, Jane Marie (ed.). *Religious Reflections on the Human Body*. Bloomington and Indianapolis: Indiana University Press, 1994.

Lingis, Alphonso. *Foreign Bodies*. New York: Routledge, 1994.

Liscutin, Nicola. 'Mapping the Sacred Body: Shintō Versus Popular Beliefs at Mt Iwaki in Tsugaru'. In John Breen and Mark Teeuwen (eds), *Shinto in History: The Ways of the Kami*. Richmond: Curzon Press, 2000.

Long, Lynne (ed.). *Translation and Religion: Holy Untranslatable?* Clevedon; Buffalo: Multilingual Matters, 2005.

Lorenzen, David N. 'Warrior Ascetics in Indian History'. *Journal of the American Oriental Society* 98, no. 1 (1978): 61–75.

Loudon, Irvine (ed.). *Western Medicine: An Illustrated History*. Oxford; New York: Oxford University Press, 1997.

Ludvik, Catherine. 'In the Service of the Kaihōgyō Practitioners of Mt Hiei: The Stopping-Obstacles Confraternity (Sokushō Kō) of Kyoto'. *Japanese Journal of Religious Studies* 33, no. 1 (2006): 115–42.

Lumsden, Douglas W. '"Touch No Unclean Thing": Apocalyptic Expressions of Ascetic Spirituality in the Early Middle Ages'. *Church History* 66, no. 2 (1997): 240–51.

McCullough, Helen Craig. *The Tale of the Heike*. Stanford, CA: Stanford University Press, 1988.

McNeill, John T. 'Asceticism Versus Militarism in the Middle Ages'. *Church History* 5, no. 1 (1936): 3–28.

Madell, Geoffrey. *Mind and Materialism*. Edinburgh: Edinburgh University Press, 1988.

Maghen, Ze'ev. *Virtues of the Flesh: Passion and Purity in Early Islamic Jurisprudence*. Leiden; Boston: Brill, 2005.

Malinowski, B. *The Scientific Theory of Culture and Other Essays*. Chapel Hill: University of North Carolina, 1944; London: Oxford University Press, 1960.

Marietta, Jack D. 'Wealth, War and Religion: The Perfecting of Quaker Asceticism 1740–1783'. *Church History* 43, no. 2 (1974): 230–41.

Masaki Akira 正木 晃, Yamaori Tetsuo 山折 哲雄 and Nagasawa Tetsu 永沢 哲. *Suteru, aruku, tsutaeru* 捨てる 歩く 伝える. Tokyo: Kosei Shuppansha, 1992.

Masson, J. Moussaieff. 'The Psychology of the Ascetic'. *The Journal of Asian Studies* 35, no. 4 (1976): 611–25.

Matsumoto Akira 松本昭. *Nihon no miira-butsu* 日本のミイラ仏. Tokyo: Rokkō Shuppan, 1985.

Mellor, Philip. 'Orientalism, Representation and Religion: The Reality Behind the Myth'. *Religion* 34 (2004): 99–112.

Merleau-Ponty, Maurice. 'The Spatiality of the Lived Body and Motility'. In Stuart F. Spicker (ed.), *The Philosophy of the Body; Rejections of Cartesian Dualism*. Chicago: Quadrangle Books, 1970: 241–73.

Midgley, Mary. 'The Soul Successors: Philos and the "Body"'. In Sarah Coakley (ed.), *Religion and the Body*. Cambridge: Cambridge University Press, 1997: 53–70.

Miller, Patricia Cox. *Women in Early Christianity: Translations From Greek Texts*. Washington, DC: Catholic University of America Press, 2005.

Miyake Hitoshi 宮家 準. *Shugendō girei no kenkyū* 修験道儀礼の研究. Tokyo: Shunjūsha, 1971.

——. *Shugendō shisō no kenkyū* 修験道思想の研究. Tokyo: Shunjūsha, 1985.

——. *Shugendō jiten* 修験道辞典. Shohan ed. Tokyo: Tōkyōdō Shuppan, 1986.

——. 'Religious Rituals in Shugendō'. *Japanese Journal of Religious Studies* 16, 2–3 (1989a): 101–16.

——. *Shūkyō minzokugaku* 宗教民俗学. Tokyo: Tokyo University Press, 1989b.

——. *Kumano shugen* 熊野修験. Tokyo: Yoshikawa Kōbunkan, 1992.

——. *Shugendō soshiki no kenkyū* 修験道組織の研究. Tokyo: Shunjūsha, 1999.

——. *Haguro shugen: Sono rekishi to mineiri* 羽黒修験: その歴史と峰入. Tokyo: Iwata Shoin, 2000a.

——. *En no gyōja to shugendō no rekishi* 役行者と修験道の歴史. Tokyo: Yoshikawa Kōbunkan, 2000b.

——. *Shugendō: Essays on the Structure of Japanese Folk Religion*. Ann Arbor, MI: Center for Japanese Studies, University of Michigan, 2001.

——. *Minzoku shūkyō to nihon shakai* 民俗宗教と日本社会. Tokyo: University of Tokyo Press, 2002.

Miyake Hitoshi and H. Byron Earhart. *Shugendō: Essays on the Structure of Japanese Folk Religion*. Ann Arbor, MI: Center for Japanese Studies, University of Michigan, 2001.

Miyake Hitoshi and Gaynor Sekimori. *The Mandala of the Mountain: Shugendō and Folk Religion*. Tokyo: Keiō University Press, 2005.

Moerman, D. Max. *Localizing Paradise: Kumano Pilgrimage and the Religious Landscape of Premodern Japan*. Cambridge, MA: Harvard University Asia Center (Distributed by Harvard University Press), 2005.

Montgomery, James A. 'Ascetic Strains in Early Judaism'. *Journal of Biblical Literature* 51, no. 3 (1932): 183–213.

Morford, Mark P. O. *The Roman Philosophers: From the Time of Cato the Censor to the Death of Marcus Aurelius*. London; New York: Routledge, 2002.

Naitō Masatoshi 内藤 正敏. *Nihon no miira shinkō* 日本のミイラ信仰. Kyoto: Hōkōzan, 1999.

Nakao Takashi 中尾崇. *Nichirenshū no seiritsu to tenkai* 日蓮宗の成立と展開. Tokyo: Yoshikawa Kōbunkan, 1973.

Namihira Emiko. *Hare, Ke and Kegare: The Structure of Japanese Folk Belief*. Ann Arbor, MI: University Microfilms International, 1979.

Nietzsche, Friedrich, Maudemarie Clark and Alan J. Swensen (eds). *On the Genealogy of Morality: A Polemic*. Indianapolis, IN: Hackett Publishers Co., 1998.

Nihon-miira-kenkyū-gurupu 日本ミイラ研究グルプ (Japanese Mummies Research Group). *Nihon miira no kenkyū* 日本ミイラの研究. Tokyo: Heibonsha, 1969.

O'Flaherty, Wendy Doniger. 'Asceticism and Sexuality in the Mythology of Siva. Part I'. *History of Religions* 8, no. 4 (1969): 300–37.

Olivelle, Patrick. *Renunciation in Hinduism: A Medieval Debate*. Vienna: Gerold, 1986.

Ōmori Tatari 大森崇 (ed.). *Nichiren no hon. Hō no yo o utsu hokkekyō no yogen* 日蓮の本―末法の世を撃つ法華経の予言. Tokyo: Gakushū Kenkyūsha, 1993.

Pease, Roger W. (ed.). *Merriam-Webster's Medical Dictionary*. [New edn] Springfield, MA: Merriam-Webster Inc, 2006.

Perkins, Judith. *The Suffering Self: Pain and Narrative Representation in Early Christian Era*. London; New York: Routledge, 1995.

Pike, Kenneth Lee. *Language in Relation to a Unified Theory of the Structure of Human Behaviour*. The Hague: Mouton de Gruyter, 1971.

Plutschow, Herbert. *Matsuri: The Festivals of Japan*. Richmond: Japan Library, 1996.

Ponzetti, James J. Jr. 'Loneliness Among College Students'. *Family Relations* 39, no. 3 (1990): 336–40.

Porter, Roy. *Flesh in the Age of Reason*. London: Allen Lane, 2003.

Pratt, Mary Louise. *Imperial Eyes: Travel Writing and Transculturation*. London; New York: Routledge, 1992.

Pye, Michael. 'Perceptions of the Body in Japanese Religion'. In Sarah Coakley (ed.), *Religion and the Body*. Cambridge: Cambridge University Press, 1997: 248–61.

——. *Skillful Means: A Concept in Mahayana Buddhism*. New York: Routledge, 2003.

Raveri, Massimo. *Itinerari nel Sacro - L' Esperienza Religiosa Giapponese*. Venice: Libreria Editrice Cafoscarina, 1984.

——. *Il Corpo e il Paradiso: Esperienze Ascetiche in Asia Orientale*. Venezia: Marsilio, 1992.

Reader, Ian. *Religion in Contemporary Japan*. Honolulu: University of Hawai'i Press, 1991.

——. *Religious Violence in Contemporary Japan: The Case of Aum Shinrikyō*. Honolulu: University of Hawai'i Press, 2000.

——. *Making Pilgrimages: Meaning and Practice in Shikoku*. Honolulu: University of Hawai'i Press, 2005.

——. 'Folk Religion'. In Paul L. Swanson and Clark Chilson (eds), *Nanzan Guide to Japanese Religions*. Honolulu: University of Hawai'i Press, 2006: 66–86.

Reader, Ian and George Joji Tanabe. *Practically Religious: Worldly Benefits and the Common Religion of Japan*. Honolulu: University of Hawai'i Press, 1998.

Reader, Ian and Tony Walter (eds). *Pilgrimage in Popular Culture*. Basingstoke: Macmillan, 1993.

Reese, William L. (ed.). *Dictionary of Philosophy and Religion: Eastern and Western Thought*. Atlantic Highlands, NJ: Humanities Press, 1980.

Rhodes, Robert F. 'The Kaihōgyō Practice of Mt Hiei'. *Japanese Journal of Religious Studies* 14, no. 2–3 (1987): 185–202.

Rhys Davids, T. W. and Hermann Oldenberg, trans. '*Vinaya* texts: Part 1, The *Patimokkha*, The *Mahavagga* 1–4'. In Max Muller (ed.), *Sacred Books of the East*, Vol. 13. Oxford: Oxford University Press, 1881.

Ricoeur, Paul. *On Translation*. New York, NY: Routledge, 2006.

Riley, Charles A. *The Saints of Modern Art: The Ascetic Ideal in Contemporary Painting, Sculpture, Architecture, Music, Dance, Literature and Philosophy*. Hanover, NH: University Press of New England, 1998.

Roberts, Tyler T. '"This Art of Transfiguration is Philosophy": Nietzsche's Asceticism'. *The Journal of Religion* 76, no. 3 (1996): 402–27.

Robinet, Isabelle. *Méditation Taoïste*. Mystiques et Religions Collection, Paris: Dervy livres, 1979.

Robinson, Douglas (ed.). *Western Translation Theory: From Herodotus to Nietzsche*. Manchester, UK; Northampton, MA: St Jerome Publishers, 2002.

Rousseau, Philip. *Ascetics, Authority and the Church in the Age of Jerome and Cassian*. Oxford; New York: Oxford University Press, 1978.

Rudolph, Kurt and R. Wilson. *Gnosis: The Nature and History of Gnosticism*. San Francisco: Harper & Row, 1987.

Russell, Bertrand. *History of Western Philosophy*. London: Routledge, 2001.

Said, Edward W. *Orientalism*. London: Penguin Books, 2003 (1978).

Sakurai Tokutarō 桜井徳太郎. *Nihon no shamanizumu* 日本のシャマニズム. Tokyo:

Yoshikawa Kōbunkan, 1974.

Sakurai Yoshirō 桜井好朗. *Nihon no inja* 日本の隠者. Tokyo: Hanawa Shobō, 1969.

Sartre, Jean-Paul. *Being and Nothingness: An Essay on Phenomenological Ontology*. London: Methuen & Co. Ltd, 1957.

Saso, Michael. 'The Taoist Body and Cosmic Prayer'. In Sarah Coakley (ed.), *Religion and the Body*. Cambridge: Cambridge University Press, 1997: 231–47.

Satlow, Michael L. '"And on the Earth You Shall Sleep": "Talmud Torah" and Rabbinic Asceticism'. *The Journal of Religion* 83, no. 2 (2003): 204–25.

Sawada, Janine Anderson. *Practical Pursuits: Religion, Politics and Personal Cultivation in Nineteenth-Century Japan*. Honolulu: University of Hawai'i Press, 2004.

Scarry, Elaine. *The Body in Pain: The Making and Unmaking of the World*. New York: Oxford University Press, 1985.

Schattschneider, Ellen. *Immortal Wishes: Labor and Transcendence on a Japanese Sacred Mountain*. Durham: Duke University Press, 2003.

Scheler, Max. *Man's Place in Nature*. Boston: Beacon Press, 1961.

——. 'Lived Body, Environment and Ego'. In Stuart F. Spicker (ed.), *The Philosophy of the Body: Rejections of Cartesian Dualism*. Chicago: Quadrangle Books, 1970: 159–86.

Schipper, Kristofer Marinus. *Le Corps Taoïste: Corps Physique, Corps Social*. L'espace intérieur, Vol. 25. Paris: Fayard, 1982.

Schnell, Scott. 'Conducting Fieldwork on Japanese Religions'. In Paul L Swanson and Clark Chilson (eds), *Nanzan Guide to Japanese Religions*. Honolulu: University of Hawai'i Press, 2006: 381–91.

Sekimori, Gaynor. 'Female Yamabushi 山伏: The Akinomine 秋の峯 of Dewa Sanzan Jinja 出羽三山神社 and Miko Shugyō 巫女修行'. *Transactions of ICES/ICO* 39, no. Dec (1994).

——. 'Shugendō: The State of the Field'. *Monumenta Nipponica* 57, no. 2 (2002): 207–27.

——. 'Paper Fowl and Wooden Fish: The Separation of Kami and Buddha Worship in Haguro Shugendō, 1869–1875'. *Japanese Journal of Religious Studies* 32, no. 2 (2005): 197–234.

Simon, Sherry. 'Translating and Interlingual Creation in the Contact Zone'. In Harish Trivedi and Susan Bassnett (eds), *Post-Colonial Translation: Theory and Practice*. London: Routledge, 1999: 58–74.

Sharf, Robert H. 'Experience'. In Mark Taylor (ed.), *Critical Terms for Religious Studies*. Chicago: University of Chicago Press, 1998:94–118.

Shilling, Chris. *The Body and Social Theory*. London: Sage Publications Ltd, 1993.

Shima Kazuharu 島一春. *Gyōdō ni ikiru* 行道に生きる. Tokyo: Kōsei Shuppansha, 1983.

Shinno Toshikazu 真野俊和. *Nihon yugyō shūkyōron* 日本遊行宗教論. Tokyo: Yoshikawa Kōbunkan, 1991.

——. 'From Minkan-Shinkō to Minzoku-Shūkyō: Refections on the Study of Folk Buddhism'. *Japanese Journal of Religious Studies* 20, no. 2–3 (1993): 187–206.

——. 'Journeys, Pilgrimages, Excursions: Religious Travels in the Early Modern Period'. *Monumenta Nipponica* 57, no. 4 (2002): 447–71.

Shiraishi Ryokai 白石凌海. *Asceticism in Buddhism and Brahmanism: A Comparative Study*. Tring, UK: Institute of Buddhist Studies, 1996.

Sonoda Minoru 薗田稔. 'The Traditional Festival in Urban Society'. *Japanese Journal of Religious Studies* 2, no. 2–3 June–September (1975): 103–36.

Spicker, Stuart F. (ed.). *The Philosophy of the Body: Rejections of Cartesian Dualism.* Chicago: Quadrangle Books, 1970.

Stephen G. Covell. 'Learning to Persevere: The Popular Teaching of Tendai Ascetics'. *Japanese Journal of Religious Studies* 31, no. 2 (2004): 255–87.

Stevens, John. *The Marathon Monks of Mount Hiei.* Boston: Shambala, 1988.

Sullivan, Lawrence E. 'Sound and Senses: Toward a Hermeneutics of Performance'. *History of Religions* 26, no. 1 (1986): 1–33.

Suzuki Masataka 鈴木正崇. *Nyonin kinsei* 女人禁制. Tokyo: Yoshikawa Kōbunkan, 2002.

Swanson, Paul L. 'Shugendō and the Yoshino-Kumano Pilgrimage: An Example of Mountain Pilgrimage'. *Monumenta Nipponica* 36, no. 1 (1981): 55–84.

Swanson, Paul and Clark Chilson (eds). *Nanzan Guide to Japanese Religions.* Honolulu: University of Hawai'i Press, 2006.

Synnott, Anthony. *The Body Social.* London; New York: Routledge, 1993.

Tanabe, George J. Jr. (ed.). *Religions of Japan in Practice.* Princeton: Princeton University Press, 1999.

Taylor, Mark C. (ed.). *Critical Terms for Religious Studies.* Chicago: University of Chicago Press, 1998.

Teeuwen, Mark, John Breen and Inoue Nobutaka (eds). *Shinto: A Short History.* London; New York: Routledge Curzon, 2003.

Thomas, Helen and Jamilah Ahmed (eds). *Cultural Bodies: Ethnography and Theory.* Malden, MA: Blackwell Publishers, 2004.

Tilley, Maureen A. 'The Ascetic Body and the (Un)Making of the World of the Martyr'. *Journal of the American Academy of Religion* 59, no. 3 (1991): 467–79.

Trivedi, Harish and Susan Bassnett (eds). '*Vinaya* texts: Part 1, The *Patimokkha,* The *Mahavagga* 1–4'. Translated by T. W. Rhys Davids and Hermann Oldenberg, *Sacred Books of the East,* Vol. 13. Oxford: Clarendon Press, 1881.

Turner, Victor Witter. *The Forest of Symbols: Aspects of Ndembu Ritual.* Ithaca, NY: Cornell University Press, 1967.

Tyler, Royall. '"The Book of the Great Practice": The Life of the Mt Fuji Ascetic Kakugyō Tōbutsu Kō'. *Asian Folklore Studies* 52, no. 2 (1993): 251–331.

Tyler, Royall and Paul L. Swanson. 'Editors' Introduction'. *Japanese Journal of Religious Studies* 16, no. 2–3 (1989): 93–100.

Tymoczko, Maria. 'Post-Colonial Writing and Literary Translation'. In Harish Trivedi and Susan Bassnett (eds), *Post-Colonial Translation: Theory and Practice.* London: Routledge, 1999: 19–40.

Vaage, Leif E. and Vincent L. Wimbush (eds). *Asceticism and the New Testament.* New York: Routledge, 1999.

Valantasis, Richard. 'Constructions of Power in Asceticism'. *Journal of the American Academy of Religion* 63, no. 4 (1995): 775–821.

van Bremen, Jan and D. P. Martinez. *Ceremony and Ritual in Japan: Religious Practices in an Industrialized Society.* London; New York: Routledge, 1995.

Vervoorn, Aat Emile. *Men of the Cliffs and Caves: The Development of the Chinese Eremitic Tradition to the End of the Han Dynasty.* Shatin, NT; Hong Kong: Chinese University Press, 1990.

Victoria, Brian Daizen. *Zen At War.* Lanham, MD: Rowman & Littlefield Publishers, 2006.

Ware, Kallistos. '"My Helper and My Enemy": The Body in Greek Christianity'. In Sarah Coakley (ed.), *Religion and the Body.* Cambridge: Cambridge University Press, 1997: 90–110.

Watson, Burton (tr). *The Vimalakirti Sutra*. Translations from the Asian Classics, New York; Chichester: Columbia University Press, 1997.

Wazaki Nobuya 和崎 信哉. *Ajari tanjō. Hieizan sennichi kaihōgyō: Aru gyōja no hansei* 阿闍梨誕生—比叡山千日回峰行・ある行者の半生. Tokyo: Kōdansha, 1979.

Weber, Max. *The Sociology of Religion*. Boston: Beacon Press, 1964.

——. *The Protestant Ethic and the Spirit of Capitalism*. Los Angeles, CA: Roxbury Publishers Co., 2001.

Weekley, Ernest (ed.). *An Etymological Dictionary of Modern English*. New York: Dover Publications, 1967.

Weisberger, Adam. 'Marginality and Its Directions'. *Sociological Forum* 7, no. 3 (1992): 425–46.

White, David Gordon (ed.). *Tantra in Practice*. Princeton, NJ: Princeton University Press, 2000.

——. *Kiss of the Yoginī: 'Tantric Sex' in Its South Asian Contexts*. Chicago; London: University of Chicago Press, 2003.

Williams, Paul. 'Some Mahāyāna Buddhist Perspectives on the Body'. In Sarah Coakley (ed.), *Religion and the Body*. Cambridge: Cambridge University Press, 1997: 205–30.

Wiltshire, Martin G. *Ascetic Figures Before and in Early Buddhism: The Emergence of Gautama as the Buddha*. Berlin; New York: Mouton de Gruyter, 1990.

Wimbush, Vincent L. *Paul, the Worldly Ascetic: Response to the World and Self-Understanding According to 1 Corinthians 7*. Macon, GA: Mercer University Press, 1987.

Winkler, Mary G. and Letha B. Cole (eds). *The Good Body: Asceticism in Contemporary Culture*. New Haven: Yale University Press, 1994.

Yajan, Veer. *A Critical Appreciation of Austerity in Ancient Indian Literature*. Delhi: Eastern Book Linkers, 2003.

Yamada Ryūshin 山田 龍真. *Aragyō: Tatoe kono inochi, kuchihaterutomo* 荒行—たとえこの命、朽ち果てるとも. Tokyo: Gendai Shorin, 1988.

Yamada Toshiaki 山田利明. 'Longevity Techniques and the Compilation of the Lingbao Wufuxu'. In Livia Kohn and Sakade Yoshinobu (eds), *Taoist Meditation and Longevity Techniques*. Ann Arbor, MI: Center for Chinese Studies, University of Michigan, 1989: 99–124.

Yoshitake Inage 吉竹稲毛 (ed.). *Kōbō daishi zenshū* 弘法大師全集. 3rd edition revised. Tokyo: Mikkyō Bunka Kenkyusha, 1965.

Yuasa Yasuo 湯浅泰雄. *Kindai nihon no tetsugaku to jitsuzon shisō* 近代日本の哲学と実存思想. Tokyo: Sōbunsha, 1970.

——. *Shintai tōyōteki shinshinron no kokoromi* 身体: 東洋的心身論の試み. Tokyo: Sōbunsha, 1977.

——. *Watsuji tetsurō: Kindai nihon tetsugaku no unmei* 和辻哲郎: 近代日本哲学の運命. Kyoto: Mineruva Shobō, 1981.

——. *Taikei – bukkyō to nihon-jin 3. Mikkyō to shugyō* 大系—仏教と日本人３: 密儀と修業. Tokyo: Shunjūsha, 1989.

Yuasa Yasuo and Thomas P. Kasulis. *The Body: Toward an Eastern Mind-Body Theory*. Albany, NY: State University of New York Press, 1987.

Zysk, Kenneth G. *Asceticism and Healing in Ancient India: Medicine in the Buddhist Monastery*. New York: Oxford University Press, 1991.

Audiovisual materials

Abela, Jean-Marc and Mark Patrick McGuire (directors). *Shugendō Now.* English and Japanese (Enpower Pictures, 2010). 1hour 28 minutes, colour.

Kitamura Minao 北村 皆雄 (director). *Nihon no meizan* 日本の名山 (Vol. 6). Japanese (Visual Folklore Inc. Japan, 2001). 1 hour 30 minutes, colour.

Kitamura Minao (director). *Nihon no meizan* 日本の名山 (Vol. 9). Japanese (Visual Folklore Inc. Japan, 2004). 1 hour 30 minutes, colour.

——*Shugen – Hagurosan akinomine* 羽黒山秋峰. Japanese (Visual Folklore Inc. Japan, 2004). 1 hour 45 minutes, colour.

——*Shugen: The Autumn Peak of Haguro Shugendō.* English and Japanese (Visual Folklore Inc. Japan, 2009). 1 hour 45 minutes, colour.

Tabata Keiichi 田畑慶吉 (director). *Yomigaeru Tōtō* 蘇る東塔. Japanese (JVC Yamamoto and Fuji Sankei Communications, 1982). 2 hours, colour.

Unknown director. *Daiaragyō* 大荒行. Japanese (NHK, 2001). 30 minutes, colour.

Yorke, Michael (director). *The Marathon Monks of Mt Hiei.* English and Japanese (Channel Four productions, 1992). 1 hour 32 minutes, colour.

Fieldwork notes

TL 240805 PFN#1: Fieldwork notes recorded during the participation in the *akinomine shugendō* retreat held at Shōzen-in/Kōtaku-ji temples, Dewa Sanzan, Yamagata prefecture (24 August–1 September 2005).

TL 240805 PFN#2: Second notebook of fieldwork notes for the *akinomine shugendō* (includes collected materials).

TL 280606 OFN#1: Fieldwork notes recorded during a short visit to Mount Nanao, near Dorogawa village in Yoshino (28 June 2006–29 June 2006).

TL 150706 PFN#1: Fieldwork notes recorded during the participation in the *okugake shugyō* (Yoshino–Kumano route), a six-day Shugendō ascetic practice held by the Tōnan-in temple in Yoshino (15–22 July 2006).

TL 250806 PFN#1: Fieldwork notes recorded during the participation in the *akinomine shugendō* retreat held at Dewa Sanzan Jinja, Dewa Sanzan, Yamagata prefecture (includes collected materials) (25 August–1 September 2006).

TL 101006 PFN#1: Fieldwork notes recorded during participation in the *hiwatari* (fire-walking) practice at Honjō shrine in Saitama (10 October 2006).

TL 010107 I#1: Brief interview of the *kaihōgyō ajari* (ascetic master) at Mudō-ji temple (part of Enryakuji complex) on Mount Hiei, Kyoto, during the rites for the first day of the year (1 January 2007).

TL 220107 PFN#1: Fieldwork notes recorded during the participation in the *samugyō* (cold practice) held by Jiga Daikyōkai, an Ontake devotees group based in Agematsu village, at the foot of Mount Ontake itself (22–24 January 2007).

TL 220207 I#1: Interview with the Jiga Daikyōkai leaders conducted in Tokyo (22 February 2007).

TL 010407 PFN#1: Fieldwork notes recorded at the end of the participation in the Spring Sesshin (*rōhatsu sesshin*) held at Tōshō-ji temple in Tokyo (27 March–1 April 2007).

TL 090407 PFI#1: Field interviews recorded during the Iwaguni *kagura*, Iwakuni, Yamaguchi prefecture. This *kagura* (sacred dance) occurs just once every seven years and includes the performance of ascetic feats (7–9 April 2007).

TL 100407 PFN#1: Fieldwork notes recorded during the Ontake devotees' Spring Festival, held at Honjō-jinja, Saitama. This is one of the few occasions in Japan where the practice of 'climbing the ladder of swords' practice (*hawatari*) is still performed (10 April 2007).

TL 130407 I#1: Interview with participants to the Spring Sesshin conducted in Tokyo (11 April 2007).

TL 170507 I#1: Second interview of the *kaihōgyō ajari* (ascetic master) at Mudō-ji temple on Mount Hiei, Kyoto (17 May 2007).

Index